BRIDGES TO PEOPLE

BRIDGES

TO PEOPLE

Communicating Jesus to People and Growing
Missional Churches in A Multi-Ethnic World

Sean S. O'Neal

Bridges To People:
Communicating Jesus to People and Growing Missional Churches
in A Multi-Ethnic World
by Sean S. O'Neal

Printed in the United States of America

ISBN 978-1-60266-268-1

For information contact the author by email:
sean@bridges2people.com

www.xulonpress.com

CONTENTS

ILLUSTRATIONS

ABBREVIATIONS

CRT   Culture Reasearch Team
DAP   Determined Action Point
DPT   Determined Point in Time

To all of those brave souls who dare to travel beyond their life
world interacting with people who may or may not
look like them and
speak the same language as they in an effort to exihibit
the compassion of
Jesus Christ through word and life. They present
the whole gospel with sincere
effort to meet life needs by bringing people into relationship with
God through knowing Jesus Christ as personal Savior,
Lord, and friend.

1

MOVEMENT MISSION AND MOMENTS

———∝∝∝———

"America is coming to be, not a Nationality, but a Transnationality, a weaving back and forth, with other lands, of many threads of all sizes" - Michael S. Laguerre

Movement

In the midst of the enviroment of "church" we the people of the church receive opportunities to get up and live in the power of Jesus Christ. His life within us causes us to move ; to go.

Go where? Go to the community, the people, our neighbors, friends, co-workers; the world. We are missionaries living in a highly populated, culturally diverse society which is thirsty and hungry for life. Jesus Christ came to give life and life abundantly (John 10:10). We as His disciples are to give life to people by sharing about Him and showing how knowing Christ in relationship sets people free.

The New Testament speaks of those who know God in personal relationship going and making disciples (Mathew 28:19). This is not a soft suggestion. It is a declarative statement that is foundational to the emergence of the church in the world. This one thing, *"Make Disciples"* is a key that unlocks the door to the vault where it seems the answer for the life or death of the church is hidden. Simply put, the church that stops going is the church that stops growing. Let that soak in deep.

The reality within a modern, post-modern, pre-Christian, people searching for an identity culture is that the successful gospel mission fulfilling existence of *"the church"* as an institution is ending. *"The church"* as a movement is re-emerging. Call it what you want, frame the arguments, write the articles and plan the conferences, keep spinning the plates, but listen, pause long enough to ask yourself one question, *"When is the last time you saw someone genuinely transformed into a sold out, committed, giving it all up, follower of Jesus?"* In fact if you are like me, it is difficult to to stay vigilant and easy to become complacent. Personally sticking my neck out, venturing off of the path of daily routine, walking with someone where they walk and just sharing Jesus with that person is challenging while living a busy lifestyle filled with activity. However, this is the calling of believers (those who know and follow the teachings of Jesus Christ). We are called to go.

Incidentally, going is not about the building, or the carpet, the sign, the worship, the visitors card, or the cheesy things we do sometimes. God is asking us to live a life among all people that shouts loudly through the way we live while we communicate to people that Jesus is real and He along with us desires to have genuine relationship with them.

This book is about going. It is a text researched and written with the goal of being a usable tool for every believer and church attempting to build relationships with people living in our culturally diverse world. It is designed to help believers share faith with people so that they will have real and authentic opportunities to connect with God through having relationship with Jesus Christ.

Often I am asked if it is possible to grow a multi-ethnic church congregation, or *"how does a multiethnic congregation develop?"*

There are some that have said, and continue to say that multi-cultural churches are an anomily or not possible. These statements are born from assumptions based on sociology and not Christology. The Bible is a multi-ethnic text, and Jesus Christ fulfilled a mission from the Father as the ultimate reconciler. Through knowing Him there is unity in the midst of our diversity. *"He is our peace, who made both groups one."* (Ephesians 2:14)

Diversity is a reality in this globally connected world in which people are continually moving. People are transnational, mobile, transient, and uniquely aware of the fact that the world is smaller than it once was. The inhabitants of earth have emerged into a global mobile urban influenced society in which centers of population continue to grow and people continually move from place to place. This population consists of people who have migrated to the cities of the world converging to form a mosaic tapestry of multi-ethnic, culturally diverse humanity in every major metropolitan area on earth.

Diversity and mobility are characteristics of this continually evolving urban society. Cities, and the areas surrounding cities, are populated with people from other places, who are representative of the population of the world. This is true in Hong Kong, London, Manila, Paris, Los Angeles, New York, San Francisco, Miami, Chicago, and many other cities throughout the world. These cities are diverse and the people living in these cities are mobile.

I observed this constant movement of people while serving as pastor of a church in the city of Chicago. After becoming pastor our congregation grew from an attendance of twenty-five to about one hundred in nine months. Then, during the following three months thirty people moved out of town. In fact they moved to different states. I looked up one day and thought, *"Where did all of the people go?"* Our church continued to grow in attendance however we had learned the reality of the mobility of people who live in and around large diverse population centers such as Chicago. This movement of people, although more visible in society today, is nothing new to the nation of the United States. It is a place where, since its inception, people have chased the fulfillment of their dreams.

Immigrant Dreams

Throughout history people have sought to improve their life journey by deviating from the path of those who lived before them and pioneering new paths to unknown worlds. Perhaps unknown worlds have an appeal of uncertainty and the possibility that the impossible may be possible. It may sound incredibly un-adult like to refer to a film for children however the animated film, *An American Tale,* effectively describes the appeal of possibly fulfilling impossible dreams. *An American Tale* has a song in which the words simply state, *"There are no cats in America, and the streets are paved with cheese"* (Kirschner 1998). This song in a children's video simplifies the dream of many people that there are no problems in America and the streets are paved with fortune. It is a great dream and vision of hope for a new life in a new place. It is a dream that we as adults watching a children's video may chuckle about. However, many people who crossed the Atlantic Ocean in the 17th, 18th, 19th, and early 20th centuries probably had a similar dream. It is the dream to come to a new place and walk on streets paved with fortune.

The stories of immigrant people are powerful and deeply moving. I have listened to the stories of Romanian immigrants who walked through the snow and broke the ice in order to swim across the Danube River to what was then known as Yugoslavia in search of freedom from an oppressive government. Haitian, Jamaican, Bulgarian, Ghanaian, Liberian, Honduran, and countless others tell their story of leaving the land of their birth in order to live in the land of the free and fulfill their *"American Dream"*. They are all in search of hope. The following quote is from an immigrant who left Ireland in search of the American Dream arriving in New York in 1914.

"I was just a farmer in Ireland, County Galway-planting and reaping potatoes, corn, cabbage, turnips, onions. 'Twas hard work, real hard work. Well, my brother and some sisters brought me out here, sent me a ticket. I was tickled to death to stay away from that hard work. I knew you could pick money off the street here. That's what I thought. [laughs.] (Morrison and Zabusky [1980] 1993, 61)."

The populating of the United States is a remarkable phenomenon. This nation, with the exception of the displaced Native American people groups and in spite of what any person could say, is a nation built upon people from other places. These people from other places have arrived with their own culture and language. They are our neighbors, our co-workers, our parents, and our relatives. They are the foundation of who we are as American people. Since the first immigrant people set foot on the soil, people from every culture in the world have made their way to the United States. They in essence have peopled the continent.

Prior to 1790, 575,000 European people made the arduous journey across the Atlantic to the shores of North America in search of something. Whether it was freedom for religious practice, business endeavors, or the desire to conquer a new frontier, people boarded ships in the ports of Europe to make the journey. Each of these people came and began to populate the North American continent bringing his or her culture, language, ethnic identity, and dream.

There were others who did not come by choice or with a dream for a better life. Prior to 1790 this included 300,000 people, who were forced sojourners brought from Africa to the shores of North America. These 300,000 were captured human beings forced into slavery, sold at auction, and transported from the African Continent through the Caribbean or directly to the United States. Upon arriving to the shores of North America they were once again sold to plantation owners, farmers, merchants, and individual families. The majority of these were brought from Africa through ports in Ghana and the Ivory Coast. According to information available from the Ellis Island American Family Immigration Center, the 875,000 pre-1790 migration consisted of 300,000 African, 300,000 English, 100,000 Scotch-Irish, 100,000 German, and 75,000 Scottish (The Peopling of America pre-1790, 2000).

Immigration was slow at first, but quickly and continually increased. A person living from the 1820's to the 1880's in the United States of America saw many changes. Life in the young country shifted drastically. Rapid change affected the lives of those living in the city and those immigrating to the United States. A historian could pick any of a number of reasons why American population exploded during this sixty-year period. The construction of the railroad, industrialization, modernization, and the California gold rush were all contributors.

The gate seemed to open even wider from 1880 to 1930. People came, and they came from everywhere. They filled New York and the multi-ethnic city formed with people from all over the world. It was as if the whole world was coming to America.

"And for millions of immigrants, New York provided opportunity. In Lower New York, one could find the whole world in a single Neighborhood" (The Peopling of America 1880-1930, 2000)

Millions of people entered the United States through Ellis Island during this period of history. Immigrants from all over the world lived and worked side by side in labor-intensive jobs throughout New York City. Others traveled to various places in America in order to find work.

People came to the United States of America to find work, create a new life, and fulfill their dreams. They often found difficulty, adversity, and their dreams slipping through their fingers like sand. Yet they came, they continued coming, and they continue to arrive today. Even with Europeans not coming to America like they once did, we see new people groups arriving who are seeking the *"American Dream"* today. Present immigration levels include both documented and undocumented persons. People are coming through the legal citizenship process, while others swim across the Rio Grande, or cross the Canadian border illegally. Still others arrive with a visitor's visa and remain beyond their visa expiration date.

According to Migration World Magazine, in 1970 9.6 million people, 4.7 percent of the population, living in the United States were foreign born. By 1990 19.8 million people or 7.9 percent of the population were foreign born. In the year 2000 this figure had grown to 28.4 million or 10.4 percent of the population of the United States were foreign born (Tomasi 2001, 12). <u>Migration World</u> also quotes the <u>New York Times</u> in its chart showing the amount of immigrants admitted to the United States in 1998: 90,000 from Europe, 220,000 from Asia and Oceania, 40,000 from Africa, 50,000 from South America, and 260,000 from North America. Immigrants, transnational Americans, sojourners, settlers, legal, illegal, documented, or undocumented: regardless of label and title they are assigned, people continue to come to this country by the thousands.

Historically the immigration process thrives in the city. However, many new immigrants are now settling in suburbs, edge cities, and rural areas of America (Appendix 1). People are moving into the United States and migrating to small town America. They are migrating to work in meat packing plants in Kansas and Iowa. They are moving to Henderson, Kentucky to process chickens at the Tyson Chicken Plant. Eight years ago Henderson, Kentucky was a rural river city on the border of Indiana and Kentucky with a majority Anglo, and minority Black American population. Today Henderson has a high percentage of new Latino immigrant residents. Nearby Sebree, Kentucky has also transitioned into a largely Latino populated community.

Dalton, Georgia, another rural American community, has been a major employer as the carpet mill capital of the world for many years. It has been a southern rural town with a large Anglo-American population. Today Dalton has a population that is 40% Hispanic (Tumulty 2001, 74). Many Mexican people have moved to Dalton to work in the carpet mills. Along with this migration of workers has come an entire infrastructure of Mexican culture.

The June 11, 2001 issue of Time Magazine was a special issue that focused on the migration process from Mexico to the United States, and the United States to Mexico. The front cover was titled "*Welcome to Amexica*". The articles inside describe border towns on the Mexican – American border, the movement of Mexican people across the border, and the new trend of American citizens retiring to Mexico. The largest minority group in the United States today is the Latino minority group (Tumulty 2001, 74). This impacts the political atmosphere of both America and Mexico. In fact future elections within the United States may be decided by the Latino vote.

Mission

This new world, which exists here in America, is in need of people to physically move among people and become missionaries to them. In 1992 our family moved to Chicago with a vision to communicate the gospel with the world through communicating the gospel among the culturally diverse population of Chicago – thus – reaching the world through reaching Chicago. We were focused on bringing the gospel to people of every ethnicity, discipling them, and praying that some would sense a call to go into ministry. Our prayer was that God would send these discipled people throughout the world with his message. We prayed that our ministry effort would have global impact through reaching people who were living in the city in the same manner that Paul's ministry affected all of Asia (Acts 19:10) when he engaged the society of Ephesus with the discussion of the gospel.

People from every culture group live in large cities and metro-politan areas. There is a great need for a missionary effort from those few who will dare to build bridges, cross rivers and attempt to reach all people living in these communities. Our world has come together, and for the first time since the world was dispersed at the tower of Babel we have the opportunity to reach the world through reaching the representation of the world living next door. In order to reach our culturally diverse population we must understand our cities, understand how these cities developed into these large masses of population, and where the population of these cities came from. We have a world of opportunity before us, and we can reach this world through reaching our community.

Bridging the gap between ethnicity, race, and nations remains one of the greatest challenges for the church in the twenty-first century. Although some have made attempts to build bridges between culture and ethnic groups and cross what are often seemingly un-crossable rivers of indifference, racism, and ethnocentrism the fact remains that Sunday is the most segregated period of time each week in American society (Dawson 1994, 130). This gap between cultures is obviously a negative reality the church must deal with. Recognition of this reality may open up the opportunity for the body of Christ to build bridges across culture, color, and language barriers reconciling people to God and one another through the presence of Jesus Christ in their lives. Since we find culture groups representing the whole world's population existing in the United States, our mission focus must include all of the people in these groups. This focus to reach the world through reaching the population living in one city is true throughout the world. Our mission focus must include every culture and ethnicity living in our community, and in every city (Bakke 1987, 133).

People move throughout the world in more ways and more often than ever before in history. In this movement of people there are opportunities for commerce, communication, and business like never before experienced. There are also great opportunities for the church – those people who follow Jesus Christ to accomplish their work – their assignment – the mission of God in the world.

The church has a divine assignment to do mission – the sharing of the gospel message with people who have yet to hear, understand, or accept Jesus Christ as their Lord, Savior, and friend. Many un-reached groups of people continue to exist in our global, mobile communities today. These un-reached people are people who do not know enough about the Gospel of Jesus Christ to make a reason-able decision whether they are to accept him or reject him. People from these un-reached groups are among those who have migrated to urban areas throughout the world including North America, Europe, and every other continent. Couple with this fact the reality that in a country like the United States the majority of people no longer attend church. In fact, we in the United States now have the first generation in existence since the nation's inception that have grown up, for the most part, "un-churched", having children of their own. These children are also "un-churched" in this, possibly, the most Christianized country in the history of the world. America has evolved from modern society to post-Modern / post Christian society and is now pre-Christian. Today America is the 3rd largest mission field in the world, and 2nd largest mission field in the Western Hemisphere (Sweet 1999, 50). Europe faces even greater challenges and opportunities having made shifts from post-Christian to pre-Christian long ago.

Unfortunately, there are many people who look at the world around them with a *"them and us"* mentality. Each group often stays within their group in order not to interfere with another group, or step out of their comfort zone. Fear keeps us from accepting the mission of God and fulfilling His Scriptural mandate to love one another. It keeps us from crossing any barrier of culture, class, ethnicity, race, or religious belief. The barriers existing in our society are not unknown to the church, and often keep Christian people separated by great distances from the communities in which they live. Many times these distances seem to be impossible to cross, and approaching these vast expanses between the church and the society is challenging. However, we as people who are called to mission by God need to develop ways to break down the barriers and build bridges of relationship that help us cross from our life world into the life world of another. The challenge of crossing the barriers and distances of culture and ethnicity, meeting new people, and talking with un-churched people can be uncomfortable, like crossing a great river that has no bridge. However, the need is present for Christian people to look at the community and build bridges of relationship across rivers of class, culture, and ethnicity. We must become like the sons of Isaachar, *"The Sons of Isaachar understood the times and knew what Israel should do"* (1 Chr 12:32). We must understand our times, understand what groups compose our community today, learn their culture, and realize our mission is to reach all of the people of every culture and ethnicity living in the communities where we live. The church is commissioned to be incarnational in the way Jesus was incarnational. The church is commissioned to live among the people in the community – commissioned to be *"missional"*.

The greatest inhibitors of crossing cultural barriers, breaking down racial walls, and building relationships with people come from fear, prejudice, preconceived notions, our childhood development, racism, and ethnocentrism. These inhibitors are rooted in a lack of understanding of how to deal with the unknown, and many times a lack of will. In order to overcome inhibitions to building relationships with others we as the church need to find the will of God, then dig deeper within ourselves and find the fortitude to accomplish His will. His will must become our will. God's mission of bringing people (His creation) into relationship with Him must become our mission.

We are much like a pioneer adventurer exploring new lands, and coming to the edge of a tremendous river. The powerful river looms ominous before the explorer. He or she fears the river, and what lies beyond it. This fear comes from the unknown. The questions may be asked, can the river be crossed? And what is on the other side of the river? Many would rather stay behind and remain *"safe"* than risk crossing into unknown territory. This is especially true when crossing from one culture to another.

Christian people must accept the challenge to build bridges of relationship between and among people groups. In order to accomplish this task we will intentionally make allowance for Jesus Christ to create deep change within us. Deep change is taking the decisive steps to consciously change our way of doing business rather than accept the mediocrity and comfort of not doing anything about our current status as people – the church. To avoid deep change is to accept a slow terminal illness in the church that will end in death (Quinn 1996, 11). Deep change can only be accomplished through a commitment to surrender to God's will and faithfully follow Jesus Christ into the world. Leaders who experience deep change will, as Robert E. Quinn writes, *"Build the Bridge as they walk on it"* (Quinn 1996, 83). In a spiritually authentic way they will commit to follow God across rivers and over mountains without having been there before.

People in the U.S., as well as, other countries look around at the current diversity of culture in society and say to themselves, *"where did all of these people come from?"* Often feeling threatened, people have been crying out for legislation and reform to end or greatly change and limit immigration processes. In former Yugoslavia we find that cultural differences and ethnocentrism turned into war. The same is true for Bangledesh, Sommalia, Ruwanda, Sudan, Israel, Iraq, and other places on earth. As culturally and ethnically diverse populations continue to explode in urban areas throughout the world people continue to migrate to the United States making it one of the more culturally and ethnically diverse population areas around the globe. America is literally an immigrant nation which in the

21st century is continually becoming a culturally ethnically diverse global nation.

This diversity can be seen as a difficult situation both inside, and outside of the church. However, we must all ask what can possibly be done to bring about friendships between people, and how can we communicate and build relationships with our neighbors who are Korean, Mexican, Haitian, or Russian? We must ask ourselves the question, is our world a world of impossible difficulty or a world filled with the ultimate opportunity for communicating the Gospel message faster and more effectively than at any time in history? The answer to this question is that our culturally diverse world is a great opportunity for fulfilling our mission.

The body of Christ in globally diverse communities such as urban areas in Europe, the United States and other urban people centers throughout the world has this great opportunity before it to share the message of Christ with all people. Those who are born again having a salvation experience with God through His Son Jesus Christ should see the difficulties of the world from a different perspective than those who dwell in the world not knowing God. Those who walk with God do not see the world as a world of difficulty and strife, but as a world of opportunity. It is a world filled with potential from every business to every home. On every corner there is potential to accomplish the task that Jesus Christ commissioned Christians to fulfill. The Scripture is clear about our mission.

"Go therefore and make disciples of all the nations, baptizing them in the name of the Father and of the Son and of the Holy Spirit" (**Matt 28:19**).

You may ask the question: *"How is the world we live in a world filled with opportunity?"* The flow of people from one place in the world to another is quite possibly greater today than it has ever been in history. As the world population grows, millions of people have become 20th century, and now 21st century nomadic travelers. People have crossed borders and oceans traveling into the unknown worlds of other nations and cultures. Living in Chicago, New Jersey, and now California our family has interacted with and crossed the paths of people from many different ethnicity and culture groups. We have worked among and ministered to people from Romania, Bulgaria, Pakistan, India, Puerto Rico, Mexico, Korea, the Philippines, Haiti, and others from around the world. We came to realize in a vivid way that virtually the whole world has come to the shores of America. This realization was not necessarily brilliant. All we had to do was look around. People from all over the world live in this country. They work hard because they know their past (where they have come from), and they see the future (where they are going). They know they can work hard and do better for themselves than their parents or grandparents did for themselves. They are determined that they too will accomplish the *"American Dream"*, as so many have.

Moments

Perhaps something significant must be acknowledged in regard to the seasons, times, and moments throughout history that have been transformational in society. Perhaps God works in everyday life and in special moments throughout time to accomplish His will, purpose, and mission. I believe there are points in time that when seized offer momentum to fuel a cause in a powerful way.

"Moments carry the momentum of the past and fuel the momentum for the future"-Erwin McManus

Moments are points in time that are windows or doorways into the future. Joshua in the Old Testament experienced a moment in his life on two distinct occasions. The first when he was one of twelve spies who ventured into the land of promise to do surveillance and report back to the Hebrew children waiting in the wilderness (Numbers 13). Joshua and one of his fellow spies, Caleb, came with recommendations to the people that this was their moment to enter their favored future in the land God promised them as a people. However, the people refused for many and various reasons. They missed their moment! A second moment in Joshua's life happened after Moses had died. God communicated to Joshua that he was to lead the people into the land of promise (Joshua 1). Joshua could have refused. He could have said, *"I'm too old"*, but Joshua seized the moment in his life and became a catalyst leader in Israel's future.

Erwin McManus dedicates an entire book (Seizing Your Divine Moment) to the subject. Rick Warren writes about this concept in his book (Your Purpose Driven Life), and Joel Osteen writes in this same flow in his book (Your Best Life Now). There is significance to the words which each of these tremendous leaders have written. God gives us each at points of time in our lives (moments) opportunity to *"seize the day"* and experience the miraculous. This era in which we now breathe the air God created is just such a point in time. We are living in a special time – a special moment in which we as the people of God have a Divine opportunity to fulfill the mission of God on the earth.

Will we, the church, become the life giving ministry God intends? The world is a great place of ministry opportunity that confronts the body of Christ (the church) with an apparent decision opportunity. Will the church stay, move, live, or die? Will we seize our moments? This is a question that many, if not all congregations will ask in the lifespan of their existence. There have been more than a few times during the past years that I have been in conversation with pastors from established churches who are facing a situation in which they have made, or are making a decision to stay in their neighborhood, or move to another location. The unfortunate aspect of this dilemma is that the majority of the time their reasons for moving are directly associated with the type of people who are moving into the neighborhood.

In an effort to safeguard family, flock, and precious property investment the church sells out, moves to the suburb of choice, liquidates in order to build, beg to pay for, and borrow against the new property so they may have their perfect church in their perfect world. Meanwhile the community left behind in the dust of the church moving van wheels is still searching for hope. These churches unfortunately miss their moments to fulfill their destiny – **their mission**.

Many times it is evident that churches are no longer going to the world, but in efforts of safeguarding the congregation run from the world. It is a, *"Get out before it is to late"*, philosophy. These situations show the need for Scriptural realignment of our thinking in the Christian community. The church should take the leadership role influencing society. We should set the example for society based on Scripture becoming light in darkness.

The church has a history of avoiding issues that have given the process of fleeing communities both credence and affirmation. We find that many churches continue the practice of running from the very communities that are crying for help, love, acceptance, and hope. As our communities change the church migrates to that place where it can find a new happy unchanged environment. One slight problem that each church is facing today is the reality that there are fewer places to run, and a congregation may actually have to change the focus of ministry in order to survive. This is a good thing. It might seem like a crisis in the church, but crisis is often the catalyst for change.

One underlying difficulty that must be addressed within each one of us, in our ministries, and our churches is the mission conflict that many church attendees possess. Many people, ministries, and churches will state that their purpose for existing is to reach their community. There are those who will live and exist with a mission that says, *"We desire to love and reach our community with the gospel"*. However, when many churches say this they are making an untrue statement. A study of the history of a church in the community will often reveal that the church may say one thing, but actually practice something completely different. We will verbally commit to loving one another and loving our community. The sad reality though is that our actions and our church's actions often say to our community that we do not care what happens. It is far easier to watch the world go by and smell the flowers, than stop and deal with the challenges. Our communities' need the hope of Jesus Christ lived out in word and action through His people. There is a great need for a mission driven church movement to emerge.

Ministry Moments in Communities of Need

Chicago is the third largest city in the United States. It has a population today of 2.8 million residents, and many undocumented residents who are for the most part seldom counted in any census.

It has been said that the windy city has the largest Polish population outside of Poland, and is the second largest Polish city in the world. The first is Warsaw. Many cultures from all over the world reside in Chicago. This internationalization of Chicago is not a new phenomenon, but a continually emerging phenomenon. The people groups today who immigrate to Chicago are different than the ones who immigrated ten, twenty, and eighty years ago. However they continue to arrive for various reasons, and face the same challenges as those who came before them.

Chicago is faced with many problems in the same way most large metropolitan areas are. While living and ministering in Chicago our family worked with people from all walks of life. During this time we found many stories of human tragedy. One story that stuck with me, and compels me to challenge churches to be who they say they are, is a story about a wonderful Christian woman. I don't know her name, and I've never met her. I have only heard her story. A homeless man named James that we worked with on Lower Wacker Drive in Chicago told us about her. I had asked James if he belonged to a church or ever attended church. James' reply was difficult to hear, but it was real. James told me he used to go to a church when this woman would come in her van, pick him and some other homeless people up and bring them to her church. The homeless people would be reverent and worship in the church with the congregation. At the conclusion of the worship service this woman would return them back to life on the street. This process took place for about three weeks. On the fourth week James and the others were awake, and ready to go to church, but the woman never came. A few days later she showed up one last time, and explained to James that the people in the church asked that she not bring the homeless people to the church anymore. This church that preached about loving the hurting could not worship next to hurting homeless people. They could not love the least, last, and lost of society.

There are those churches that exist who love and truly show love. Their vision is real, and it lives in their church and community as they do real ministry touching real people with real problems in their community. One such church was located at the corner of Broadway and Foster in Chicago. Pastor Vic, the Senior Pastor, built a church through prayer and love that reached sixteen culture groups and people from every walk of life. One particular man that came to church each week was George. George was a homeless man. He would come to worship service, sit on the pew, and get warm in the winter or cool in the summer. Many times George would sleep through service however, the church loved him. One particular Sunday George showed up for Sunday-School. In fact, he made his way upstairs into the Teen Sunday School Class and sat down. The Sunday School Class had been studying foot-washing, and on this day the teacher planned for the class to do what Jesus did and wash one another's feet. They were in this process when George came in and sat down. George took off his shoes to get his feet washed. Now, you can imagine what a class of teenagers thought at this moment. Well, imagine what people in your Sunday School Class would think, and do in this situation. Pastor Vic happened to walk into the class when all of this was happening. Without a second thought, he went over to George and knelt down. He had the teacher bring a pail of water and a towel. Pastor Vic washed George's feet that day. They had to change the water two or three time because of the dirt, but the pastor didn't care how dirty George's feet were. He loved George with the compassion of Jesus Christ.

In order for a church to become what God desires, it must be willing to go where God sends it, remain where God puts it, and love those who God sends in the midst of it. In essence, to believe something is wonderful, but that belief has no power until we do something about it. Belief alone is powerless. Even the Gospel cannot save the world without someone to profess the Gospel. Think about the church that has written on its sign, "we love our community", but when the homeless man comes by, they send him away hungry. There may even be some pious person in the congregation that is able to keep the hurting person away from the pastor because he or she is preparing to deliver a message from God, or keep them from the congregation that is preparing to receive what God has for them. This scene is too familiar in too many churches. It is also sad.

As a congregation learns about the community, and studies the history of the community and the church, the congregation will be confronted with the issues of previous failure, success, and future strategy. Questions will need to be asked, and answers will have to be found. The congregation will have to decide why they exist, who they are, and who they desire to become. Each church should examine its mission, vision, and values. They must understand themselves in order to become who God wants them to become. The church faced with community change needs to understand they will have to change in many ways to reach all of the people in their community with the message of Jesus Christ.

Compassion inspired by the passion of the cross experience of individuals and congregations can inspire the desire within these people to seize each opportunity they have to follow God's plan for humanity. The fact is that congregations can effectively communicate the gospel message to all people of all ethnicities and cultures living within their community. This task can be accomplished through the congregation developing ministries that reach all people, and learning principles and strategies for building bridges of relationship among all people of every culture and ethnic group living within their community and life world.

This book is a resource for Christians living within and ministering among the ethnically and culturally diverse community to use for gaining a better understanding of how to connect with people in relationship in order to reach them with the gospel. It is my primary objective to put into your hands usable tools that are easily understood and implemented in order for you as a Christian, ministry leader, pastor or church planter to accomplish this task. Effectively reaching all people living in the culturally diverse community is possible. Church leaders, church planters and people can be equipped to empower and lead churches to accomplish this task by ministering to people in ways that meet their whole life needs. The greatest measure of success in accomplishing this task is that people from every ethnicity and culture existing within the community receive Jesus Christ as personal Lord and Savior, becoming disciples, and sharing Jesus with others.

The text begins by focusing on the theological significance of proclaiming the good news to all people by pointing to the fact that God's mission in the world is to bring all people into relationship with him. With a theological foundation established the text highlights the fact that it is God's will that churches grow, illustrates a viable plan for developing multicultural life giving churches, and tools of historical and demographic research for the purpose of growing churches. Chapter five talks about relationship and introduces the concept of building bridges from people to people. This concept includes five relationship bridges Christians existing in culturally diverse environments can continually work toward building. These bridges include:

1. A bridge from the churched world to the un-churched world
2. A bridge from the believer to the unbeliever
3. A bridge from culture/people group to culture/people group
4. A bridge from belief system to belief system
5. A bridge from person to person

Chapter six reflects on the fact that communication is a key to successful presentation of the gospel to people. Developing communication, observation, and relationship skills will help Christian people to reach beyond knowing who lives in their community to knowing the people in their community. Chapter seven focuses on developing a viable vision strategy for a church congregation. Chapter eight directly addresses leadership with an emphasis on development of people into leaders who are indigenous to the community or culture group. Chapter nine is a summation focusing on the fact that multi-cultural church ministry is possible, necessary, and Biblical. We must understand our times, understand what groups compose our community today, and realize our mission is to reach all people.

2

REACHING THE NATIONS:

FULFILLING THE MISSION OF GOD BY FULFILLING GOSPEL MISSION WITHIN CULTURALLY DIVERSE COMMUNITIES

A ny theological understanding of the city and especially the culturally diverse community must begin and end with the fact that it is God's desire to bring the people of all nations who live on the earth into relationship with Him. Reaching these communities provides tremendous opportunities to evangelize the world's population. This opportunity to evangelize the world through evangelizing the culturally diverse community is a strategy of reaching all people based on Paul's work as a missionary. Especially significant to this strategic thinking is the scriptural witness in Acts 19:10 of Paul's work in Ephesus being the means by which all areas of Asia heard the gospel. The church existing in or being planted in the culturally diverse community can greatly facilitate the fulfillment of

God's plan to reach the nations by reaching the people of the nations living in their community, preparing, and then sending those who are motivated by God to go into all of the world. These churches need to conceptualize the fact that God does indeed desire to reach the nations (Gen 12:3), and they are God's most strategically placed vehicle for making His desire reality.

God has established His plan through covenant with Abraham making Israel a nation to reach the nations. He has secured His plan of salvation for all people through His only son Jesus Christ life, death, resurrection, and Jesus' establishing the nation of God as the nation of all nations. He has finalized His plan to reach the nations in establishing the church as the catalyst of His hand in the world proclaiming the good news of Jesus Christ to all nations, thus building the nation of God. It is on the foundation of this understanding that the strategic implementation of the mission of God to reach the nations through evangelizing the culturally diverse community is developed.

Reaching the nations

The single powerful thread that weaves through time as the primary theme in the history of the world is the fact that God desires to reach all people of all nations. This is God's mission in the world. Since the fall of Adam and Eve in the garden (Gen 3:6-7) God has masterfully worked to make His mission to bring people into relationship with Him reality. In fact the Bible epic highlights events that occur as a witness of God working out His plan to reach the nations and also gives examples of strategic ministry that we may endeavor at doing in order to accomplish this task. God has placed and continues to place people on divine pathways where they may choose to fulfill their destiny and thus fulfill His plan. It is evident from the pathways of the people of God that His plan to connect with all (Gen 12:1-3) and bless all "ethnic and national groupings" of the earth (Holladay 1988, 221) has been fleshed out in history and continues to be fleshed out as the people of God step forward by faith in the same manner as Abraham (Heb11:8-10) accomplishing God's will now and in the future. In the Old Testament redeeming the nations begins with God's covenant with Abraham.

Covenant with Abraham

God began strategically reaching the nations with the covenant He made with Abraham (Glasser and McGavran 1983, 33). After being in Egypt during a famine, Abraham travels north into the area he had camped in after originally migrating from Ur. Bietzel describes this area as being near Bethel and AI (Bietzel 1985, 92), the Zondervan Pictorial Encyclopedia of the Bible Vol. I edited by Merrill Tenney describes this place as the Negev or South Country (Tenney 1976, 1:21). The Place Abraham returns to is a place he had been to before. The covenant itself is recorded in Genesis Chapter twelve verses one through three:

> "Now the Lord had said to Abram, Go forth from your country, and from your relatives and from your father's house, to the land which I will show you: And I will make you a great nation, and I will bless you, and make your name great; and so you shall be a blessing; and I will bless those who bless you, and the one who curses you I will curse. And in you all the families of the earth shall be blessed (Gen 12:1-3)."

The covenant is referred to, and affirmed by God in Genesis 15:5 and 13-21, 18:17-19, and 22:17-18.

Abraham's life was renewed by faith in God, and through him God made a promise of a great nation, and great blessings for his people. The people of Abraham were the people of God placed on the earth to bring others into relationship with Him (Costas 1995, 27). They were a nation designed to reach the nations (Gen 12:3). The importance of Abraham in the fulfillment of God's plan is clearly evidenced in scripture. He is mentioned more than forty times in the Old Testament and more than seventy times in the New Testament (Tenney 1976, 1:21).

In the scripture text of the Old Testament and New Testament the plan of God to reach the nations is fleshed out as God's people struggle with their faith, the practice of their faith, and their mission from God. In the account of Jonah we find a man being sent by God to the city of Nineveh who did not want to go there. God called Jonah to preach His message of repentance from sin in Nineveh. Jonah ran from the city because of his own personal issues, which included ethnocentrism, fear, and pride (Jonah 1:1-3). Many times throughout history the church has been influenced by the same issues Jonah was influenced by. Jonah churches have fled neighborhoods, cities, and geographical areas based on the skin color of people, their fear of people who are different than them, and their inability to intentionally love people who have not achieved the same socio-economic status as them in life. God needs Jonah churches to become Jesus churches in society loving the poor, the broken, the outcast, and most of all proclaiming the gospel message to all people.

Nineveh was not an isolated city. God had compassion on other cities and nations throughout the Old Testament. He spared judgment on Sodom for a time after Abraham petitioned Him to help the people of Sodom by allowing any who might be righteous in Sodom to leave the wicked sinfulness of Sodom's society prior to the destruction that was imminent (Gen 18:22). God blessed Persia through Daniel, Egypt through Joseph (Gen 41:53-57), saved His people through Esther in Persia (Esth 8:8-17), and then encouraged the nation of Israel to bless Babylon the city of their captivity as recorded in Jeremiah by planting gardens, allowing their children to marry Babylonian children, building homes, and praying for the peace of the city (Jer 29:5-9). God continuously showed His love for the nations as He often spared life, and as He sent the nation of Israel to the nations to bless them by bringing them to Him. His work through the nation of Israel flows through history from Abraham to Jesus, and then to the crucifixion-resurrection event. It is this point in time that God's plan to redeem the nations becomes a viable reality. It is a viable reality because of the incarnation of God through Jesus Christ being born into the world (Phil chapter 2). In Jesus Christ the possibility to accomplish what could not be accomplished primarily through the flesh of humanity alone becomes reality.

Redemption for all nations

Continually throughout scripture it is clear that God was working through the nation of Israel (the offspring of Abraham) to reach the nations (Costas 1995, 27). His effort to reach the nations leads through the pathway of time to the cross. It is the cross that represents the ultimate plan for the redemption of humankind. Through Jesus Christ the covenant made with Abraham is completed and renewed in the ultimate action of God rewriting the citizenship requirements for entry into His nation. The new membership criteria are concerned with the heart, and centered on having a right relationship with God through knowing Jesus Christ as personal Lord and Savior (John 3:16). Under the new requirements the nation of God is not only a nation reaching other nations, but is a nation made of all nations unified together by the single unifying factor of relationship with Jesus Christ, the Messiah. It is in Jesus Christ that unity of culturally diverse sinful humanity is possible.

"The fallen condition of the human race was so acute and the need for redemption so great that only the incarnation of God and the atonement of the cross could avail to provide for the salvation of His people (Glasser and McGavran 1983, 37)."

It is in Jesus Christ, who is the central figure of all of history, that God is building a nation of all nations, a people of all peoples, and a family of all families. In the nation of God every culture, language, and person can be seen.

In fact, Jesus was multi-cultural in His lineage cited by Mathew (1:1-6). In His divinity He was fully God. In His humanity he represented the whole of the human experience in that His human genetic code was multi-cultural. The lineage of Jesus Christ (Matt 1:1-6) included Rahab from Jericho, Ruth the Moabite woman, and Bathsheba the Hittite (Bakke 1997, 121-126). God in His infinite wisdom worked with the whole of humanity through His only son Jesus to reach the whole of humanity (all people). God's nation is a movement of all people who call Jesus Christ Lord. It is this nation of all nations that is painted by scripture in the glimpse of the future shown in Revelation 7:9-10.

The church: the hand of God in the world

The nation building effort of God's nation redeemed through the presence of Jesus Christ is commissioned to the church. In establishing the church, Jesus assigned the Divine mission of God to the church, *"To go into all of the world and make disciples"* (Matt 28:19). He then promised Divine authority and power for the church to accomplish His mission in the person of the Holy Spirit (Acts 1:8). God's hand is present in the establishment of His church as the catalyst to reach the nations with the message that eternal salvation is possible through knowing Jesus Christ.

It seems that often in the history of the church society has influenced the church more than the church has influenced society. One of the saddest realities of societal influence on the church in the 20th and now 21st century is the evangelical church's failure to do justice, and the Ecumenical church's failure to maintain the infallibility of scripture including the fact that salvation is only possible through knowing Jesus Christ as personal savior (John 14:6). A failure to hold to the whole truth of the gospel has resulted in a distinct division of theological thinking between ecumenical churches, and evangelical churches.

A Well Balanced Theology of Ministry

It is in the light of the whole text of scripture that well balanced theology of ministry is established. It is ministry that touches the whole life of individuals. A well balanced theology of ministry holds the fact that Jesus Christ is the only way a person can receive salvation as its primary basis. However, well balanced theology includes the facts that God loves all people, cares for the life situation of people, and is interested in them as whole persons. It is theology birthed in the compassion of Christ, and the compassion of Christ involves helping people. J. Paul Landry writes,

"Social action is integral to the mission of evangelism. As Jesus went about doing good (such as healing the sick and feeding the hungry) and preaching the kingdom, he did not label one as spiritual and the other as temporal. There was no establishing priorities or polarizing them. All his words and works were essential to his ministry to humankind's total well-being. If the church is true to its calling it will emulate the ministry of Christ when he was here on earth. Like his, our ministry is to be a full-orbed and concrete expression of love and service to persons (Balda 1984, 54)."

It is vital to the transformation of people that the church develop ministry that ministers to the spiritual and physical needs of all people (Greenway and Monsma 1989, 175).

New thinking has emerged among many evangelical churches. Many evangelical churches are becoming interested, and motivated to help people with their life needs as well as their spiritual needs. Many churches have awakened to the fact that ministry involves more than verbal message, and actions of compassion often speak louder than words.

The mission of God is to bring sinful humanity into relationship with Him through knowing His son Jesus Christ as personal Savior. The primary work of the church is to carry out the mission of God by proclaiming the gospel to all people. Along with the primary goal of proclaiming the mission of God that all people be saved is the fact that God cares for the whole person of humanity and therefore it is important that the church also care for people and minister to them completely.

If all the church does is preach the gospel then it is living half of the gospel. God called people to first live for Him. Therefore it is the responsibility of the church to live the gospel and living the gospel means being God's presence in the world fulfilling His mission of bringing all people to Him in relationship and also feeding the poor, and healing the brokenhearted. The theology of the church must be compassion driven and well balanced. Well balanced theology of mission always has the primary goal of bringing people into relationship with Jesus Christ.

A Biblical Vision for Ministry in the Culturally Diverse Community

Understanding the opportunity of the multi-cultural church begins with understanding God's compassion for all people, the city, and the culturally diverse community. God is in the people business. He loves people. There is evidence in history and scripture of his love for people, cities, and communities. He cares and therefore the church that is fulfilling His mission will care.

God's compassion for people

Each person who is born is made in the image of God. Creation of human beings began with God forming Adam in His image (Gen 1:26). According to Anthony Hoekema this is the "most distinctive feature of the biblical understanding of man" (Hoekema 1986, 17). God created humankind in His image, and fellowshipped with Adam and Eve each day in the garden (Gen 3:8). God loved the relationship He had with humanity; He loved humanity. They were his creation, and perhaps after Adam and Eve committed sin God grieved tremendously because their relationship had been severed by sin. God loved humanity so much He planned for their redemption in spite of their sin.

> "Because of his fall into sin, man has in one sense lost the image of God (some theologians call this the narrower or functional sense). Instead of serving and obeying God, man is now turned away from God; he is 'man in revolt'. In the work of redemption God graciously restores his image in man, making him once again like God in his love, faithfulness, and willingness to serve others. Because human beings are creatures, God must restore them to his image-this is a work of sovereign grace. But because they are also persons, they have a responsibility in this restoration-hence Paul can say to the Ephesians, 'Be imitators of God'(5:1) (Hoekema 1986, 10)."

The *Imagio Dei* is powerful in that human beings are not God but are created in His image and through Jesus Christ they can have relationship with God.

It is in the cross-compassion of Jesus Christ that enmity between people is abolished. Intentionally coming together in relationship through Jesus is to affirm the reconciliation power of what Jesus did for mankind. It is this reconciliation power that is the cornerstone of successful ministry in the culturally diverse community.

Developing multi-cultural life giving churches exemplifies the work of Jesus Christ in its fullest. It is a testimony of the salvation, and transformation power of Jesus Christ. Paul believed in the multi-cultural church. In fact Rod Cooper states,

> "The apostle Paul, in all of his missionary journeys, did not plant one homogeneous church. These churches were made up for poor, rich, young, old, and ethnically diverse people (Perry ed. 2002, 155)."

The multi-cultural church of the New Testament included all people. They worshipped
the risen Christ together in unity (Bakke 1997, 140). It is this ministry endeavor that exemplifies God's love for people living in the culturally diverse community like no other church ministry. When people of all cultures worship together it is powerful in that it truly reveals God's compassion for people.

God's Compassion for the City

God loves people and most people live in or around large cities. Today cities have exploded into city centers, edge city, and suburbs. There is little distinction between cities in leaving one and entering another. It is vital to the success of Christianity for the church to minister to the urban community. This must take place with the biblical mandate for urban ministry as a driving force. The compassion of Christ is the motivator behind this type of ministry.

The city is an important element in society that is full of life. This is due to the individuals, groups, processes, businesses, and other activities that take place every second of every day in the city. We associate the city with many things; such as government, business, crime, danger, wealth, poverty, and fast paced lifestyle. As we come to the realization that there is a tremendous amount of activity that takes place in the urban area we may begin to understand the great potential for ministry in every area of the city. People of every ethnicity, and culture live and work in and around the city. Ministry from the richest person to the poorest, regardless of race or cultural heritage, centralized in ministry centers located in every metropolitan statistical area in the world can be the greatest force of evangelism in the world in this century.

Society is in a dilemma in handling, and effectively dealing with the issues of life present in cities. The answer for the city is the practical and spiritual ministry of Christ's love. God has concern for the city. The word city is in the Bible (RSV) 1,227 times (Dubose 1978, 101). David Claerbaut states that there is a biblical mandate for urban ministry (Claerbaut 1983, 17 and 18), and it is important that the church embrace this mandate.

In the preface of his book, Urban Ministry, David Clarebaut quotes Amos Hawley's definition of a city.

"The city is a 'Permanent, relatively densely settled and administratively defined unit of territory, the residents of which gain their living primarily by specializing in a variety of non-agricultural activities (Claerbaut 1983, 12)."

In scripture we see the city as a place of evil and a place of good. The reason the city is a sinful place is because the world is full of broken people who exist in a sinful state. As long as there are broken people in the world there will be broken cities. People need to receive redemption from their sin and be lifted out of the effects of sin in their lives. In this same manner cities need to receive redemption from their brokenness, and be lifted out of the effects of sin. In Babel we see man's attempt to become like God. This attempt is birthed in the sinful desire of man to be great (Gen 11). In Jerusalem, Ephesus, and Corinth we see God working through people to reach people with His plan of redemption in order that people would have the opportunity to have relationship with Him.

It is the responsibility of the Body of Christ (the church) to pray for the peace of the city, and work toward the redemption of the city by transforming people one person at a time. It is the hope of the believer that one day there will be a new city (Linthicum 1991, 192). This hope is the great motivator for Christian people doing ministry in this broken world. The City of God is a place that will be, but is not yet a reality. Therefore it should be the goal of ministry in urban environments to transform the fiber of the city (Jer 31) by changing lives. Changing lives in this regard is taking people from the darkness of sin to the freedom of Christ through knowing Jesus Christ who willingly gave His life so that this would be possible (John 3:16).

This transformation takes place one life at a time. The challenge of the church in the city is life redemption that results in redemption of the city, its structures, practice, and life systems (Linthicum 1991, 192). Scripture is clear that we are to love the poor and feed the hungry. Jesus read Isaiah chapter 61 with authority in Luke chapter 4:18-19. Jesus spoke with authority because He came with authority, and did the very things that Isaiah 61 states. He set free the captive, gave sight to the blind, and made the lame to walk. We must live in our communities with the presence of God in our lives and walk in the authority of God setting captive people free through the life changing power of His presence.

God's compassion for the culturally diverse community

The fact that God desires that all people be reached and that He is so serious about reaching the people of the earth that He sent His only Son to die a brutal death on a cross should be the single most definable factor as to why churches should develop theology based on scripture that is intentionally focused on bringing all people in their community to conversion opportunities. A theological strategy that has as its primary focus reaching the people of all nations living in the North American context must be built on the foundation of the history of God's work in the world, and drawn from the biblical text. This biblical theology as previously noted has as its core value the fact that God desires to reach the nations. God's desire to reach the nations is seen in God's covenant with Abraham, the birth, life, death, and resurrection of Jesus Christ and the establishment of the New Testament Church which is building the nation of God (Glasser and McGavran 1983, 104).

In North American culturally diverse communities reaching all nations means reaching all cultures living in these culturally diverse communities with the gospel of Jesus Christ that brings heart change as well as life change. The multi-cultural church is a biblical model of ministry in which the compassion of Jesus Christ and the commission of Jesus Christ intersect. The compassion of Christ in people crosses the barriers of culture and race through His reconciliation power. His reconciliation power is the only power that makes unity in diversity possible among people.

"There is no argument that evangelism is one of the key purposes of the church. Yet the very nature and impact of the church upon society is evidenced in the church's ability to do something society cannot do, namely have unity in the midst of diversity. Jesus emphasized this unity in John 17 and John 13:34-35 (Perry ed.2002, 154)."

There are some who misrepresent Scripture to justify segregation, and diminish the possibility of multi-cultural ministry. Yet there is no Scripture taken in the context of the whole text of scripture that provides reasonable evidence for such justification.

"The New Testament gives no evidence that the church focused on a homogeneous mentality of establishing churches according to people groups. Instead, the principle was that of the heterogeneity. The word heterogeneous means 'consisting of dissimilar or diverse ingredients or constituents; mixed' according to Webster's Dictionary (Perry ed. 2002, 155)."

Jerusalem

People who were Jewish were not necessarily the same ethnicity, they did not speak the same language, nor did they all live in the same places. They were scattered throughout the geographic regions from Jerusalem to Rome. This is evidenced in the Acts chapter 2 experience in Jerusalem where Jewish people who were, "Parthians and Medes and Elamites, and residents of Mesopotamia, Judea and Cappadocia, Pontus and Asia, Phyrgia and Pamphylia, Egypt and the districts of Libya around Cyrene, and visitors from Rome, both Jews and proselytes, Cretans and Arabs (Acts 2:9-11)" were present. (Balda 1984, 32). Jesus proclaimed a vision that included taking the gospel to people in Jerusalem, Judea, Samaria, and throughout the world in Mathew 28:19 and in Acts chapter 2 we see the presence of the Holy Spirit move among those gathered on a rooftop in Jerusalem so obvious that in the vicinity around the building people were greatly impacted. The New Testament church was birthed in the midst of the culturally diverse community (Bakke 1997, 139). It is therefore unreasonable to limit the presence of God's power by targeting one culture group in a community where more than one culture group is present. God desires to reach all people and has commissioned the church to fulfill this task. In fact, look at Paul. He was consistently developing church ministry that crossed cultural boundaries.

"The apostle Paul, in all of his missionary journeys, did not plant one homogeneous church. These churches were made up for poor, rich, young, old, and ethnically diverse people (Perry ed. 2002, 155)."

The Bible gives clear examples of ministry that exemplify the presence of Christ among diverse people bringing them together in unity and sharing His compassion with the world as people accept His commission. These examples represent the working of God's plan to reach the nations by reaching local communities through which there is global impact. The reality of Scripture is that God loves all people and desires that all people be saved. He desires to reach the culturally diverse community with His gospel and He works through the community to reach the world (Perry ed. 2002, 114).

It is in the culturally diverse community that the multi-cultural church becomes a possibility. God's compassion for humanity includes all people being saved, transformed, and walking in the light of Scripture. This is Christian community exemplifying the diversity of man connected together through the power of Jesus Christ in unity. God loves all people (May 1990, 96). It is the will of God, 'That none should perish'. The people of God include all people from every culture who accept Jesus Christ as personal Lord and Savior (May 1990, 88).

Salvation – Salvation is through the work of Jesus Christ on the cross (Morris 1992, 56). The salvation experience of an individual happens as an event in their life. This salvation event takes place at a particular point in time. Salvation is not a process but the point in the life of a person where they acknowledge, accept, and receive the grace of God through the presence of Jesus Christ in their life. It is the acceptance of Jesus Christ that provides grace for the individual through the work that was completed in the life, death, and resurrection of Jesus Christ (Stott [1958] 1971, 90-91). God's compassion for people is evident in His willingness to send His only Son Jesus to make salvation possible (John 3:16). It is salvation that provides the opportunity for people to have relationship with God that was made impossible by the sin of Adam in the garden, but is now possible because of the blood of Jesus Christ that was shed in order to cover sin. It is the event of salvation that provides redemption from sin (Morris 1990, 150).

It is God's plan that His people bring people to Him through proclamation of the gospel; thus bringing salvation to people. It is having the passion of Jesus Christ that compels the people of God to action in which they attempt to prevent people from hell (an eternity without God). Tomlinson writes,

> "When we fully realize the value of souls, the awfulness of hell, and have attained such a love for Jesus that His words will sink into our hearts like stones into water, then and not until then will we really awake to the full responsibility that is now resting heavy upon us. We are so slow! Millions are dropping into hell that could have been rescued while we are studying and planning what to do (Tomlinson 1984, 42)."

God works with people by working through people to communicate to people (Morris 1990, 56). It is His plan that all receive salvation, and people will not hear about Jesus unless someone tells them about Him. The plan of salvation is accomplished by people sharing Jesus with people, and those people receiving Him.

Life Transformation – God's compassion does not end with salvation. His compassion extends beyond salvation in the lives of people (Greenway and Monsma 1989, 175). Jesus healed the blind, sick, and lame. He transforms the lives of people, spiritually, and physically. Transformation is the process of people being lifted by the power of the Holy Spirit and through the action of the local church in the community. Understanding life transformation is primary to understanding God's compassion for people. The Christian religion in its true fulfillment of scripture and representation of Jesus has a twofold goal, 1. bring people to the cross, and 2. transform them into people who represent Jesus in this world (Balda 1984, 23).

Transformation of the individual is both a point and a process. It begins in the life of the individual at the point of salvation, and continues after salvation with the process of the individual continually striving to become like Jesus Christ. This process of becoming like Jesus Christ is not intended to be a lonely process accomplished by individuals by themselves but it is in fact accomplished within the community of believers. The church (body of believers) is to become life transformers of individuals and the community (Balda 1984, 54). The church is called to love one another (John 14) and be a representation of the power and presence of the compassion of Christ. It is important to note that personal transformation leads to community transformation.

Community Transformation – The greatest testimony of community transformation in the culturally diverse community happens when the church congregation represents the community and is worshipping together in the unity of Jesus Christ (Perry ed. 2002, 111)." Community is important to the Christian believer's process of becoming like Jesus. Christian community within the culturally diverse context exemplifies the compassion of God for all people (Greenway and Monsma 1989, 22). The gospel liberates people from sin and liberated people live like they are liberated. They no longer act like they once did. As the people of God Christians have the divine opportunity to live in community relationship that can not be understood by people who are not Christians (Lingenfelter 1998, 17). John Stott states that unity in Christ is where, "Men remain men, women remain women, Jews remain Jews, and Gentiles remain Gentiles. But inequality before God is abolished. There is a new unity in Christ (Stott 1979, 102)."

Fulfilling the mission of God through reaching the culturally diverse community

Today in North America we live in a culturally diverse society. The European Anglo descendent population of the United States is becoming less and less of a majority. The diversity of American society is in fact a reflection of world population. The cities of North America reflect the foreign mission fields. It is exciting to think about the possibilities of evangelization among many people groups and cultures in the cities across North America. Our ethnically and culturally diverse communities are places of great evangelism opportunity. Reaching people groups who live in these communities can also be a strategic key to reaching the world.

Those persons who believe mission exists only outside the boundaries of North America accept a model of mission which fails to minister to people next door and especially those in large urban areas. Sending missionaries from America throughout the world has worked effectively in the evangelization of the world. Many churches have experienced phenomenal growth outside of the United States, and Christianity is truly reaching every area of the globe in a powerful way. Although this is the case it is interesting that the church sends a missionary to an airport located in a culturally diverse megalopolis within the United States to fly somewhere that he or she does not know the language, culture, context, and many times can not legally go in order to proclaim the gospel. Is it possible that there is a strategy, which is biblically based, and often overlooked that includes reaching the world through reaching the culturally diverse community?

Perhaps, God utilized the diverse peopling of the North American Continent to establish the Ephesus of the modern world. It is in this new diverse world that many cultures of the world have come to be represented in its population, and the gospel is freely preached. It is quite possible that these diverse population centers are vital to the completion of God's mission. Paul reached out to people in the cities he traveled to and in which he lived. He witnessed people who were immigrants, citizens, and travelers receive Jesus Christ and share their faith. He was aware of the significance of effective evangelism within diverse population centers and we have opportunities to follow his leadership path in pursuing the strategic evangelism of people living in these communities today.

Onesimus is an account of one such immigrant person in scripture. Onesimus the runaway slave of Philemon finds his way to the city. While in the city Onesimus meets Paul, is introduced to Jesus Christ, and accepts Jesus as personal savior. Paul then sends Onesimus back to Philemon and encourages Philemon that Onesimus will be of benefit to the entire community because he is now a follower of Christ. Paul sees the sending back of Onesimus as an opportunity. In this same manner it is perhaps an opportunity that immigrant people who are converted and discipled may travel home, or elsewhere proclaiming the gospel message (Bakke 1997, 165).

A theology of multi-cultural ministry has as its foundation God's compassion for all people, and His compassion includes the cities where people live. He inspired strategic models of evangelization of the world through evangelization of the culturally diverse community represented by Antioch, Corinth, and Ephesus in scripture, and He continues to be the significant inspiration available to those who desire to communicate His message to all people.

Antioch

Antioch was a city with a population between 500,000 and 800,000 residents. It was the third largest city in the Roman Empire. The largest cities were of course Rome and Alexandria (Tenney 1:1976). The Antioch church is quite possibly the most culturally diverse church in early church history. Paul spent time in the church in Antioch and perhaps this is where Paul learned of the effectiveness of a church that reaches all people living in the culturally diverse community. In Antioch there is significant growth of the church, and the church has an obvious impact on the community. It is interesting that in the midst of this large cosmopolitan city a multicultural life giving church is birthed and grows impacting the community so powerfully that the followers of *"The Way"* in Antioch are called Christians for the first time (Keener 1993, 354).

This is evidence of the tremendous impact the church had in the community. However the greatest evidence of the culturally diverse community at Antioch being impacted by the gospel is the cultural diversity present in the congregation. This diversity is reflected in the leadership team of the Antioch church.

"When he came to this city-center church, Barnabas built a pastoral team that consisted of:
Simeon the black (an African)
Lucius of Cyrene (A North African)
Manean (possibly a slave of Herod's father)
Saul of Tarsus (native of Asia Minor, the land bridge to Europe)
Barnabas himself (from Cyprus)
(Bakke 1997, 145-146)."

Antioch is a powerful example of God's continued mission to reach the nations being accomplished through the church in the culturally diverse community. The ministry there is a strategic example of how the church can reach the culturally diverse community and have such a powerful impact on the community that a change in thinking occurs in the lives of people.

Corinth

Another example of the church being effective in reaching the culturally diverse community and growing as a multi-cultural congregation is in Corinth. Corinth was a city built on commerce. The Isthmus of Corinth was utilized by ships as a short cut over land from the Aegean Sea to the Adriatic Sea. It was therefore a trade route city where people of various cultural, religious, and socio-economic backgrounds lived, visited, and worked. It was strategically located and as the shortcut on the trade route it became a center of trade, industry and what Tenney describes as "commercialized pleasure" (Tenney 1976, 1: 960). It was a culturally diverse city which included Greek people, Jews, Italians, Orientals, Romans and others (Tenney 1976 1: 961).

Great difficulties eventually arose within the ministry in Corinth. Paul dealt with issues in his letters to the Corinthian Church that included Gnosticism, Jewish law, immorality, pagan worship, and division. These issues were challenging for the new church, and are more than likely indicative of issues that may arise in large urban trade route cities in the Roman world. Corinth had a population of up to 200,000 free people, and possibly 5,000 slaves. As a seaport, Corinth was a meeting place of all nationalities and it offered all of the attendant vices (Tenney 1976, 1:961). However, "But where sin abounded, grace did much more abound (Romans 5:20)". In the environment of this culturally diverse, pagan, immoral city, the church is established. It is in this culturally diverse city that Paul proclaims the gospel to all people and once again the hand of God can be seen working through the church to accomplish His mission to reach the nations.

Ephesus

Quite possibly the greatest strategic example in scripture of effective ministry within the culturally diverse community is shown in Ephesus. Paul spent a great deal of time in Ephesus as compared to the rest of his ministry (Witherington 1998, 572). It is in Ephesus that Paul lives out the most successful strategy for evangelism evidenced in his ministry. His ministry there, represents evangelism of people of various cultures and belief systems, and the redemption, development, and sending out of people into the world carrying the gospel message.

Ephesus was a city that had thrived as a port of trade but due to land erosion the harbor filled in with topsoil. By the time of Paul's life in Ephesus (Tenney 1976, 2:326) the temple of Diana (goddess of fertility) had become the primary source of commerce, and population in Ephesus (Tenney 1976, 2:238). Paul intentionally moves into and ministers the gospel among people of Ephesus who are pagan and immoral people. In fact, it would seem that Ephesus would be hostile to his message of the risen savior Jesus Christ (Tenney 1976, 2:238). After all, the Ephesian people and those traveling to Ephesus to worship pagan gods in a temple representing religion that has priests and formality may not appreciate Paul speaking about the son of a carpenter born in a borrowed stable, who was rejected by his own people, crucified, placed in a tomb, resurrected, and ascended into heaven. Even more controversial would be the message of knowing Jesus Christ in relationship being the only way to know God.

It is into this environment that Paul boldly goes. Paul did what many churches today avoid. In fact many churches run from the type of environment that Paul purposed to work in. Churches often run from cities and culturally diverse communities to suburbs embracing policies for ministry that encourage and justify isolation and segregation. Paul, strategically targeted the people of Ephesus, and through reaching the people of Ephesus the message was proclaimed to people living throughout Asia. Reaching the city becomes the key to evangelism success both for the city and for the entire region of Asia (Bakke 1997, 157). The city becomes the "amplifier of the Gospel" (Bakke 1997, 157).

"When Luke reports that 'all the Jews and Greeks who lived in the province of Asia heard the word of the Lord' (Acts 19:10), he is not saying that everyone in Asia heard, but that the gospel was heard all over Asia. Paul penetrated the city; the gospel did the traveling. The city has always functioned like the woofer and tweeter of an amplifying system. For the first time in American history (as of 1990) more than 50 percent of all Americans live in thirty-nine metro areas of more than one million persons. Clearly, we need more than ever to learn from Paul how to penetrate cities (Bakke 1997, 157)."

When our family moved to the city of Chicago this biblical strategy of fulfilling the mission of God in order to reach the nations became our mission statement for ministry in the culturally diverse community of the city. We established our ministry among the nations with the goal of evangelizing the world through evangelizing the city. It was this passion driven by the mission of God that inspired our ministry among Romanian, Hungarian, Haitian, Pakistani, Italian, East Indian, Latino, Anglo-American, African

American people and others. We went to the city to reach the city, and prayed that through reaching the city God would send workers into His harvest field throughout the world.

In Ephesus Paul ministered in one area yet accomplished the success of the gospel throughout the entire region. He remained in one place and the message spread all over the area. His ministry powerfully impacted all of Asia. "Paul apparently remained in Ephesus, but the gospel spread all over the province even to the Lycus Valley including the rest of the seven churches of Rev. 1:11; 2; 3 (Gaeblin 1976, vol. 9)."

Ministry intentionally focused on reaching the people living in the culturally diverse community is biblically correct ministry effort that intentionally targets all people. What is not biblically correct, but has been most often socially accepted are strategies that isolate the church from society, and segregate people culturally from one another. It is God's will that all people be saved and not perish. Perish in this sense is not physical death, but spiritual death for eternity. Salvation is the process of a person doomed to eternal death receiving eternal life. Paul's strategy is anchored in the commission of Jesus Christ in Mathew 28:19 and driven in the power of the Holy Spirit to empower the people of God through His presence, and convict the sinner of his or her sinfulness.

It is in the establishment of the church in Jerusalem, Antioch, Corinth, Ephesus, and others that God gives us, the church a picture of the implementation of the strategy of reaching the world through winning the cultures in large urban areas. Scriptural accounts of the gospel crossing barriers and reaching people are a theologically sound model for strategically reaching people in a culturally diverse community. God worked through the cultural diversity of Jerusalem, Ephesus, and Corinth. Peter, Paul, and others utilized the preaching of the gospel in these communities to reach the nations. God's love for people as well as His love for the city includes redemption and life for people as well as the city, and communicating the gospel message in the city means reaching all people of all cultures who live in the city celebrating the unity of Jesus Christ in the diversity of God's creation.

The goal of ministry in the culturally diverse community is not to build heaven on earth, but to work toward growing the kingdom of God. Understanding the reality of freedom in Christ is the reality that man can reject God and there will continue to be broken people who do not know Christ in the world until the atmosphere is changed by God. The struggle of the church is a struggle that has reward. At the present time the people of God are sojourners like Abraham looking for a city whose builder and maker is God. Understanding that this journey is one of looking for the city of God but not yet experiencing the city of God is important to the inspiration to continue to work at fulfilling the mission of God to reach all nations.

The world view of a sojourner includes the realization that the population of the world is without hope, except that hope which is in Christ Jesus. Understanding the dilemma of the world and the great commission which Jesus Christ has given us, we will go to the whole world (every nation) and preach the gospel message. We will make disciples, and bring all those who will come, to Christ.

God has and continues to work toward accomplishing His mission in the world to reach all people from all nations. He began His redemptive plan with the covenant He made with Abraham, sealed the successful outcome of His mission through His son Jesus Christ, and is working through the church to continue to reach the nations. He loves all people and He desires to reach all people from the nations. The church reaching the population of the culturally diverse community will reflect the population of the community as it gives life to the community by giving Jesus to people. These churches will experience growth and their growth will reflect the diversity of the community being redeemed through the presence and power of Jesus Christ.

3

GROWING THE
MULTI–CULTURAL LIFE
GIVING CHURCH

———— ∞∞∞ ————

U ndertaking the task of growing a church, whether planting
a church or growing an existing church is never an easy
task. Church growth is challenging, however it is not impossible.
Unfortunately many churches in America today are not growing, but
are declining in population and will close in a few years unless there
is a dynamic change in the way these congregations do business.

Today, 335,000 church congregations currently exist in America.
Unfortunately, 80% of these churches have plateaued or are declining.
Thirteen churches a day are organized, and thirty-seven churches
a day are closed. At this present rate of the 335,000 churches in
America one-half will be closed in fourteen years (Malphurs [1992]
1998, 32 and 35).

"After nearly two decades of studying Christian churches in America, I'm convinced that the typical church as we know it today has a rapidly expiring shelf life (Barna 1998, 1)."

The great commission is the primary mandate of the church, and bringing people into relationship with God through knowing Jesus Christ as personal savior and Lord is the fulfillment of this mandate. In order to fulfill this mandate the church must become relevant to people living in their community. Being relevant does not mean equating the gospel with other religions or belief systems (syncretism) as some church organizations have done today. Becoming relevant to people is the process that provides communication of the message to people in ways they understand. It is in this effort to reach people that the church becomes the living force that God intends it to become. The church grows by giving life to people.

Growth in local church ministry is often too focused on what happens in the church building on Sunday morning. The Sunday worship experience is important. It should be exciting, and powerful. It is a place for the congregation to experience fellowship, celebrate in worship, and introduce non-Christian people to Christ. Sunday worship should be well planned, and well done. However, church growth does not completely happen because of what is done on Sunday in worship. The work of growing the church is done throughout the week. What happens on Sunday is a result of what takes place Monday through Saturday.

Church growth is biblical

Since the moment in time that Adam and Eve exited the garden as a result of their sin, God has worked through the lives of people to bring people back into right relationship with Him, and with each other. The goal of the church is to help people find God through relationship with Jesus Christ, develop relationships with God's people, and show people who do not know God the way they can know Him. The church community is the community of faith where people come together, celebrate their relationship with the living God, and celebrate their relationship with one another through Jesus Christ. Church growth is focused on accomplishing this task.

I recently listened to a lecture given by Bill Hybels at the Willow Creek Church Contagious Evangelism Conference. Hybels made this statement regarding the local church, *"The hope of the world is the local church."* Hybels' statement is powerful. It identifies the fundamental success of Christianity in the world being the local church giving eternal life to people through Jesus Christ, and meeting the whole life needs of people.

The whole-person focused life giving church is the key to people finding Jesus Christ as personal savior, being developed in the Christ life, growing in their community relationships, and going out into the community to bring others to Jesus. The church that is a growing life giving church is reaching people, keeping people, growing people, and sending people. It is a place where people come together in a community of faith, worship God, and have their whole life needs met.

The community life of the church is a powerful model of the living compassion of Jesus Christ. The New Testament church experienced this compassion of Jesus Christ as they "valued people over possessions", (Keener 1993, 330) and they shared in community life with their table fellowship (Keener 1993, 330). The church fed the poor, preached the gospel, and expressed their relationship with Christ through their compassion toward people. It is powerful that they went beyond their group and reached out to meet the needs of others (Acts 2:42-46).

The church has gone through many periods of struggle, oppression, and persecution, yet the church still stands strong as the sole great light in this dark world. Although many have tried there has not been a successful effort thus far that could remove the church's presence in the world. Jesus declared that he would build His church (Matt 16:18), shared the pathway to knowing His Father (John 14:6), gave instructions to His Apostles to go into the whole world (Matt 28:19-20), and promised to send power for them to accomplish this task in the presence of the Holy Spirit (Acts 1:8). Clearly based on scripture it is God's will and plan that churches grow.

Church growth is possible

Although it is God's will that churches grow, the future of the church in North America is seen by some as hopeless. Many churches are declining, and many have already closed. The situation that the church faces is one that can only be helped by the local church doing self-analysis, and changing the way it does business if it desires to become a growing church.

"The church in North America is not in good shape. A study of various sources reveals that a large number of churches have leveled out or are declining, and many are dying (Malphurs [1992] 1998, 32)."

Traveling to many different churches gives a visiting minister a unique perspective of what is happening in a local church, and an ability to make an initial assessment of the church quickly. I can say from personal experience, identifying whether a church is growing, plateaued, or declining is something a visiting minister can many times accomplish within moments of visiting a local church. This identification is possible by making observations of the building, the people, their worship, their approach to preaching, how they minister to children, and how they treat guests.

If a church building has paint peeling on the front doors, the curtains are in disrepair, the restrooms smell badly, people are unfriendly, worship is not well done, and the preaching lacks passion, the church is more than likely not growing. Although none of these factors absolutely determine if a church is growing or in decline, these factors help a person to formulate a picture of where the church may be in its life cycle. A dying church is usually very distinguishable from a growing church. Growing churches exhibit life. Even if the building is not the greatest, a growing church is alive and there is a level of excitement in the church. More in-depth analysis, including interviews of the pastor, church members, numerical data, etc. will help a person to better identify if a church is growing, plateaued, or declining. The exciting news is that after visiting numerous churches I can say that although many are plateaued or declining there are many that are growing.

When a leader and people join together with God, utilizing effective church growth strategies and loving people with the compassion of Jesus Christ that ministers to the whole person, churches grow. Growing a church takes faith, fortitude, and function. Faith is the ability to see what isn't there. Fortitude is the ability to keep working when no results are visible, and function is doing what should be done. A growth oriented church must act like a growing church.

Church Growth is Powerful

Church growth is powerful. The church is the place where lives are transformed from the ugliness of sin into the beauty of the Christ life. It is a place that people can come to find encouragement and hope. They bring their friends to church; partnering with the church to help them to find eternal life.

The church is not just another human movement. It is a movement that is alive with the power of God. This movement was brought to life with the resurrection of Jesus Christ, and remains alive today through His presence and power (Morris 1986, 150). God can change the heart of human beings, and a healthy church grows as human beings are changed (Ezek 36:26). Seeing people change is exciting. It is powerful watching people walk out of darkness into light through the presence of Jesus Christ in their lives. Growing churches facilitate this life change in all that they do as organizations. Life is evidenced in their mission, vision, and core values. They are determined to grow, and they know the alternative to growth is death. "Robert Schuller says, *'One thing is certain: a church must never stop growing, when it ceases to grow it will start to die'* (Wagner 1984, 103)." Growing churches are soul winning, life changing, whole person focused churches. They win people to Jesus, they are growing churches, and this is powerful.

Building Growing Churches

A growing church will experience three types of growth including biological growth, transfer growth, and conversion growth. Biological growth happens when babies are born to people in the church. Transfer growth represents church members moving from one church to another (Rainer 1993, 21-22). It is important to understand that just because someone claims a church affiliation, or worships in a church it does not mean that they have a relationship with Jesus Christ. Therefore, hidden within transfer growth may also be a segment of people who have attended church all or part of their lives but never accepted Jesus Christ into their life until visiting another church that explained the gospel to them in a way they comprehended. Since they were members of another church they transfer their membership, but in actuality the goal of the life giving church is that at some point in their process they find the message of Jesus Christ in the church which surpasses polity, membership, and tradition. They find Jesus for themselves, and their lives change. Conversion growth members are those which find Jesus Christ as their personal Lord and Savior through the ministry of the church body (Rainer 1993, 21). This type of church growth is the most exciting. Salvation growth motivates church people to action. When church people start seeing non-church people finding Christ through the church, something happens in the congregation. Salvation growth is contagious, and it should be contagious. The visionary point leader (the pastor) of the church is the key to salvation growth happening as a normal part of what the church is doing.

Wholistic Church Growth

Growing the church in the culturally diverse community is perhaps one of the greatest challenges Christianity in the North American context faces today. As the North American context continues to become more and more diverse communities change and churches are confronted with the decision to change. Reaching culturally diverse communities with the gospel is also the greatest opportunity the church in America has to accomplish powerful New Testament ministry. Growing churches in these communities means the church will have to change its methods of ministry.

Historically most evangelical churches bring people into the church building three times on a weekly basis. The doors open for Sunday-School, Sunday morning worship, Sunday Evening Worship, and Wednesday Evening Bible Study. This tradition continues for many North American churches although some are opting out of Sunday-School and Sunday evening worship. This method of church ministry has primarily focused on the individual as a spectator, and learner. People sit and watch as leadership does the ministry. Pentecostal churches have historically been more experiential, but have evolved in many locations to a sit and watch church model. The spectator, sit and watch model, centers on a cognitive experience. It is a method where the mind is developed, and the soul secured through salvation, but the whole life of a person is not impacted. It is in this traditional model that individuals have been able to successfully compartmentalize their life into areas of God conscious lifestyle and areas that do not honor and please God. The Compartmentalization of the gospel and a focus on cognitive learning have together opened the evangelical church to what is often deserved criticism. The criticism is that the evangelical church is a cognitive experience that never deals with the whole person and therefore preaches a gospel with no evidence of redemption and lift for the person and the community within which the church is located.

In general, churches often develop ministry that targets a particular aspect of the person. Some churches focus on excellent teaching ministries that develop biblical knowledge in people. Some churches focus on the physical well being of people by meeting their physical needs. The church should be concerned with ministry to the whole person. This means the church will become a center for hope that deals with the whole person (Richards 1975, 66), and growing churches will be most successfully accomplished by whole-person focused ministry. This is especially true in the culturally diverse community.

The church must help each person grow in faith and life. A powerful model for church growth involving faith and life has been developed by Orlando Costas called the Wholistic Model of Church Growth. According to Costas, wholistic church growth includes numerical growth, organic growth, conceptual growth, and diaconal growth.

Numerical growth has both negative and positive aspects. The negative aspect of numerical church growth is the fact that churches can become numerically driven. In fact many churches are so numerically focused that nothing else matters in their endeavor to fill the church building with as many people as possible. I have been to numerous conferences and meetings where the question, *"How many people are you running?"* is the first question fellow ministers ask when they see me. There are also positive aspects of numerical growth. One positive aspect of numerical growth is that numerical growth data is tangible. It is visible, and can be analyzed by comparing it with previous years (Shenk 1983, 102).

Organic growth is the growth of a church's life systems. It includes the integral structure of the church that provides the care, nurture, healthy relationship development and logistical process of operating the church. It is organic growth that focuses on assimilation of people into the body of the church and closing the back door of the church. Creating an atmosphere that will minister to peoples life needs when they enter the place of worship includes the appearance and layout of the building, nursery, and people care (Shenk 1983, 102). It is important to remember the saying, *"People don't care how much you know until they know how much you care"*.

Conceptual growth is that aspect of church growth that focuses on developing the mind of the individual. It is cognitive growth that is accomplished through teaching ministries such as Sunday-School, and Discipleship classes. Conceptual growth develops theology, and the ability of the individual to analyze the churches fulfillment of the great commission. A church whose members experience little or no conceptual growth is often theologically weak and members of the church are vulnerable to false doctrine. I recently heard a pastor describe some local churches as being a mile wide and an inch deep. Shallow theologically weak Christians are developed by placing little emphasis on conceptual growth (Shenk 1983, 102).

Diaconal growth is the area that is historically the weakest area of the Pentecostal evangelical church. It is the compassion in action growth of the church. Diaconal growth is the church visibly living in the community by meeting the needs of the community. Diaconal growth includes all that the church does to be active in the community sharing the love and message of Jesus Christ. Diaconal ministries may include feeding the hungry, helping people deal with their life needs, and other life issues. The wholistic model is powerful. It is a model of church growth that includes reaching people, keeping people, growing people, and sending people into the community with the gospel message.

Reaching People

Reaching people is the fundamental number one priority of the church. It is the primary reason for the existence of the church. Reaching people involves bringing people into relationship with God through knowing His Son Jesus Christ as personal Savior and Lord. Numerical growth directly correlates to the concept of reaching people as a primary aspect of church growth. However, reaching people focuses specifically on winning people to Jesus Christ. Although numerical growth includes biological growth, transfer growth, and conversion growth, reaching people places the highest emphasis on conversion growth. As such conversion growth includes the goal of winning children born to church people (biological growth) to Christ by presenting the plan of salvation to them, and providing them the opportunity to receive Him as their Savior.

Keeping People

Keeping people is the aspect of church growth that includes sharing in the life experiences of people as they grow in their faith walk, and caring for people by meeting their life needs. There is a level of meeting life needs in each aspect of church growth. However, keeping people focuses on providing people care through the ministry of the church that helps people feel the family connection of church ministry, and see their children cared for in the love of Jesus Christ. Keeping people is the area of ministry where the church intentionally focuses on opening the front door and closing the back door. It includes developing a real and effective assimilation process for grafting people into the body of Christ.

An assimilation process includes the effectiveness of worship, friendliness of people, and level of excellence with which the ministry is approached. It is the conscious effort of the church to build community in the church. It includes the development of the church structure, government, and people care ministry. It is what Costas describes as organic growth. Keeping people involves touching a person's life when they walk through the door for the first time and consciously creating an atmosphere for them to connect and become active in the life of the church.

Growing People

The growing people factor of church growth targets the development of their knowledge of Scripture, theology, the defense of their faith, and the offense of their faith. Traditionally growing people is accomplished through Sunday School, and classes developed to train people in scripture truth. Today, there is a shift in thinking that has influenced many churches to be more mobile with training by moving cognitive training or the conceptual growth development of people (discipleship) into homes, coffee shops, and work places outside of the walls of the church (third places). Mobility discipleship allows a higher level of partnering organic growth and conceptual growth together. Mobile discipleship opportunities are often accomplished through home meetings and small group ministry in which fellowship learning, and evangelism happens. Regardless of how the growth of people is accomplished it is important that people are encouraged, and facilitated to grow in maturity in their spiritual and biblical knowledge in the church.

Sending People

Sending people is the aspect of church growth that focuses on the growth of the church in the world community outside of the church. It is that place where people who have been reached begin reaching. The true success of people becoming Christians is seen when they grow in their faith to become soul winners. Sending people into the community to do ministry has positive impact on the community and accomplishes diaconal growth in the community.

Diaconal growth is the ministry of the church in the world. It is intentionally focused outreach with faith expectation that lives will be changed, but without the expectation that the church will gain materially in some great substantial way for their giving in the community. In other words it is ministry investment in the community without guarantee of some tangible benefit to the church.

Many churches that do effective sacrificial diaconal ministry have members that from time to time question the benefit of homeless ministry sponsored by their church, or feeding ministries in their church. They question these ministries because they have not released themselves or their money completely to God. Often what people give has strings attached, because of this they see strings attached to everything the church does. These people expect a *quid pro quo* for everything they do as a church. Ministries that hold on to their resources, give with strings attached, and only do enough to receive the warm fuzzy feeling of guilt relief are like the man in the parable of the talents (spoken by Jesus) who buried his talent in the ground (Matt 25:18).They have buried the opportunity that God has given them. The church that is determined to grow in becoming a sending church (diaconal growth) will be found with their resources invested in the work of the kingdom changing the world with the compassion of Jesus Christ upon the return of Jesus Christ.

Reaching, keeping, growing, and sending people into the community is the growth of the church that is accomplished by ministering to the whole person. Ministry to the whole person takes intentional effort on the part of the church. It is accomplished by the church being a wholistic growth focused church that gives equal attention and effort to the numeric, organic, conceptual, and diaconal ministries of the church. Becoming a wholistic growth focused church will greatly facilitate the church in the culturally diverse community to reach the community.

Transition Churches

Churches in North America need help; although many may not admit this fact. It is evident with 80% of churches either plateaued or declining something must be done. Churches typically don't just wake up and decide to do something. Usually it takes someone or some event to wake them up, and motivate the church to action. Revitalizing or turning around the local church is not an endeavor that happens quickly. Change takes time. People typically do not like change and pastors who move into the church that needs to change often find resistance and opposition to change. I have heard more than once in conferences that it takes four years for a pastor to become the leader of the church. Today, it may take up to six years for the pastor to become the leader of the church. Whether it takes four years or six years to become the leader, leadership is a key to turning around a plateaued or declining church.

The church that exists in the culturally diverse community or the community that is in transition from one culture to multiple cultures will be confronted with decision opportunities that will determine the church's ministry success in the community, and their future as a church. As the church's population departs from the community, the church will have to decide whether to depart also, or stay in the community. The natural tendency of churches has often been to leave their community. Ray Bakke describes this departure of churches from cities in the 1960s in his book, *The Urban Christian,* as fleeing the city (Bakke 1987, 55-57).

Theories of justification for the church leaving the community have been offered by good well intentioned people. Those ominous words, "the neighborhood is changing" have caused many churches to board "Jonah's ship", and run from "Nineveh" (Jonah 1:3). The sad reality of this history in the church is that the Nineveh communities' churches run from are in great need, and the vehicle God designed and called to meet the needs of these communities, the church, is missing in action (Bakke 1987, 138).

It is a challenging dilemma with no simple answer. In fact, just because a church remains in a community does not mean they desire to reach their community. They may have stayed in the community because they do not want to leave the building, or they do not have the financial means to move. The community may change so fast that the church hasn't had a chance to consider how they will respond to their changing community. The church that stays in the transitioning community will come to the realization of their need to change in order to survive, and be effective at accomplishing God's mission in the community. The church in transition who desires to minister effectively to its community and grow must intentionally develop a vision strategy for reaching the community. Developing a vision strategy will help a church see the community more accurately, do self-reflection in light of what God says in scripture, and be motivated to action. The church ministry that is determined to be a growing church reaching the culturally diverse community will have legitimate opportunities to fulfill their vision.

Planting Churches

Church planting is perhaps one of the most challenging ministry endeavors, yet it is one of the most rewarding. When planting a church is well planned, and done with excellence it is probably the most effective method of bringing people into relationship with Jesus Christ available. Peter Wagner is convinced that church planting is powerful. In fact, Wagner states that church planting is the *"single most effective evangelistic methodology under heaven* (Wagner 1990, 11)." It is bringing new life into communities by providing opportunities of evangelism among people who have not yet been reached with the gospel.

People in general are not motivated to plant new churches. Few people are motivated to make the great sacrifices necessary to plant a new church. It takes great commitment to plant a church.

"Church planting will indeed be a method for church growth that will take many believers from their comfort zone; but Christianity was never meant to be a business as usual faith. The early church was always on the cutting edge of reaching people for Christ. Even when persecution broke out against the church, Christians scattered throughout Judea, and Samaria. They shared their faith and started churches as they fled (Acts 8:1-4) (Rainer 1993, 209)".

Typically I have observed five methods by which churches are planted, including 1.prayer meeting church planting, 2.church split church planting, 3.partnership church planting, 4.if we start it they will come church planting and 5.cell church planting.

Prayer Meeting Church Planting – Prayer meeting church planting is perhaps one of the greatest church planting methods utilized in history. In fact many churches started as a result of home prayer meetings. Historically, many pioneer church planters who utilized this method of church planting were women compelled by God to pray. Often after their prayer meetings grew from small groups to small congregations the praying women who started the prayer meetings would call church leaders and ask that a trained pastor be sent to lead the group. One example of this type of prayer meeting church plant is the Narragansett Church of God in Chicago. The Church of God (Cleveland, TN.) was introduced to the city of Chicago in January 1928. Two ladies with a vision started the first services by having prayer meetings in a rented storefront. Amelia Shumaker and Martha Zimmerlin started these first meetings in a storefront located at 1491 Larrabee Street. On October 10, 1929, the church was set in order by John H. Jones. Nine members were taken in. In late 1929 the church moved to a new location at 2407 W. Madison. Then in 1930 State Overseer E.L. Simmons came to the church. Simmons baptized and added seventeen new members to the church. In 1933 the first Sunday-School was organized (Biography of Martha Zimmerlin). Although prayer meeting church planting is a simple strategy in which people have prayer in a home, apartment or storefront as the primary method of bringing together a group of people who will form a core group that grows into a church body, it has been an effective way of accomplishing the gospel mandate.

Church Split Church Planting – Church split church planting can be and often is looked at only from a negative viewpoint. However, it is important to focus on the fact that God works in spite of people to accomplish His will. In the same manner that Paul and Barnabas parted ways there are instances in the church that people part ways and new churches begin (Acts 15:36-41). Church split church planting is normally not intentional, and is definitely less than ideal. When churches split there are usually hurt feelings, division, and pain. Therefore, it is important in these situations to make efforts at reconciliation, peace, and forgiveness of both congregations involved.

Partnership Church Planting – The ministry partnership church planting model happens when an established church partners with a church planter to plant a new church. This model is also called mothering a church. Partnership may include money for rental of worship facilities, tithing of membership, providing leaders and teachers, curriculum, and other needs for the new church by the partnering church. Partnership church planting is a powerful method of church planting because of the strength the new church gains with the partnership church backing it up. The new church does not have to struggle by itself. It can draw from the strength of the established partner church in building its foundation and strategy for growth.

One example of how partnership can help the new church is in financial backing. The ability of the new church to lease or purchase property is greatly facilitated by having the backing of an established partner church. Financial institutions normally require a minimum of three years financial records from any church applying for a loan. This is quite difficult for a new church for two reasons; first, a new church will only have records for the time they have been in existence, and second the first three years of financial records for a new church will more than likely show their inability to repay a loan more than their ability to repay a loan. Unfortunately, financial institutions do not loan money with faith promises as collateral. Therefore, if the partnership church is willing and able to sign for, or co-sign for banking needs the new church's financial stability will be greatly enhanced.

If We Start It They Will Come Church Planting – If we start it they will come church planting is probably the most difficult method of planting churches. This is the method that includes renting a building with little or no people as a core group, putting up a sign, and waiting for people to come to the new church. Some leaders who utilize this method of church planting pound the pavement, meet people and bring them to Jesus. Some just go to the rented facility and wait for people to show up.

When a person says they are going to plant a church often times this is the picture that comes to mind. The fact is in today's society just because we start a church does not mean people will come. More than likely they will not come to a new church just because it is there. Starting a church with a small amount of people or no people by renting a building, putting up a sign and having service will take money, patience, and time. The church plant can be successful, but quick success is not very likely. Getting the most out of the investment of time and resources should be a legitimate goal of any church planter. When looking at church planting models there is a model that accomplishes more success in far less time than any other model. This model is the cell church model.

Cell Church Planting Model - Clearly the most effective and successful model of church planting is the cell church model. The cell model is especially effective in the urban culturally diverse context.

"When we look at a large urban area, we wonder how the gospel can penetrate into all those apartments, barrios, people groups, and neighborhoods. It is through structure that the task is divided into smaller pieces and made more doable (Neumann 1999, 62)".

Cell evangelism connects with people in their life world and provides opportunities for effective communication of the gospel message to be accomplished. According to Joel Comiskey, "Cells are open, evangelism-focused small groups that are entwined into the life of the church (Comiskey 1998, 17)" Ralph Neighbor's magazine, The Cell Group Journal defines cell group ministry as,

"A spiritual cell group is very similar to a biological cell. Followers of Jesus Christ edify one another and increase the kingdom by sharing their lives with unbelievers. New leaders are raised up from within the group to grow and expand the ministry to a hurting world when the group multiplies, and the process repeats itself (Cell Group Journal Spring 2002, 3)."

Well accomplished cell ministry will have growth results that are qualitative. Growth results of cell ministry also have the potential of tremendous numerical growth or quantitative growth. This is a great possibility because cell ministry is evangelism driven. Healthy cells are reproducing cells (Comiskey 1998, 26). If cell groups are not instilled with the passion of evangelism, no longer see evangelism a priority, or focus their efforts on fellowship, they are unhealthy, ingrown, and no longer valid.

The initial work of planting a cell church ministry takes time. Results do not happen over night. However, when the foundation of the cell church plant is well laid tremendous growth becomes a possibility in a short amount of time. Cell ministry groups grow in such powerful ways because people are connected together in a community that has personal touch in their people care. The primary mission of the cell is to bring people to Jesus Christ (Comiskey 1998, 21).

Developing the Multi-Cultural Life Giving Church

Once a church determines to reach the culturally diverse community or a church planter is going to plant a church in a culturally diverse community decisions must be made regarding how the church will reach the community incorporating their desire and effort into vision strategy that correlates their vision with their actions. Prior to beginning the planning process it is important for the church to look at key models of cross-cultural ministry. There are two key models for doing effective ministry in the culturally diverse community. These include the multi-congregational ministry model, and the multi-cultural church model.

Multi-congregational ministry model

The multi-congregational approach to reaching the culturally diverse community involves the primary church congregation establishing ministry to one or more other culture groups by providing worship facilities for them to have worship services. This approach to ministry in the culturally diverse community can be inspired by the primary congregation seeking a culture group to minister to or by a culture group desiring a place to worship making a request to the church. In either case everything should be detailed, negotiated, and planned up front. It is important that the primary congregation pastor evaluate his or her congregation and discern who will be the best person to communicate to another culture group. This person can serve as a member of a committee that will facilitate the process of developing the best relationship in the beginning with each group the church provides facilities for worship. The Church of God (Cleveland, TN.) Indiana state ministry headquarters developed a written agreement form to be signed by each culture group a church provides a place of worship (Appendix 2). This type of agreement may be helpful to the multi-congregational ministry church.

Renting Relationship Model

The renting relationship model is a method of reaching the community by opening the church to other groups for worship opportunities by offering some area of the church facility for rent. This structure allows a people group with a different culture / ethnicity than the primary congregation to minister to the people within their culture in their language, and in a contextualized manner that is often more effective than one culture going to another culture. Opening the church gives culture groups opportunities to worship in a church facility when they are not able to purchase their own facility (Ortiz 1996, 66-69).

The renting relationship model is an easy way for a church to feel benevolent without any sacrificial commitment to intentionally changing who they are as a church in order to become what they need to become to reach all of the people in their community. The danger of the renting model is the landlord and tenant trap. God did not intend the church to be in the real estate business. God calls the church to be in the relationship business.

Relationship Partnership Model

While pastoring in Chicago we developed two Sunday culture group worship services with a verbal agreement of how each group (including the primary congregation group) would operate. In this structure the primary congregation is reaching their community by facilitating the planting of new congregations. These congregations usually consist of first generation immigrants who speak very little or no English. Their worship services are normally done in their indigenous language (Rainer 1993, 212). These groups may or may not organize as fully functioning churches but they represent key ministry opportunities for reaching the community.

The local congregation who chooses (as the primary congrega-tion) to plant other culture group congregations without also inten-tionally creating a culturally diverse friendly worship service fails the primary congregation and the other culture group congrega-tions. This is especially true when the culture group congregation's worship services are not in English, but in their indigenous language. Doing multi-congregational ministry as a way to remain segregated in worship fails the primary congregation in two specific ways:

The primary congregation has a tendency to end up as the landlord and the other congregations as tenants. Although the new groups, as tenants, may help with utility expenses, and property maintenance needs the relationship connection between the primary congregation and these groups must be compassion driven. Without compassion, relationships can strain and dissipate into nothing more than business associations.

The primary congregation becomes an island never really connecting with the community. Without community connection the primary congregation does not reach the community and may cease to exist.

This approach also fails the culture group congregations in two specific ways:

1. Their children have no where to go. If they do not want to worship within their cultural tradition and language, and the primary congregation does not welcome them, they have no one to turn to, and no where to go.
2. When in-migration of first generation immigrants ceases in the community, the congregation will decline into non-existence.

It is for these reasons, approaching the multi-congregational ministry model is best accomplished with a strong commitment to ministry partnership and an intentional openness to culturally diverse ministry. Ministry partnership between congregations of differing cultures is accomplished by developing real Christ-like relation-ships that handle the difficulties of life and remain intact.

There are four ministry partnership principles that are foundational to developing a partnership relationship strcutre of multi-congregational ministry. These are 1. relationship, 2. life support, 3. future priority, and 4. leadership. The primary goal of developing a partnership relationship multi-congregational ministry structure is to develop a wholistic model of ministry that is evidenced by tangible qualitative and quantitative church growth.

1. Relationship – A commitment to relationship between congregations is exhibited by them intentionally planning relationship building and partnership commitment opportunities for the congregations. Partnership opportunities include having designated celebration worship services that include all of the congregations who utilize the church property. These opportunities may be planned for the first Sunday evening, every fifth Sunday evening, monthly, or quarterly at a designated time. In these celebration services each group should be included in the planning, and administering of the service. This means that all groups should be represented in the worship service both in the congregation and on the platform. Another partnership opportunity is to develop a prayer ministry that includes all of the groups praying together on a weekly basis. There is power in prayer and when people agree together in prayer a deep heart connection is formed between people (Prov 27:17).

One of The greatest relationship opportunities available to the church is the church fellowship dinner. Breaking bread together builds community relationships. Organizing a monthly multi-congregational church dinner where each culture prepares their indigenous food and all people share together is powerful. Seating must be intentionally planned. It should be organized in a way that families of different cultures sit together. This kind of intentionality may be uncomfortable at first, but being intentional does not usually mean being comfortable. Relationship building happens when people meet in koinonia settings.

2. Life Support – Life support is a commitment of partnership in helping people with their life needs. Life support is not intended to mean that the church will become an institution of welfare. Life

support simply means a commitment to work together supporting life. Life needs in the multi-congregational church may include financial planning, food resourcing, clothing, housing assistance, job placement, English as a second language classes, Immigration and Naturalization Service assistance, education, training, and other life areas. Life support is partnering together to help people with their life needs.

3. Future Priority – Future priority is making future generations a high priority of ministry. It includes a commitment of congregations to partner together in youth evangelism, youth discipleship, and youth celebration ministries. The primary church can reach out and help other culture congregations in the area of youth ministry in a powerful way. The youth born to first generation immigrants, and first generation immigrants who are youth need opportunities for worship that appeal to their life needs as they struggle for new identity. Partnering together churches work to evangelize the youth growing up in and around the church.

4. Leadership – A leadership commitment is the commitment to partner together in developing indigenous, whole person focused, life-giving leaders. Leadership is essential, and the continued improvement of leadership skills in the life of each leader is essential to the success of the local church. Congregations can partner together to help develop leaders from within their own groups. These leaders will better understand the context, and needs of people than leaders who are imported. They will be the catalyst that grows the church congregation in the future.

Multi-Cultural Ministry

The multi-cultural church model is a ministry model that has a high priority of intentional reconciliation of culture groups. It is a church ministry where worship, discipleship, and membership include people from all cultures who are living in the community (Smith 1994, 33). Multi-cultural ministry is not a new experience in the Pentecostal church as much as it is often a forgotten experience in the Pentecostal church. A key attribute in the early history of the first meetings of the 20th century Pentecostal church was cultural diversity in worship. Harvey Cox describes this scene at Azusa Street in Los Angeles, California in his book *Fire From Heaven*,

> "In retrospect the interracial character of the growing congregation on Azusa Street was indeed a kind of miracle. It was, after all, 1906, a time of growing, not diminishing, racial separation everywhere else. But many visitors reported that in the Azusa Street revival blacks and whites and Asians and Mexicans sang and prayed together. Seymour was recognized as the pastor. But there were both black and white deacons, and both black and white women-including Lucy Farrow-were exhorters and healers. What seemed to impress or disgust visitors most, however, was not the interracial leadership but the fact that blacks and whites, men and women, embraced each other at the tiny altar as they wept and prayed. A southern white preacher later jotted in his diary that he was first offended and startled, then inspired, by the fact that, as he put it, 'the color line was washed away by the blood.' (Cox 1995, 58-59)."

Unfortunately as the church grew societal influence disintegrated the multi-cultural experience of Asuza Street into the accepted structure of segregation in North America.

It is important to note that the goal of the multi-cultural church is not to assimilate all cultures into one new culture, but the goal is to provide a place of worship and community for all people. It is a worship experience that celebrates the unity of Christ in the diversity of God's creation. Very often people who are motivated by multi-cultural church ministry are people who are experiencing or have experienced the cultural assimilation process.

Cultural assimilation as a process is a fact of life that can not be avoided in North America. Immigrant people have children, and grandchildren who are in a process of assimilation. There is a television commercial produced by the Leadership Conference on Civil Rights that shows people of different ethnicity stating their name and ethnicity, and then stating they are American. "*I'm half Arabic, half German, - I'm an American", "I'm a Spanish Irish Jew – I'm an American", and "I was born in Madison, Wisconsin – I'm Lebanese American".* This commercial highlights the diversity of American people. It is unfortunate that many people who were born in America do not remember or know much about the land and culture of their ancestors. Another primary goal of the multi-cultural church is to help people in their assimilation process while encouraging them to embrace their culture so as not to forget their culture.

In June of 1992 my wife Shyrel and I took a trip to the city of Chicago that changed our lives. At that time we were living in Evansville, Indiana. We had been part of a church plant ministry team for approximately two years. We were also in the process of receiving a foreign missionary appointment. During our weekend in Chicago God impressed our hearts with an overwhelming sense of compassion for the people in Chicago. We sensed direction from God to move to and minister among the population of culturally diverse people living in Chicago.

After moving to Chicago we began working with culture groups immediately. We primarily worked with youth who were first and second generation immigrants to the United States, most of whom arrived in Chicago at a young age and were rapidly assimilating into North American culture. Our goal was to build bridges to them and help them to find God and not reject their culture. We involved young people in activities including feeding the homeless, youth discipleship, and other ministry opportunities. We worked to affirm the cultural heritage of these youth while helping them to find Jesus Christ as their personal savior. We also worked with them helping them to find their identity as immigrant people in their new world. We intentionally worked to avoid "Americanizing" them while not pushing them to remain in their culture. This ministry effort was difficult, but needed among young immigrants and children of immigrants. It is a careful balancing act that brings the gospel message to young people while not pushing them to lose or keep their culture. It is a ministry in which the minister becomes the Shepherd who doesn't drive the sheep, but guides the sheep around the dangers of their new world helping them to develop into the person God desires them to become.

The multi-cultural church model includes the four principles of the multi-congregational relationship model (relationship, life support, future priority, and leadership) and more. The multi-cultural congregation must focus on giving people life, intentional reconciliation, and empowering people to do the work of ministry.

Giving People Life – Giving people life is powerful. Jesus said I have come to give you life and life more abundantly (John 10:10). Just as Jesus came to give life, the church must give life. The church is the body of believers who are the presence of Jesus Christ in the world. It is through the church that Jesus accomplishes His work. There are many people in the culturally diverse community who need someone who will give them opportunities for life in knowing Jesus Christ, but will also care for their needs as well as their soul (Matt 25:35). People, especially newcomers to the United States have many needs. They are in need of someone to give them a hand and lift them up. They are in need of life lift as well as redemption from sin. The life giving church provides opportunities for redemption and lift of people living in their community.

Reconciliation - Reconciliation is the intentional effort by people to come together in Christian relationship through the compassion of Jesus Christ. Multi-cultural community worship is not a possible reality without Jesus living in the hearts of people. We are all different culturally, but through His presence we are one. It is through Jesus Christ that unity in diversity is a possibility. It is through Him we can be reconciled, because He provides the greatest opportunity for forgiveness, freedom from the past, and life. We as people are too often wrapped up in what we do instead of who we are. As people redeemed by Jesus Christ we are different but in Christ we are the same, we are diverse but through Him united, and we are unique but united; we are one in Christ.

Empowerment - A culturally diverse church that does not represent the diversity of the church in its leadership is not a church that can be considered culturally sensitive or authentic. A commitment to winning people to Christ in the culturally diverse community is one that will include empowering those who come to Christ. Empowering people includes developing them, training them, and releasing them to do the work of ministry. Empowering a person is giving them opportunities to do what they have never done, go where they have never gone, and be what they have never been before for God.

Walking into the multi-cultural church that is empowering people an observer will see people of different ethnicity and cultures serving as ushers, on the worship team, in the choir, receiving the offering, and moderating the service. The presence of cultural diversity will be obvious in the multi-cultural church. The multi-cultural church is a place of excitement in which all people are welcome from every culture.

The Multi-Cultural Life Giving Church

The multi-cultural life giving church includes being a multi-congregational relationship oriented church, a multi-cultural church and a multi-generational church. It is a church ministry that ministers to the whole life needs of people, and people groups. This ministry effort includes understanding the history of people, their culture, and their present life situation.

Growing the multi-cultural life giving church..

What should a multi-cultural life giving church look like? Many diagrams and models can be drawn describing the multi-cultural church but the key to developing a multi-cultural life giving church is to develop ministry that meets the whole life needs of all people living in the culturally diverse community. Meeting needs of all people will include each culture group, and each age group. It also includes ministry to the churched and un- churched. The multi-cultural life giving church is a church which joins together a multi-congregational model and multi-cultural model of ministry. A diagram of the multi-cultural life giving church will perhaps look something like this:

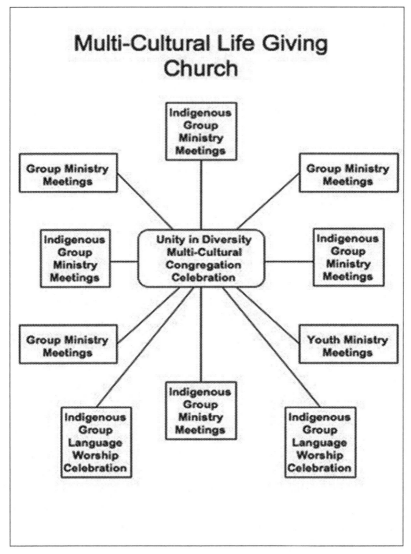

Fig. 1 Multi-cultural Life Giving Church Diagram

This diagram shows a church ministry that exists as intentional ministry targeting specific groups and is connected together through relationships, and unified celebration worship opportunities. It is one church with many members who are receiving ministry specifically targeting their felt needs. The multi-cultural life giving church includes ministry to each language group and each generation.

Indigenous Language Group Home Meetings – These meetings are designed with the same goals of cell ministry; relationship and evangelism. It is in these meetings people can experience close community within their culture group, hear the gospel in their language, and network with other people from their culture group about finding work, housing, medical care, immigration needs, life back home, and other needs.

When we began working with Bulgarian people in Chicago we started Indigenous Language Group Home Meetings in two Bulgarian homes. We came to these meetings in everyday clothes, worshipped together, drank coffee together, and prayed for one another's needs. After praying together we just talked and helped facilitate people with meeting their needs for work, housing, immigration, etc. These group meetings facilitated the numerical multiplication of our Bulgarian ministry in a few months. We soon began a ministry among people from Mexico living in the community. We utilized this same home group method of ministry to grow the Mexican ministry. The indigenous Language Group Home Meeting is a powerful place of people connection. People are more open with their life needs when they are comfortable, and meeting in homes is often more comfortable than meeting in the church building.

Group Ministry Meetings – Group ministry meetings are similar to Indigenous Language Group Home Meetings except they are conducted in a primary language in the society in which the church exists. For example, if the church is located in the United States the primary language in most of the country is English, however if the church is located in Paris the primary language will be French. The format of the group ministry meeting is the same and the process the same as that of the indigenous Language group meetings. These group meetings utilizing the primary language of the community are more likely to be culturally diverse as they are planned by location more than language. Again these meetings are a powerful way of introducing people to Christ in a non-threatening atmosphere.

Youth Ministry Meetings – Most church youth ministry meetings are conducted in the church building. However, youth meetings can also be conducted in homes, at bowling alleys, pizza places, or somewhere else. Praying in a public place may be awkward for young people, but meetings can include some element of fun on a regular basis. The youth ministry home group meeting facilitates 1st, 2nd, and 3rd generation youth in developing relationships with culturally assimilated North American youth. Remember young people go to culturally diverse schools and speak English every day. It is important to provide opportunities for them to make a God connection within their peer group environment. The multi-cultural life giving church model provides a tremendous opportunity for youth from non-North American cultures to worship with those who speak English; the same language they learn in school. Building strong community among 1st generation, 2nd generation and North American born youth is not just a noble thing to do it is a way to connect them with Christ in the community that will have eternal value.

Indigenous Language Group Worship Celebration - These worship opportunities are conducted in the group's indigenous language. This is the worship experience developed for the 1st generation immigrant. These worship opportunities must be approached with the same level of planning, and preparation as any other worship service. These Indigenous Language Group services are not intended to be different churches. They are developed as different worship opportunities for people within one church.

Unity in Diversity Multi-cultural Worship Services – This worship service is intentionally designed to be culturally diverse. First generation non-English speaking worshippers are welcome, and translation systems can be provided to facilitate their language needs. However, the focus of the worship service is to celebrate the unity of Christ among the diversity of culture. This worship experience is a great opportunity for 2nd and 3rd generation immigrant people to celebrate in worship together in the multi-cultural community.

Multi-cultural Language Celebration Services – The multi-cultural language celebration services are special planned times of the entire church body coming together to worship God. These special services include each group participating in worship celebrating their culture, and language as they worship God together. These services may also include a dinner celebration after the service in which each culture group brings food indigenous to their culture.

While serving as pastor of a multi-cultural church I preached in each indigenous language group worship service at least one time a month. I administered the Lord's Supper, dedicated children, and visited people in the hospital. I also led indigenous language group home group meetings and developed strong relationships with them. These efforts at ministry were intentional efforts. It was our church's vision to remain as one church in order to have such close relationship that the 2nd generation would not leave their language group worship service and have nowhere to go. We decided to build a church community that they connected with, and would always see as a place where their needs were met.

Leadership development was another priority of all that we did among these language groups. We appointed a Bulgarian ministry coordinator, and a Spanish ministry coordinator to lead and help pastor these groups of people. Developing leaders within these groups was a key to ministry success among these groups, and long term vision in the multi-cultural life giving church must include developing indigenous leaders.

Developing the multi-cultural life giving church is accomplished by intentionally creating an atmosphere that encourages the diversity of people coming together in unity through the presence and power of Jesus Christ in their lives and in the community. Creating an atmosphere may include the physical presence of the building such as hanging flags from various countries, indigenous artwork, and color schemes. However, none of these create the atmosphere in and of themselves. Creating an atmosphere that encourages diversity begins with heart change that is demonstrated by action. How people act is determined by who they are. How people live is determined by their commitment to who they serve. Growing a multi-cultural life giving church is possible and powerful through the presence and power of Jesus Christ.

Power to Grow

Human effort in growing churches is vital, needed, and an absolute. However, it is important to focus on the reality that growing churches is God's work, and as such human effort can ultimately accomplish very little without God. It is the Holy Spirit that draws people to God (John 6:44). Through people God is accomplishing His will of bringing people into relationship with Him. Timing and approach are important, strategy planning is necessary, but without the presence of the power of God nothing effective will be accomplished. He is the power source (Zech 4:6). The Azusa street revival that is attributed as the launch pad of the modern Pentecostal movement took place in a little rented warehouse storefront building that had no sign, no newspaper advertising, or no organized publicity campaigns. By all standards of strategic church planting this meeting could never be successful. Yet the revival exploded and grew in a powerful way (Cox 1995, 56-57).

Historically the Pentecostal church is a movement that holds the power of God being present in the lives of people as a high core value of their faith. Even for early Pentecostal believers experiencing God was not a dry solemn event, but a living relationship where the individual felt the power and presence of God in their worship. The fact is Pentecostal, charismatic, and third wave churches not only believe God can change lives, but these congregations expect God to change lives. It is with this confidence that Pentecostal churches have grown, and continue to grow. (Sweet 1999, 209).

This is not to imply that the only growing churches are Pentecostal churches. However, a church that is alive with the presence of God in worship has a tremendous growth potential. A living church is concerned about the future of people's souls, and celebrates the power of God's presence in their lives. Celebrating the power of God's presence in an individual's life is the celebration that they were once lost but now they are found. It is a celebration of, *"victory in Jesus"* like the old hymn says. Growing churches is biblical, possible, and powerful. Churches can grow and should grow. Growing churches are soul winning, life changing, whole person focused churches.

God worked through Paul the Apostle on Mars Hill to convince people through the power of the Holy Spirit in spoken word (Acts 17:34). He worked through Peter on the day of Pentecost through the presence of the Holy Spirit and changed a multitude of lives (Acts 2). The power of God has not changed throughout eternity. He still has the power to change lives, and it is His power that makes church growth possible and powerful.

Church growth is not only a possibility for the traditional one culture church, but church growth can happen in the culturally diverse community. Church growth in the culturally diverse community can be effectively accomplished by developing multi-cultural life giving churches. The multi-cultural life giving church is a reflection of God's power of reconciliation, redemption, and lift in the lives of people. It is a church that reflects the action of God's compassion through the lives of people. The multi-cultural life giving church represents the diversity of cultures living in the community, because it is communicating the gospel with meaning to all people in the community.

4

COMMUNITY MINISTRY IN A
CHANGING WORLD

———— ∞∞∞ ————

The world we live in today is filled with movement, excitement, life, and energy. The global community is transcending borders, barriers, language, and culture. Our world is fast paced, technology dependent, and diverse. Modernization has facilitated society becoming further disconnected, and more driven to obtain prosperity, power, and fame at a faster rate than ever in history. Success in today's North American context is not only to accomplish a certain level of economic well being in one's life, but it is to accomplish a certain level of economic well being by a certain age in life.

In this global society things are constantly changing. Immigration, migration, transnational citizens, and people flow is constant. One thing that can be counted on is change. People are moving, technology changes daily, new science, new breakthroughs, and life continually offer new challenges.

Successfully reaching the community through local church ministry seems to be seldom accomplished. Realistically, there are many keys to reaching communities with the gospel message. Every day someone develops a new slogan, creates a new tool, writes a new book, and originates a new program that seemingly is the key to great growth and achieving ministry success. Unfortunately, many, if not most of these latest and greatest resources are contextual in focus and what worked in the context from which they came often will not work in another context.

It is important that the church identify basic tools for developing the church in the community, and learn how to utilize these tools successfully. Two tools that transcend any specific community context and are viable for the church, regardless of the context are demographic research and historical research. Utilizing these two tools will help the church gain a complete understanding of the people living in the culturally diverse community. The data from demographic research and historical research will not help the church to change, unless the church interacts with the data. This interaction of the congregation with historical and demographic research is necessary, and exciting. It is at this interaction point that the need to develop vision strategy can be fully understood.

Understanding the data alone is not enough cannot be over emphasized. It is one thing to hold data in your hand, but another to do something with the data. Analyzing data collected will help the church congregation gain revelation of who they are, and who lives in their community. This revelation will lay the foundation and prepare the congregation for a decision process. In this decision process the church will be confronted with who they are as a congregation, decide who they will become in the future, and who they will reach. This decision process will also allow the church to decide what level of investment they will be willing to make in becoming a catalyst for God's kingdom.

The first step for the congregation to take is to be proactive with all of the data collected. Based on their research data they will be able to see into the future to some extent and gain an understanding of where the community is at, and where it is going. Understanding their community and the transitions happening in the community in the future gives the church the opportunity to decide their future. A church congregation will have to decide whether to stay in the community, or move out of the community. If the congregation decides that business as usual is ok it is not a major dilemma for anyone other than the church. The congregation simply knows who they are, and they are satisfied. The major dilemma for the satisfied congregation is the fact that their community will inevitably change, it is very likely their congregation will never grow, and more than likely the church will eventually die.

Fig. 2 Results of Churches That Do Not Change

For the church that dares to be different, wants to take positive steps toward reaching the people in their community, and desires transformation there is hope. This church will be willing to take steps to respond to their community, and will have hope to fulfill its potential.

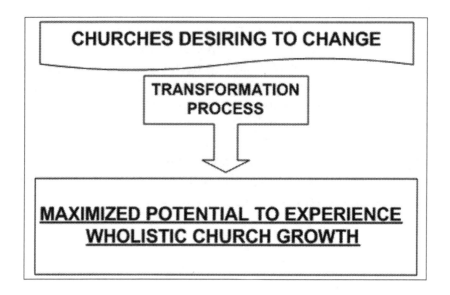

Fig. 3 Churches Desiring Change

Choosing to remain and live in a changing community is choosing to no longer do business as usual, but to be willing to think outside of the box. Deciding to stay and change is making the decision to become intentional about doing things differently. This means that the congregation will deal with their own issues of racism, ethno-centrism, compassion, and commitment to be what God desires them to become. The congregation will walk where it has not been, or as Robert Quinn writes, *"Walk naked into the land of uncertainty"*. This will take determination and great faith (Quinn 1996, 3).

Demographic Research

One of the key starting points to painting the picture of the community population and church congregation is demography. It is the process of understanding the population in a certain community at a given time. Demography is the scientific study of human population, its size, its composition, dynamic life-course processes that change this composition (birth, death, marriage, migration, etc.), and relationships of population composition and change within social and physical environments (Anderson and Yaukey 2001, 379). In the church it includes research, documentation of the findings of this research, and analysis of the data from the Christian perspective. In other words the Christian person will ask the question what does demographic data show me about people needs of the people living in the community? Demographic data will reveal areas where ministry can be targeted to produce greater effectiveness of ministry in a community. As an applied science it is important that demographic research is not research that is done for research sake. It is research that has beneficial meaning for the local church.

Demographic research is something we all do, and most of the time, we do not even realize it. At any given moment in time you may find yourself checking out the people around you. Your observations of people may include people in the mall, the line of the grocery store, students in a child's classroom, the people in a restaurant, or in a neighborhood (Anderson and Yaukey 2001, 379).

When you go to church, or especially when you visit a church for the first time, you look to see who is there. If you have children, you may look around to see if there are other children present who are the age of your children. You may also see if there are other adults who are your age. It may interest you to know what median age, income level, and education level exists among the congregation. These observations take place continuously throughout the world in which we live every day. Each time we walk into a mall, grocery store, church, club, school, and community we look around to see who is there. This process is demography. It is seeing who is there, who is living in the community, and who is in need of ministry.

Demography is important to businesses, schools, government, and church ministries. It is the research and analysis of people making up a certain community's population. By doing demographic study we can get a preliminary observation of who lives in our community. Demographic information will tell us what people live in our community, and provide other limited information about them. This information will give us a "scratch-the-surface" view of what people live in the communities of our church. It will give a preliminary view of their ethnicity, income level, education, family status, average age and other information. Understanding these preliminary observations will help a church to begin the process of customizing ministry to meet the felt needs of people living in the community.

Demographic research includes data collection and analysis. Unfortunately, demographic research for many pastors and people is an unknown concept. Census data is something they are not interested in analyzing. The census is seen as something only for the government to do once every decade, and for the most part means very little to people or their church. As far as they are concerned, *"That is business stuff, and we are here to be spiritual."* Unfortunately, this lack of desire to know about the community directly relates to a lack of vision for ministry.

Demographic data is vital to effective vision planning. However, in regard to demographic research, it is important to note that demographic data is not a vision in itself, but a tool for the pastor, missionary, church planter, church, or ministry to use in order to help them accomplish a realistic vision for the community. This is true in any context. In fact, without an understanding of the community's past, and the present demographics, it will be next to impossible to develop a meaningful ministry vision for the future.

Researching and analyzing demographic data, will help the church to target the people among whom it ministers. For example, gaining the knowledge that ten years ago a community consisted almost exclusively of middle-income white Anglo-Saxon protestant families, and today the community has the same population in number but has transitioned culturally will help a congregation to understand the need to transform in order to reach the newer, more diverse community. Let us say, for example, that the people who now make up the population (ten years later) are 30% African American, 20% Hispanic, 5% Asian, and 45% white Anglo-Saxon protestant. In this case, we see that these percentages of people represent a community with much different interests and needs than the community of ten years ago. Suppose through the study of census data it could be noted that the community has a single parent population of 20%, or in other words two out of every ten people is a single parent. This type of information will also greatly assist the church in planning ministry that will meet the needs of people in their community.

Another aspect of demographic study is analyzing the data in order to understand the growth rate of the community. Growth in the field of demographics can be either positive or negative. Whether there is a decrease in population, or an increase in population the rate of increase or decrease is considered growth. In other words growth can either be positive or negative and it's still considered growth. An analysis of the rate of growth in a community will help an individual to understand if the community is experiencing positive or negative growth during a certain period of time. A more detailed and in-depth study of demographic data will show where growth (negative or positive) is occurring. There are at least six areas of data that need to be researched and analyzed when doing demographic research. These include migration, mortality, birth rate, finance, home ownership, and community/city planning.

Migration - Are people migrating (moving from one place to another place) into the community or out of the community? Studying growth rates and factors involved in migration will help an individual or church person to understand the "people flow" into and out of the community or ministry area of a particular church. Understanding who is moving into and out of the community will help strategic ministry planning to be possible by the church.

Mortality - Who is dying and at what rate? Are people dying from age, sickness, accidents, or crime? How is the mortality rate affecting the rate of growth in the community?

Birth - How many births are being recorded? How is the birthrate affecting the rate of growth in the community? If the rate of birth is significantly high this indicates there are many adults of child bearing age, and ministry to young families may be a strong felt need.

Finance - How many banking institutions and credit unions are located in the community? Are banks willing to loan money within the community? Are business owners establishing themselves in the community? All of these factors affect the community. Often a community in decline economically will have few banking facilities and little or no new business development. However a growing community will evidence new business, such as new restaurants, banks, and retail stores.

Home Ownership - What is the percentage of home ownership in the community? What is the number of multiple family buildings compared to single-family homes? Are people buying or renting?

City Planning - What are the city/community plans for the community in the future? Find out what permits are being granted, attend zoning meetings, and become involved in what is happening in the community planning process.

Accomplishing Demographic Research - Doing demographic research for the church community can be accomplished in various ways. The church pastor or people do not need to earn a high degree in sociology in order to accomplish the majority of data collection and analysis that is needed for the average local ministry. (Anderson and Yaukey 2001). There are two or three practical, doable processes of research that each church can embark on that will help them to collect, analyze, and evaluate data in an effective way.

Practical Steps to Doing Demographic Research
It is important to understand demographic research is not the ultimate word or final say about a community. In fact by the time most demographic data is compiled the community will have changed to some degree. Demographic research is therefore research which is continuous in the sense that population is fluid. People constantly move, die, and new births are recorded.

However, as Christian people doing research on the community in order to more effectively serve the community, we need to accomplish two specific things: 1) studying the most current census data available, creating a snapshot in time of the community, 2) visually observe the community (community observation) in order to understand better who is in the community and verify the census data. This will include how the community appears to have changed since the census data was gathered, and what things we may need to address in the future as a congregation in the community that are only obvious through observation.

Studying Census Data - The United States Census Bureau has a wealth of demographic data that is easily accessible through their website, www.census.gov. It is a good exercise for the researcher to open the Census Bureau's website browse, and investigate the website in order to learn how to use the site. Many data sets are available that are useful for researching the community. Data can be accessed by zip-code, city, county, and other specific data sets can be located such as the Hispanic population in a particular county. It is important to understand that census data will be most accurate immediately following the release of the data, and less and less accurate each year after the data is released. Since the census happens every decade, it is safe to say that the data will be the least accurate in the ninth and tenth year following the release of the data. Reports can also be generated by zip-code, city, and state. Other parameters may be defined in order to select specific areas or groups referred to in the census data.

Community Observation - Visually observe the community in order to understand better who is in the community, and verify the census data. This will include how the community appears to have changed since the census data was gathered and what things the church may need to address in the future as a congregation in the community that are only obvious through observation. This level of observation is not intended to be at the deep level of ethnographic research or participant observation. Doing community research is primarily focused on covering the ground of the community in a short amount of time in order to establish who is in the community. Community observation can be accomplished by walking through the community with our eyes open. In other words we are intentionally looking at the community to see who is in the community. A person may believe they have an understanding of their community because they drive through it all of the time. However as busy people we can drive *through* a community every day and not notice what is happening *in* the community. As people living in the community we become like the frog in the boiling pot we learned about in biology class in high school. The frog in the pot does not notice the pot getting hotter if the heat is turned up slowly, but the frog thrown into the boiling pot will jump out immediately realizing the heat. Observing the community will help the church leader to understand in a greater way what is happening throughout the community.

Community observation will include observing people in everyday places such as the grocery store, Laundromat, library, and local eating establishments. An example of this is to observe playgrounds at restaurants like McDonald's and Burger King to gain an understanding of the ethnicity, culture, and approximate age range of parents and children living nearby. Similarly, diners, bowling alleys, and drug stores will provide a picture of adults living in the community. Another important aspect of observation is looking at ethnic grocery stores and restaurants. This will provide a picture of what people groups may have significant populations within the community, and what people are moving into the community (in-migration). Another important place to look for new immigrants is the day labor or temporary service companies.

Congregation Research - Another aspect of demographic research will include looking at the congregation itself. Thus far in this writing, demographic research, and the steps for doing demographic research have focused on the community existing outside of the church. However, it is equally important to research the congregation itself. Knowing the average age of the congregation, birth rate, mortality rate, migration into, and migration out of the congregation are all important factors in understanding who is in the congregation as compared to who is in the community.

Another important piece of congregational research is the rate of numerical growth of the congregation. Although healthy church growth is not based solely on the numbers, when analyzed, numbers help the researcher gain further understanding of the church. Numeric growth of the church must be viewed in light of:

Individual Salvation Experiences
Migration

Birth Rates and Mortality

A church may exist in a dying community and numerically the membership attendance of the congregation never seems to change, but it may be a growing church. For example, if a church consists of 100 people who are worshipping members: (members who regularly attend and financially support it) during a 2-3 year period, who gradually die or move out of the area, but at the end of the 2-3 year period the church still has 100 worshipping members, then the church has had a significant rate of growth that is not immediately evident. This church actually would be considered a growing church. Society today is mobile and transient. Many times the church will have to take in three people in order to gain one. Researching the demographic data of the church will help to identify the viability of what the church has been doing, and begin to show areas that need improving.

Demography will help the local church congregation, church planter, pastor, and missionary to connect with the community. This community connection will begin with the knowledge of who is in the community, who is moving into and out of the community, and what the needs of people possibly are.

Understanding what is going on in our world today is key to reaching our world. Who is coming to our neighborhood? How is the population shifting? What is the past, present, and future of our community? These are the questions each person with the slightest conviction of fulfilling the Great Commission should ask and answer. Of course, it is one thing to ask the question, it is another to find the answer. Demographic research will help the congregation begin to determine immigration and migration patterns in their community. Who were the first people in the community, the next people in the community, and who is coming now?

In order to reach the community, a church needs to know who lives in their community. It is important to learn who lives in the community, is moving into the community, moving out of the community, and know the rate of population growth. A second important research the congregation must undertake is a historical research. The congregation needs to know the history of their community as well as the history of their congregation.

Doing Community History Research - Historical research in the community should include researching of city planning, meeting city officials, utilizing the local library, and talking to people.

City Master Plan – What plans does the city have for our community? What permits for construction are being applied for, approved, have been applied for in the past, in the present, and future? City planning, urban development, or the fact that there is no development taking place or planned are all indications of a community that is growing, currently on a plateau, or in decline.

Meet City Officials - Meet the mayor (if possible) or city commissioner/alderman – ask about resources for community history. After being appointed pastor of the Narragansett Church of God in Chicago there were many things to accomplish in the first few months. This is always the case when taking on the task of moving in, getting to know a congregation, and being their pastor. However, within the first three months I called and scheduled an appointment with the Alderman of our Ward. He was very kind and welcomed us to the community. I was surprised to learn that I was the first pastor of our church he had met, and he had been the alderman for eight years. I suppose one could say that it is his responsibility to meet the people in the community since he is elected by the community to represent the community. It is far better though, to be intentional and seek out the politician. In fact, the alderman helped our church sponsor a community block party and helped us get approval for our church sign.

Local Library – Check with the librarian on local church history, community, and history. The local library will have newspapers and other resources that will help provide the church with historical data of the community, and possibly the church.

Talk with People - Talk to people who have been in the community for a while. Talk with long time neighbors of the church. Also talk with business owners. Business owners know business owners and they often have knowledge of things that have happened in the community historically. This is especially true of local business owners more than business managers. Some places you may find good community history data are the funeral homes (funeral directors), corner restaurant – diner, tavern owner-proprietor person, mom and pop owned businesses, real-estate agents, residential and commercial, local police officers (precinct captain), sheriff's office, school teachers, and school administration. When talking with people it is important to ask what their view of the church is today, have they ever known anyone who attended services before in the church, and what they feel the church should be doing in the community to help the improve the community.

Developing Questions – Questions developed in advance will be more effective than questions thought of during an interview. Questions developed prior to any interview will also help a researcher to stay focused on the task and stay within a pre-determined time frame. The researcher should listen more than talk, but keep the conversation flowing. When utilizing a committee to do research it may be helpful to prepare research questions for them and prepare some guidelines that will help keep them on track.

Some guidelines may include:
1. Present yourself well
2. Be friendly
3. Be time conscious
4. Treat people equally
5. Buy a cup of coffee, or a soda

Sample questions may include:
1. How long have you live in the community?
2. Describe the community
3. What changes would you make?
4. What is the history of the community?
5. Who are the local government officials?
6. What do like most about the community?
7. What do you dislike most about the community?

Historical research of the local church

- **Church Members** - Start with the church members. The most readily available source of information for anyone researching the history of a local congregation is local church members. Begin asking people questions, and searching for answers.
- **Recorder of Deeds Office** – Research the deed of the church, Plot of Survey, and Site Plan. This will verify when the church was purchased, the land area, and original plans of the church building construction.
- **Church records** - Research old check books, business meeting minutes, -School roll books, and photo albums. Valuable information can be gained by looking through this material. In a sense, this work will be investigative and not comprehensive. However, research data gained from this process will help reveal the historical picture of the church.
- **Denominational records** - Denominational publications may contain articles and statistics about the local church and churches that have existed in the community throughout the history of the denomination. This information can be helpful in confirmation of other data gathered. It may also be helpful in finding new information.
- **Local Newspaper Records** - Information about the church and the community may be found in newspaper articles. Matters of public record are normally recorded in local newspapers and will assist in identifying dates of construction, permit approvals, and other civil matters pertaining to the church. Newspaper articles may also be located that pertain to events in the church.
- **Previous Pastors** - Call and interview former pastors and members. Often these people are not available, or perhaps not easily found. However, they may provide a wealth of information for the researcher studying the history of the church.

This chapter has focused on two specific tools for ministry that to some level transcend context, and help to lay a foundation for identifying the needs of the community today, the past history of the community, local church history, and where the church is today. These tools are demographic research and historical research. Understanding the history of a community and the demographics of the community's population presents the church with the opportunity to build relationship and communication bridges to people living in the community. Building people bridges is important and powerful for the church desiring to reach their community with the gospel of Jesus Christ.

5

BUILDING PEOPLE BRIDGES

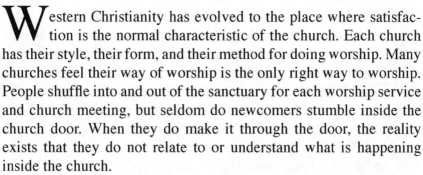

Western Christianity has evolved to the place where satisfaction is the normal characteristic of the church. Each church has their style, their form, and their method for doing worship. Many churches feel their way of worship is the only right way to worship. People shuffle into and out of the sanctuary for each worship service and church meeting, but seldom do newcomers stumble inside the church door. When they do make it through the door, the reality exists that they do not relate to or understand what is happening inside the church.

There is a gap that exists between the church and the world. Call it a canyon, a broad space, or distance. Robert Lewis uses the term chasm. The world does not relate to the church, and the church seldom tries to relate to the world (Lewis 2001, 23). The church it, seems, has fallen asleep and is no longer relevant to the world.

Perhaps this is why Tom Rainer reports that 41% of the American population attends church regularly and the rest of the population does not. Fifty nine percent of the United States population does not regularly attend church. They are un-churched. They are lost (Rainer 2001, 23).

Imagine what an un-churched person thinks about Christians. Most Christian people probably attend church once, twice, or three times a week. They get up on Sunday morning get dressed, drive, walk, or ride to church. Along their journey they pass numerous households, people in the street, at the store, McDonald's, Hardees, diners, Dunkin Doughnuts, and other places doing their Sunday morning activity. The Christian person arrives at their church and enters a place where they find comfort. They read from Scripture, they sing, they give their offering and tithes, they listen to someone talk, they pray, and then go home. This scene to the un-churched person may possibly look like this: *Members of that Christian club go there (to the church) every Sunday morning. They enter the building and speak using words I have never heard, greet one another, and sit down in their seat. The seats aren't numbered, but each person seems to know where his or her seat is located. The music begins and the members sing. They read from a book, meditate, pray, pay their dues, listen to a man or woman talk, meditate again, greet one another again, and go home. They say all people are welcome but I don't feel like I fit. I don't feel welcome.*

Is it possible for people to feel welcome in most churches in America? If the church is going to be relevant in the world, the church will have to build bridges of relationship to those living in the world. Robert Lewis in his book, The Church of Irresistible Influence, writes about the church becoming relevant in doing evangelism to the world. Lewis writes, *"Without its own bridges to the world, church life – in time – fades into isolation, self congratulation, and finally, irrelevance (Lewis 2001, 31)."*

Geographically, bridges connect places; however, bridges of relationship connect people. People bridges are connection points we build between people. In essence, a people bridge is a relationship. Building people bridges is something we all do to some extent in our lives every day. However, most people only build bridges to people they have to build in order to live their life. They talk to people who live next door, possibly look like they look, and speak the same language they speak. People develop bridges to people out of necessity and convenience.

In spite of this, the fact remains that God has a greater calling for His people to fulfill. Christian people have a mission given to them by Jesus Christ to go into the world and make disciples. In order to accomplish this mission the Christian person will have to intentionally build bridges of relationship and communication to people. This is the process of crossing from one's own life world to another person's life world and sharing new life. It is the process of God building bridges through people to people in order that they might build a bridge to Him.

Building people bridges is a challenge, but a necessary task in fulfilling the Great Commission. There are five people bridges that churches existing in the culturally diverse context in America need to continually work toward building. These bridges include:

1. A bridge from the churched world to the un-churched world
2. A bridge from the believer to the unbeliever
3. A bridge from culture/people group to culture/people group
4. A bridge from belief system to belief system
5. A bridge from person to person

A Bridge from the Churched World to the Un-churched World

Few churches in America today try to relate to, or understand those, who do not attend church. Perhaps there are many reasons for a lack of interest or effort on the part of the church in relation to the un-churched. After all, the task is challenging. It requires effort, and people are often busy trying to survive the complexities of the world themselves without being concerned for someone else to the extent that it might interrupt their life. In order to build a bridge from the churched world to the un-churched world, it takes hard work, intentional effort, and good planning. It is a task that requires an investment of time and resources.

Today America has evolved into un-churched nation. Pre-modern thinking gave way to modern thinking sometime in the middle of the twentieth century, modern thinking evolved into post-modern thinking, and post-modern thought has saturated society with the greatness of humankind and the uselessness of religion. The result is a nation that is post-Christian, and not interested in God. Remember, according to Tom Ranier, "Only 41 percent of Americans attend church services on a typical weekend." (Ranier 2001, 33). Post-modernity has influenced America.

Post-Modern, according to Tony Jones, is the period of societal thinking following the modern era of thought born in the Industrial Revolution. In a sense, modern society built the world, and post modern society has asked why? Author Elmer Towns and Warren Bird in their book, Into The Future, and Tony Jones in his book, Postmodern Youth Ministry, refer to the example in the text written by J. Richard Middletown, and Brian J. Walsh, Truth is Stranger Than It Used To Be: Biblical Faith in A Postmodern Age, to describe post-modernity compared to modernity and pre-modernity. (Jones 2001, 20) and (Towns and Bird 2000, 70).

> "Three baseball umpires in an imaginary conversation, Pre-modern... "There's balls and there's strikes and I call them as they are" Modern... "There's balls and there's strikes and I call them as I see them" Post-modern... "There's balls and there's strikes and they ain't nothing until I call them (Middleton and Walsh 1995, 70)"

The separation of generational values and thinking that exists in society is evident throughout the United States among all groups of people. According to George Barna, there are multiple generations, each with a different world-view existing in American society. These generations include the groups known as Seniors, Builders, Boomers, Busters, and Mosaics (Barna 1998, 71). Each of these generation groups see the world differently and exhibit different felt needs. They like different music styles, clothing styles, hair styles, and have different value systems. They see the world differently and their world view has affected the fabric of the American popular culture.

A generation ago United States society was known as a Christian society and has traditionally been understood to be a society based in Christian values. However, values were challenged with modern thinking and significantly changed with post-modern thinking (Sweet 1999, 50-51). Ethics once seen as black and white, like ink on a page, have blended into gray. Right and wrong are relative and people often do not accept truth as reality. This post-modern world finds American society in a post-modern state of mind. The fact is, in this post-modern world, the United States has found itself becoming a post-Christian society (Barna 1998, 68).

Gaining knowledge of people groups living in the United States is a task that begins with understanding the characteristics of today's American population. There are three significant characteristics evident today in American Society. They are 1. a popular culture shift from a churched society to an un-churched society, to post Christian society, 2.generational separation, and 3.the mainstreaming of cultural diversity in America.

1. <u>A popular culture shift from a church world to an un-churched world</u>

A popular culture shift has occurred in the United States from a churched society, to an un-churched society, and now to a post-Christian society. It was not too many years ago that people in the United States were generally thought to attend a church service on the weekend as a normal part of their weekly schedule. Of course, the primary day of the weekend most church people have attended worship services traditionally has been Sunday. Today, tradition is not what it once was. People no longer speak church vocabulary well; they do not know church language. People in American society no longer view or understand "church" as a normal process of life. The American population has walked down a road toward a post-Christian destination, and their journey has been successful (Sweet 1999, 50-51).

Aubry Malphurs and George Barna describe the post-Christian perspective of the Baby Buster generation in the same manner. This generation group has little or no concept of God. Their life process includes modern thought. They are un-churched, and their children are un-churched (Malphurs [1992] 1998, 38). Consider that millennials, the generation following Xers, born starting in 1982, were twenty years old in 2002, and now possibly having children of their own. If a millennial person having children is un-churched, like their Buster parents and Boomer grandparents, their children will be the fourth generation removed from a churched society in America. They will be un-churched. In fact they are part of a post-Christian Society.

> "When I was a kid in the 1950's, people's minds were still naturalized in Christianity. If you breathed air, you knew who a 'Pharisee' was, or what it meant to call a city 'Sodom and Gomorrah' (Sweet 1999, 45)."

We are living in a post-modern world and have moved from a society where people have knowledge about a Judeo-Christian God into a post-Christian world where people question the concept of God

> "The pastoral team at Trinity Church in Columbus, Ohio, 'retreated' to Indianapolis for the NCAA 'March Madness' basketball playoffs. The ubiquitous guy with orange hair and a homemade 'John 3:16' sign was under the basket at the other end of the court. Seated directly behind the pastoral team were two well-dressed couples debating what the 'John 3:16' sign meant. Reduced to guessing, one thought it must be an ad for a new restaurant in town. The others dissed that idea since 'who would send someone out with orange hair and a hand drawn sign to advertise anything?' Another thought the 'John 3:16' sign might be a signal to someone to meet John on the third floor, stall 16. Talk about clueless. They were totally in the dark why anyone would be holding a sign with those words on it (Sweet 1999, 45)."

American society has become a post-Christian, multicultural, multi-ethnic, multigenerational mission field, many times stumbling in the dark, like a person waking up in the middle of the night in an unfamiliar hotel searching for a light switch. The American population is lost in the dark. America is a mission field and America needs missionaries.

Looking at the United States and realizing it is now a post-Christian society that is the third largest mission field in the world, will cause a Christian person concerned with the mission mandate of God, to scratch his or her head and wonder, "What can possibly be done?" In fact, a significant question that must be considered is, "At what point does a post-Christian society become a pre-Christian society?" Regardless of the answer to this question, a people, society, or culture who no longer serve or seek God (post-Christian), and a people, society, or culture who have not yet found God, are both without God and in need of a messenger who will understand them and communicate a gospel message that finds meaning in their heart.

2. Generational Separation

Church ministry has focused within the walls of the sanctuary for too many years. The church stands as the lighthouse to the world preaching hope to the hopeless and help to the helpless; however, many times the helpless and hopeless do not fit into the right image of the church. They do not speak church language and; therefore, do not understand the church's message (Sweet 1999, 53). This is true regardless of culture.

The growing church today will be a church of multiple ministry efforts. Church folks need to understand that in planting and growing breathing, living churches whether an existing congregation, a church in a transitioning community, or church plant, ministry has to become multi-faceted. People today have many options to choose from in life. Along with this fact is the reality that society is experiencing separation of generations. Although these generation separations are most distinct among Anglo-Americans, generation separation affects all culture and ethnic groups in the United States at some level.

People are offered many, many choices today. Therefore, in building bridges to people, two things are important to consider. First of all, church ministry should offer some choices and options to both churched and unchurched people to experience God. Secondly, the message must remain intact. Options in presenting the message do not result in optional messages as some today propose. Commitment is a low priority among people, while variety, something new, and somebody different drive people from church to church looking for the hottest, most interesting thing. What is happening according to George Barna is,

> "Church attendance. Overall attendance at Christian churches has slumped somewhat; people are going less regularly; and are becoming more selective. Worship remains an art that most people have tried – and tens of millions continue to invest in each week. However, nearly one-fifth of all church-goers now attend more than one church, usually on a rotating basis, in order to meet their spiritual needs and satisfy their theological curiosity (Barna 1998, 18)."

People are not getting what they feel they need in only one church. People are very often going to more than one church at the same time. Baby Busters and Millennials are going to different churches, and different places, to meet their needs than their parents and grandparents did. The church should consider offering multiple faceted ministries in the worship experience that are meeting the felt needs of people.

We are living in a mosaic thinking world today and ministry effort will need to be adjusted to reach the generations of people existing in society including Millennials, Mosaic thinkers, Baby Busters, and those who are coming on the horizon. We have gone from a one-dimensional world, to a two-dimensional world, and now a three-dimensional world.

People today do not necessarily think salvation is the only way to heaven. Yet the central thing we offer, the main thing we offer people to find and know God, is our Sunday morning worship service. The thing in the church that we have put all of our energy into is Sunday morning worship. We do not need to diminish our efforts at worship but we need to enhance efforts in other opportunities for worship.

People are looking for hope, help and love; but, many have never been to a church. They do not know where to begin.

If a person is to look at the history of the early church, the question can be asked, "why Sunday?" Our emphasis on the Sabbath in some ways has taken precedent over our emphasis on salvation. This has happened as church growth has continually been determined by how many warm bodies are in the pew on Sunday instead of how many people are coming to Christ. The church has to come to the understanding that youth, and adults today, are not tied to the 11AM worship service in order to meet God.

3. Mainstreaming of cultural diversity in America

A one generation, one culture targeted church is on its way to the grave in most growing, and especially, culturally diverse communities. A church may be early in a dying process. Perhaps it even has a significant attendance; but, if the congregation in the culturally diverse community consists of one generation from one culture, the future of the church is in jeopardy.

In 1992, I visited an Italian Pentecostal church on a few different occasions. The congregation was made of primarily first generation Italian immigrants. They spoke Italian in church, sang in Italian, and prayed in Italian. However, the median age of the congregation was approximately 60. There were no children, no grandchildren, and no young people whatsoever. I asked some of the people one day where the younger people were. They told me their children attend an English speaking church, or not at all.

What was once considered urban is no longer tied to the geographical boundaries of the city; but urban characteristics of diversity and modernity are seen throughout the fabric of United States society. Diversity has been a city thing, but today, diversity is a fiber of mainstream society in America. With an understanding of the changing characteristics of American society, the researcher begins to understand that doing ministry in the same manner it has done in the past, will not be effective in the present, or future. As bridges are built from the churched world to the un-churched world, it is important to consider what is happening in the world and strategically plan accordingly.

A Bridge from Believer to Un-believer

The New Testament model of evangelism was very personal much of the time. There were times of proclamation when Paul would stand on the steps of the synagogue and preach. In Acts 19:9, he rented the school of Tyrannus in Ephesus in the afternoons to teach and preach the message of the Messiah; and, when he stood on Mars Hill at the Acropolis (Acts 17:22-23), he proclaimed that he personally knew the unknown God, Paul publicly proclaimed the gospel. Proclamation is an important part of evangelism in Scripture. However, there is clearly guidance in Scripture that the message of the Messiah is a personal message carried by believers to unbelievers in person. Jeremiah 29:7 encouraged the people of God to build houses, plant, marry, have children. This is an admonition to believers that they flesh out their faith in an unbelieving community in order to bring people into direct contact with the creator God Adonai.

In the New Testament, believers are encouraged to go from house to house and break bread together (Acts 2:46). Breaking bread together is something Christians have become very good at doing. However, "together" in the Christian world has come to mean exactly that: Christians breaking bread together with Christians, also known as fellowship. I know from my personal experience as a Pentecostal Christian, the Pentecostal church has mastered fellowship. Christian people are fellowshipping people, and church dinners are a normal process of church life. In fact, we often joke around about how we love to eat. There is great community building power in fellowship. Breaking bread together is a powerful experience, and there is great significance to the spiritual intimacy attached with eating together. God affirmed this in ordaining the Lord's Supper (Communion) as a powerful experience of fellowshipping with Christ by remembering what He accomplished on the cross (I Cor 11:23-26). The fact is, personal relationship must be established in order to communicate to people, and having a meal together is a powerful way to build relationships and communicate.

The believer must see the need, feel the burden, and sense the passion to actively engage unbelievers with the gospel message. Being a silent witness is simply exemplifying Christian character throughout the process of living life. It is that level of life where we, as Christians, exemplify the fruit of the Spirit; love, joy, peace, longsuffering, meekness, kindness, etc. (Gal 5:22) Being a silent witness is a given in Christianity. It is understood that Christians will be Christ like. Every believer, as he or she becomes more and more like Jesus Christ, exemplifies more and more the attributes of Jesus Christ; and, thus becomes a greater testimony to the world of Jesus Christ.

Boldness to do the work of evangelism is not a natural phenomenon within human beings. There is significance to the presence of the power existing in the person of the Holy Spirit. The guts to evangelize is born in a hunger from the heart of God to see all people have a relationship with God through His Son Jesus Christ. Tom Rainer speaks of this evangelism burden in terms of developing a Theology of Lostness. A Theology of Lostness is that driving force not only to see all people saved, but also to keep them from an eternity in hell. It is the understanding of John 14:6 that there is only one way to salvation, and that way is through Jesus Christ (Rainer 2001, 158).

Building a bridge from believer to unbeliever includes an understanding of God's mandate for His people to reach the lost. Throughout scripture, God continually brings the understanding through His people that He desires people to know Him in relationship; thus He desires that none should perish. Ezekiel 3:18 shows the significance of God's servants going to those who are lost

"When I say to the wicked, 'You shall surely die; and you do not warn him or speak out to warn the wicked from his wicked way that he may live, that wicked man shall die in his iniquity, but his blood I will require at your hand.

(Ezek 3:18)."

Isn't it amazing that throughout history God has utilized his people to speak His word to humankind. People have been, and continue to be, His vessels of ministry in this world. In Mathew 28:19 Jesus gives the mandate to His disciples to go into the entire world and make disciples. Jesus tells the disciples they are to be proactive in engaging people with His message. Of course, He does not leave His followers in a state of weakness. He plants the seed in their heart that they would soon receive Divine power in the presence of the Holy Spirit in their lives to be witnesses of Him (Acts 1:8).

God expects His followers to be "Fishers of Men" (Matt 4:19, Mark 1:17). This means being fishers of people by having scripture knowledge and skill which is developed through the knowledge and practice of doing evangelism among people. The problem with our fellowship in the church is the fact that it is most often only in the church. Evangelism has lost a great deal of significance as a priority in the daily life of the believer. Today, in America, the national conversion ratio of how many church members it takes to reach one person for Christ in a year is 85:1. This ratio reveals a great need for believers to build bridges to unbelievers successfully (Rainer 2001, 23).

A Bridge from Culture to Culture

In order for evangelism to be effectively accomplished in communities that are ethnically and culturally diverse, the church will need to build bridges from culture group to culture group. The process of building bridges from culture group to culture group is a process that includes elements of understanding ourselves and understanding those to whom we are building a bridge. Eugene Nida developed what he called the Three Culture Model of Missionary Communication as a means to communicating the gospel message from one culture to another culture. According to Nida there are three elements included in effective missionary communication. Nida's elements are the Bible culture, the sender culture, and the respondent culture. The Three Culture Model of Missionary Communication looks like this in diagram form:

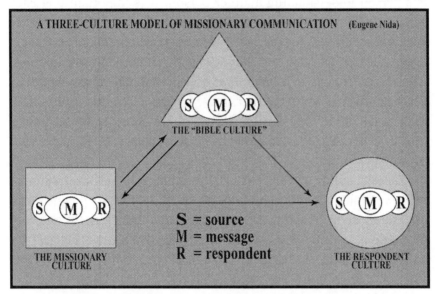

Fig. 4 A Three-Culture Model of Missionary Communication

According to Nida's model the sender of the message, or in the theme of this writing, the builder of the bridge, has to understand scripture in the sense that it is written in cultural context.

A. Understanding Bible culture

The gospel is written in the context of culture, but the message transcends culture. Understanding this is understanding that the goal of studying scripture in context is to understand why scripture deals with the issues it deals with in certain situations, and how it deals with these issues. The "why" of scripture truth is that element of scripture that goes beyond culture, or exists in spite of cultural context. Gaining a deeper understanding of the Bible within the culture it was written allows the messenger to understand that the Bible is always seen through the eyes of culture.

B. Understanding ourselves

There is a need for the sender of the message to understand who he or she is, what matters to them, and what they see as truth in relation to the gospel. Knowing oneself is a vital key to one person understanding another person. It is important that each person understand that just because he or she is talking to people does not mean that people are hearing and comprehending what is being said. Ligenfelter and Mayers say, "A common error in cross-cultural ministry is to assume that people understand us when they hear our words" (Lingenfelter and Mayers 1986, 79). Individuals need a self understanding of who they are in order to communicate to other people. Understanding oneself is vital to successful communication.

Understanding oneself is only possible with self-examination. Self-examination begins with looking at who we are as people. Who we are as people includes our history, our family traditions, our perceptions of life issues, and our personality traits. The greatest difficulty we have is that it is very challenging to realize the extent that our culture molds who we are.

In addition to self-examination, each person needs to deal with the isms in their life. The isms of American society are racism, ethnocentrism, elitism, and sexism. These are the three ism's each individual, growing up in the United States, must uncover and deal with in his or her life. This process is necessary prior to building bridges to culture groups, other than the sender's own culture. These three isms will possibly need to be dealt with more than once as cross-cultural tensions bring hidden feelings to light. As these feelings come to the surface they must be brought under submission. Like the Apostle Paul each believer must bring his or her life under subjection every day (I Cor 9:27).

These isms are not new to the world. Racism, ethnocentrism, elitism, and sexism have plagued our world especially, the country of the United States for many years. Unfortunately, world history is filled with accounts of oppression of one group of people against another. Tribal warfare, clan feuds, and battles of people based upon their difference in cultural, religious, and moral values are a fact of history. These conflicts are a part of history; and, unfortunately, are part of the present, also.

Racism

Struggles between people in America are nothing new to America. Even from this country's beginning people were oppressed on this continent. This continent has experienced a history of difficulty in relationships that continues to overshadow our society today. It wasn't too many years ago (1992) that Rodney King stood before television cameras, with the city of Los Angeles in flames, and made his profound statement, *"Can't we all just get along?"* The tensions of racism, ethnocentrism, and elitism effect the way people think and feel. These tensions are not new and must be placed within a historical frame in order to gain a full understanding of the shadow that has been cast over America.

First, Spanish Conquistadors, explorers, and priests oppressed indigenous peoples in what would become Florida, New Mexico, California, and the country of Mexico. Then the French, Dutch, and British who were also colonial oppressors came. Each group arrived with their own set of values, cultural norms, and belief systems. Each fought to conquer one another and each oppressed the indigenous people groups of the Americas, often in efforts to "Christianize" the heathen. Eventually, these indigenous peoples were removed from the landscape either by death, ethnocide (ethnocide – the destruction of a people's culture carried out on a systematic basis) (Howard [1983] 1986, 445), or deportation.

Even after this destruction of people groups indigenous to this continent, oppression on the continent was not over. Dutch slave traders brought people captured primarily from West Africa to Caribbean Islands, including Haïti, Jamaica, Puerto Rico, and others. Many were brought to Elmina Castle in Ghana. It was there that they were placed into the cargo holds of slave ships bound for the Americas. Upon arriving on the Caribbean Islands, they were sold to the highest bidders who included plantation owners, farmers, and the wealthy elite. They were then transported to their new homes bound in chains with no hope of freedom. They were strangers in a foreign land brought to this land in bondage. These were days of great pain and misery for peoples from the African continent who were the slaves of well off European settlers.

Shame causes people to forget things in history of which no one can be proud about. It is shame that causes people to forget about the plight of people indigenous to the Americas (Native Americans) and the bondage of people brought to this continent in chains in order to serve those in power over them as slaves. The shame and guilt associated with the history of the United States of America is something for each person who is an American citizen to give thought to. Learning from history includes learning from the victories of the past, and it also means learning from defeat.

Fortunately, many attempts at healing the hurts of the past and righting the misery of injustice have been successful along the way. The dream of the Declaration of Independence, "That all men are created equal," has driven humble men to accomplish great feats for justice and freedom. Freedom is, in essence, the ability of an individual to determine his or her own destiny. This cause of freedom drove farmers, shoe makers, and pilgrims to become patriots in the war of Independence. It inspired Abraham Lincoln, a man who had failed at everything he ever tried, to campaign for the presidency with a vision to emancipate people from the chains of slavery. Freedom inspired Lincoln to write these words in his address at Gettysburg:

"Four score and seven years ago our fathers brought forth on this continent a new nation, conceived in liberty, and dedicated to the proposition that all men are created equal. Now we are engaged in a great civil war, testing whether that nation, or any nation so conceived and so dedicated, can long endure (Morison 1994, 469)."

Although Lincoln was by no means a perfect man, his vision for freedom cost him his life. The triumph of his death is that the dream did not end. Even as the century turned from 19th to 20th, and pre-industrial to industrial, many picked up the pen of freedom with which Lincoln penned his words.

Irish peasant immigrants fled the horror of famine, starvation, and tyranny in their homeland only to find, upon their arrival in New York City, life just as difficult as what they left behind. They were welcomed, upon their arrival, with signs saying, "Irish stay out", or

"No Irish welcome here". It is a fact that millions of people arriving on the shores of America of every culture, color, and creed have not found an easy way or a promised land. In spite of their challenges, people have somehow heard the cry of the beat in their heart to live as free people free to choose their own destiny. Although the oppression, discrimination, difficulties, and obstacles have hindered many, many more have climbed out of bed morning after morning with only a few hours of sleep to begin their work day of two or three jobs because they are driven by the fact that they are forging their destiny. They are free people.

It is this driving force to live free that drove European outcast immigrants in the early part of the 20th century to survive. It caused Japanese men and women to see beyond the fences that confined them in the 1940s during World War II to a world where they would live free. This driving force is that thing that caused Black Americans to seek complete freedom from the indignity of the American apartheid that existed from the time of the Emancipation Proclamation until the Civil Rights Act of 1964 and beyond. It is this force of freedom that caused Dr. Martin Luther King Jr. to pick up the freedom pen, and 100 years after Abraham Lincoln addressed Gettysburg pen these words which he spoke on the Mall at Washington D.C. in 1963:

> "Fivescore years ago, a great American, in whose symbolic shadow we stand today, signed the Emancipation Proclamation. This momentous decree came as a great beacon light of hope to millions of Negro slaves who had been seared in the flames of withering injustice. It came as a joyous daybreak to end the long night of their captivity. But one hundred years later, the Negro still is not free; one hundred years later, the life of the Negro is still sadly crippled by the manacles of segregation and the chains of discrimination...(King 1993, 1-3)."

King finishes his famous speech with these lines:

> "And when we allow freedom to ring...we will be able to speed up that day when all of God's children – black men

and white men, Jews and Gentiles, Catholics and Protestants will be able to join hands and to sing in the words of the old Negro Spiritual, 'Free at last, free at last; thank God Almighty, we are free at last' (King 1993, 31-33)."

Freedom in America is an almost, but not quite yet, fact of life. The remnants of racism are still present, and perhaps racism is more of an issue in our society than is acknowledged or recognized. The fact is that racism is an issue we, as missionaries to American communities, will confront.

This is why each person must deal with his or her own issues. Each person has to confront the isms in his or her own life. Racism does still exist today. In the same manner that few people want to talk about slavery, or the ethnocide of Native American people, many people are very uncomfortable with the fact that racism continues to be a fact of American life in many communities, and in many individuals. In fact, if the subject comes up among Caucasian people, some completely deny its existence, some accept the issue as reality, some change the subject, and others try and justify their position, sealing the fact that they are racist without even realizing it.

The effects of racism can be seen in three specific ways today in society. These are overt racism, systemic racism, and response racism.

1. Overt racism is blatant open racism. It is the clearly identifiable injustice of an individual or group in power acting against another individual or group not in power. It is vivid in the sense of hood wearing Klan members, Arian Nation members, or a restaurant not serving an individual because of the color of his or her skin. In America, the largest color group, and strongest power group, is the Caucasian people group. Racism in the United States is primarily and historically known to be a white people against black people issue; but, in essence, it can be any group who is not in power being diminished and oppressed by the group in power.

2. Systemic racism is most often not readily recognized. It is that subtle form of racism that creeps along as part of the fiber of society which is often not exposed or seldom acknowledged. Systems, organizations, and political institutions are most often the primary

perpetrators of systemic racism. It is in institutions that systemic racism develops. Systemic racism is noticed when institutions exact race-neutral policies (such as stopping certain programs under the guise of controlling big government while allowing other programs to continue), and the results of the policies overly affect those not in power who are typically non-white.

3. Response racism is a direct product of racism, and is very dangerous. It is like a hidden infection that grows until it can not be hidden anymore. According to Joseph Barndt racism is racial prejudice plus power (Barndt 1991, 28). Response racism is the reaction to the action of racism. It is the emotion that has been exemplified in periods of history through inflicting violence on people such as happened during the Los Angeles riots. Very often the result of response racism is a hatred of an entire people group that generates violence in which innocent people are injured. This is the case in the Middle East today. One people group has experienced such great oppression from another people group that the oppressed people kill innocent people with little moral regard for life.

Ethnocentrism

Have you ever been in conversation with a group of people who talked about another group of people saying, "We are better than they are" or "Aren't they weird?" "Our group is better than that group", is the hidden cry in the heart. Ethnocentrism may or may not include issues of power. It does, however, include issues of pride. A little cultural pride is not necessarily negative in and of itself; but, when one group overtly influences another group to do it their way because it is the "right" way, it is negative. Ethnocentrism may occur in ethnicity groupings because it is culturally defined. Ethnocentrism is the interpretation of the behavior of others in terms of one's own cultural values and traditions (Howard [1983] 1986, 445). People groups often look down on other groups.

Elitism

A third ism each person will deal with in his or her life is elitism. Elitism happens when a person feels he or she is better than someone else due to class differences or sometimes birthright. Everyone needs a compassion test once in a while. I remember growing up and hearing some people in the church make fun of homeless people and poor people from time to time. The truth is that very often people have negative thoughts about other people who are poor, broken, or homeless.

How should a Christian feel when they meet a homeless person in the street or in the sanctuary? Israel didn't handle the situation correctly at one point in their history, and too often the church falls far short of where it should be in dealing with broken people. Ezekiel spelled out the sin of Israel as being synonymous with the sin of Sodom in Ezekiel 16:49. "Because they did not love the poor"…God brought judgment upon them. Today in our society we find a similar situation. Most of society has little compassion for those who are homeless and see them as people who just do not want to work.

A homeless person finds filling out a job application challenging because they have no address, and they have no phone for a perspective employer to contact them. Homelessness is a place of being stuck. It is that place in life where a person has little or no hope for the future much like the man at the gate of the temple in Acts chapter 3. Lame since birth, he was stuck at the gate begging for money.

Sexism

Sexism is defined (according to Webster Dictionary) as prejudice or discrimination based on sex; especially discrimination against women. Sexism in society is most commonly expressed toward women. It may include overt actions which keep women in subservient roles in the society or church in which they live. We as people must deal with our own issues of sexism in our lives. This affects us as females, males and as we approach people of culture groups other than our own.

1. Females – There is a tendency for those in society who have been oppressed to adapt their mannerisms, actions, and lifestyle to avoid the harsh reality of being oppressed. This may include becoming silent among groups of people avoiding the possibility of being hurt rather than being the individual God has called them to become interacting with their environment offering input to their environment. As the gender who is most often the object of sexism,

women must deal with the issues of self-worth, confidence and work toward being visible as equal persons of worth created in the image of God.

2. Males – Each person of male gender must deal with their own issues of sexism. This includes the man confronting his development as a person, view of women in society, in the church, and in leadership. Men are the perpetrators of sexism in society. There are some men who try to deflect this reality by pointing to women who assert themselves as individuals created equal by God as being feminists in the most negative sense. However, the reality is sexism does exist, men are the primary persons exhibiting prejudice and oppression against women, and men must deal with this ism in their lives. Acknowledgment of sexist attitudes and feelings will provide the opportunity for repentance and subsequent reconciliation in the life of a man.

3. Our approach in working with people from other cultures It is important to learn about how cultures other than our own view women. Understanding the roles of women and how sexism is exhibited in their will help a person approaching the culture to be more effective in doing ministry among that culture. Working among a culture in which sexism may be overt and sometimes even violent can be quite challenging. While working to reach people in such a culture with the gospel message, cause life transformation in the lives of people, and remain sensitive to the cultural traditions the work of the person building a bridge to the culture is a challenging balancing act.

Reconciliation

Overcoming our learned behaviors of thinking we are better than someone else begins in our relationship with Jesus Christ. As we become like Jesus, we will desire to help the hurting and love those who are outcast. Those who have resisted becoming like Jesus Christ have a Christian experience which has never grown beyond the embryo stage. Allowing God's love to flow through a life is the key to destroying the yoke of sin that says we are better than other people because they are worse off than us. The greatest way to deal with our isms, and the results issues of racism, ethnocentrism, elitism, and sexism in a person's life, is through the presence and power of Jesus Christ as the reconciler of people.

Reconciliation begins in the heart, and true complete reconciliation is only possible through Jesus Christ. Raleigh Washington and Glen Kehrein are two men who dared to do what very few people will do. Washington, an African-American man, and Kehrein, a Caucasian American man, intentionally moved to the Westside of Chicago to build a model of reconciliation that showed through Jesus Christ people could come together. They founded their ministry on the scripture 2 Corinthians 5:16-21. Washington and Kehrein speak of reconciliation as a Christ centered principle, and focus on Him as the ultimate reconciler. As the song says, "He is our peace, and He has broken down every wall", Jesus has torn down the walls of separation.

Understanding that Jesus is the ultimate reconciler, each believer should follow His example and become people of reconciliation. Reconciliation must become a core value of the church; but, it will not be a core value of the church until it is a core value in each person's life. In order for reconciliation to become a core value, an individual must deal with his or her own feelings in regard to racism. This is true for the oppressed and the oppressor. It is one thing for a person to have a parking lot relationship with another person, but a family room relationship should be our priority in relationship building with one another.

The reality of the church is that many have accepted their racism as the natural order of humanity. Statements have been made by people, ministers, and scholars that people of different ethnicity and culture shouldn't come together. However, in the United States, people who live in a diverse community work together, go to school together, and live in neighborhoods together. Why then shouldn't people worship together also? This strategy of spiritual separation has been very effective in many places in keeping the church the most segregated institution in American society (Rainer 1993, 259). In order for the church as an institution to change, people have to change.

In their book, <u>Breaking Down Walls</u>, Washington and Kehrein write about eight principles of reconciliation they have developed.

These are powerful principles that each Christian should learn to live by. However, it is important that we all bend our knee and pray for forgiveness of any racism issues we have in our lives, or have had in our lives. Without deep heart change through repentance of sin these principles have no real power. It is possible to find redemption from the sin of racism, and people who desire to build bridges to people can become reconcilers through intentional effort, self examination, and repentance (Washington and Kehrein 1993).

C. Understanding the respondent culture

The final element of the Three Culture Model that Nida introduced is that of the respondent culture. Knowledge about the respondent culture is critical for two primary reasons. First of all, people's knowledge of the respondent culture will assist the sender in knowing how to approach the respondent. Secondly, knowledge of the respondent culture will increase the opportunity for effective communication of the message of the gospel.

How we approach people is important. It is vital to evangelism success. J.H. Bavink describes Approach Theories as relevant to the missionary endeavor of crossing from one culture to another culture. How an individual approaches another individual impacts the outcome of their encounter (Bavinck 1960, 89). Lingenfelter and Mayers discuss two powerful elements to cross-cultural ministry that are profound and important in building bridges from culture to culture. These are basic values, and becoming 150% persons.

Basic values are values which are present in every culture. Understanding these basic values will help an individual to develop his or her approach to people from other culture groups. Lingenfelter and Mayers refer to Edward Hall's list of ten primary message systems found in culture. These are temporality, territoriality, exploitation, association, subsistence, bisexuality (differing modes of speech, dress, and conduct), language, learning, play, and defense (Lingenfelter and Mayers 1986, 27). Lingenfelter and Mayers further develop the concept of cultural traits that each culture group exhibits in their theory of basic values. They describe twelve key elements in their model of basic values which are broken down into six contrasting points. These are:

a) Tensions about time
b) Tensions in judgment
c) Tensions in handling crisis
d) Tensions over goals
e) Tensions about self worth
f) Tensions regarding vulnerability

Tensions about time

Ligenfelter and Mayers describe time oriented people as those who feel the highest priority in any event is that the event begins on time and ends on time. Event oriented people are more interested in the event than when it begins or ends. While pastoring in Chicago, our church grew from two Sunday worship services each Sunday to four worship services each Sunday. Our Sunday schedule included Sunday School at 10AM, a multi-ethnic / multi-cultural service at 11AM, a Bulgarian language worship service at 1PM, a Spanish language worship service at 3PM, and a multi-ethnic / multi-cultural service at 6:30PM.

The church's greatest time tensions were experienced during the 11AM worship service. The church sign advertised that our service began at 11AM, but we usually started around 11:15AM. Most Sundays I would begin preaching around 11:50, and finish about 12:15PM. We then had prayer around the altar area and most often prayed the benediction between 12:30 and 12:40PM. Following the benediction, my wife and I would stand at the exit and shake hands with everyone as they departed the church after each service. After the 11AM service, one couple would always shake my hand and say, *"Pastor, if we would start on time we could end on time"*, and every Sunday I would smile, thank him, and tell him we would try to do better next time. We also had a young couple from a different culture than this man who would stop each Sunday as they left the church and say, *"That was a great service Pastor, but it would have been better if you had preached longer."* This couple almost always arrived at the church after I began preaching. As we shook hands, I would smile, thank them, encourage them to arrive a little sooner, and assure them we were doing our best to accommodate everyone's schedule in the most workable way. Both of these couples were right in their perception of time according to their culture. One was from a time oriented culture, and one from an event oriented culture.

The western world is focused on the clock. This focus on the clock almost reaches the level of obsession at times. The first opportunity I had to leave the United States and visit another country was in 1985 after graduating from high school. At the grand old age of eighteen, I boarded an airplane along with nine other people from our church. We flew to Miami, changed planes, and then flew to Port-Au Prince, Haiti. The trip was exciting, but very challenging. Our challenges did not come from language barriers, Haitian food, or worship styles. Our challenges came from our perception of how things should be done.

I remember our greatest challenge, and our group's greatest frustration that week, was our tension with time. We left our home in America and traveled to a culture that had no concept of our time oriented culture. This frustration was first directed at the missionary, and then at one another. Our missionary host told us he would pick us up at a certain time, and then he wouldn't show up until two hours later. Our group became very impatient with him.

We would go to the church for the evening service by 7PM, and sit alone in the church for an hour and a half until people began showing up for church. I didn't figure out the concept of time in Haïti until my second trip to Haïti. During my second trip to Haïti, we were working in a church in Gonaive putting fluorescent lighting in the church. During this installation process I asked a man for the time. He gave me a strange look, and then told me he didn't have a watch. It was then I realized that very few people had watches. I learned that people in that area of Haïti knew when to get up in the morning because the sun came up, and church members knew it was time to go to church when the sun went down.

Our group did not have an understanding of Haitian culture and their concept of time. It was because of our group's lack of understanding of Haitian culture, and lack of willingness to understand the culture, that tension over the issue of time was a problem of our group and trip. Building bridges from culture group to culture group comes with challenges. As people come together to worship in a culturally diverse church there are tensions that arise. Each tension has to be handled with love, wisdom, grace, and strength. In the multi-ethnic / multi-cultural church one of the tensions that has the potential to be of great difficulty is time.

Tensions in Judgment

North American society, speaking in generic terms, is a working society, and hard work is a high value. Although Americans, in comparison to many countries, today may seem lazy, historically American people are known as working people. They in many ways tend to separate their lives according to the activities they do. Every part of their life is often compartmentalized. Work time, personal time, family time, and church time are periods of time when the individual is dedicated to that particular activity. People who compartmentalize their lives often struggle to relate to those who look at life as a whole process.

Many cultures approach life as a whole. They do not compartmentalize their lives into specific areas, but live life as a whole. How we approach life affect our judgment and influences our decision making process. The understanding that people from different cultural backgrounds than from our own have different ways of making decisions is an important fact of knowledge for anyone working among different culture groups. It is important to learn how each group makes decisions in order to include the group in the decision making process in the church. This affords each group partnership in the life of the church.

Some cultures are matriarchal (the matriarch is the decision maker), some are patriarchal (the patriarch is the decision maker), some are individualistic (the individual makes their own decision), and some are group oriented (the entire group makes the decision). Understanding that there are differing decision making processes, and learning about them in order to develop a decision making process within the life of the church that everyone can live with, is important to the success of the church.

Tensions in handling crisis

In April 2001, our family had the opportunity to do ministry training and to minister in Jamaica. We flew from Atlanta to Montego

Bay, Jamaica. When we landed at Montego Bay, our host gathered our small group, we gathered our luggage, and we followed him to the place at the airport that our ride would pick us up. We waited two hours for our ride. Our family was fine with waiting. By this time in our ministry we were culturally sensitive and were not overly anxious about a wait.

Our ride eventually arrived and we embarked on our journey. Our group of eight people fit into two vans and made our way from Montego Bay up into the mountains toward Mandeville, Jamaica. About half way through our journey, we drove around a deep ravine along the side of a mountain and our van developed a slight problem. Our host Daniel looked up and asked inquisitively, "Isn't that our tire?" Daniel asked this question as our tired rolled past us down the road and the van dragged the ground. Our driver stopped the van and we all piled out onto the road. By the time my feet hit the ground there were already approximately twenty people standing around the van staring at the passenger side rear of the vehicle. I spoke up and asked Daniel, "What will we do? It seems like everyone turned and looked at me at the same time and said, "No problem man!" People handle problems and crisis differently. In this example, I never dreamed that the van could be repaired, but the next morning the van was rolling.

Tensions over goals

Lingenfelter and Mayers describe tensions over goals as the tension that exists between task oriented people and person oriented people. According to them, task oriented people focus on tasks and principles, find satisfaction in the achievement of goals, and accept loneliness and social deprivation for the sake of personal achievements. Whereas person oriented people focus on persons and relationships, find satisfaction in interaction, seek friends who are group oriented, and deplore loneliness.

When building bridges from one culture group to another, it is very important to understand that element of an individual or people within a culture that directs their thinking. Understanding what directs the thinking of an individual and people will lead a person to understand how they set goals and why. Understanding how and why people set goals will help the missionary person to maneuver in forging the way into the darkness as culture groups working together.

When I first moved to the city of Chicago to work among first generation youth from different culture groups our greatest success was among the Romanian and Hungarian youth. In particular, we found success among the Romanian people in a great way. However, in working with the Romanian people, our success eventually exposed tension in our goals. The board of the Romanian church had a different goal in mind about our role in the ministry than we did.

We started a youth meeting each Thursday night in January of 1993. Our meeting started with twelve youth the first night we met. Our goal was first to build relationship with and among the youth of the church, and second to bring Romanian youth into relationship through Jesus Christ. Our small meetings grew numerically to twenty, thirty, fifty, and eventually seventy-five to eighty each Thursday evening. We were extremely excited about what God was doing within the group. However, not everyone shared our excitement. There was a feeling among some that we were not doing what we were doing correctly.

Remember, our goal centered on building relationships with one another and with God. We started each class with twenty minutes of fellowship. We then spent twenty minutes talking to each other. We then sang choruses, heard a Scripture message, and prayed together. Each night became an exciting and powerful night of ministry. I later came to find out that there had been an expectation by a few individuals in the church that the youth should enter class quietly and sit for an hour with their hands folded in front of them as I lectured. There were tensions present over our goals.

Recognizing tensions in goal setting might occur is a powerful way to avoid or prepare for possible future ministry stress. When building bridges of relationship from one culture group to another, these tensions may not be seen until individuals find themselves in the midst of turmoil. When this type of tension is present, it is necessary to pause in the process of working to accomplish our goal in order to evaluate, educate, and elevate. Evaluation of cultural tensions from every perspective is essential to gaining an understanding of what is causing and how to alleviate the tensions over setting goals. Resolving cultural tensions over setting goals is a process that also includes educating people about the goals being set and understanding that education is a two-way process. In other words, the person who is educating is also receiving an education. A third ingredient, in a formula resolving tensions over setting goals, is to elevate other individuals above oneself. Very often in life, some things are not worth fighting about. Many times cultural tensions can be resolved by the dominant culture releasing ownership of an issue and focusing on relationship by elevating other individuals above themselves. Evaluating our priorities is a priority in resolving tensions over goal setting (Lingenfelter and Mayers 1986, 90).

Tensions over self worth

Self worth and societal status are ascribed to people in some way in most societies and cultures. In British society, there is great prestige ascribed to being a part of royalty. Along with royalty in England often comes wealth, favor in job placement, and a high level of respect. In the country of Haïti there was historically a color classification in the society in which the lighter a person's skin color the further he or she could rise in the society. India's caste system is a challenge for any outsider to understand, but building bridges to people in India is a process doomed to failure without knowledge of where people are placed in society according to the society structure. Lingenfelter describes his work among Yapese people in Micronesia as illustrating the importance of understanding the tensions of self-worth and how people view themselves in society (Lingenfelter and Mayers 1986).

There are two specific things that are relevant regarding the self-worth of people in building bridges between cultures in North American society. First, any person attempting to build a bridge from their culture to another culture needs to be conscious of how people are perceived within that culture regarding their societal status. How does their culture view them? Second, there is a need to understand that in the United States the lives of newcomers are very often turned upside down. Many immigrant people find themselves in a situation that their world has changed in every possible way.

Obviously, most immigrants have to learn the American English Language. They also experience change in the food they eat, and often, the clothes they wear.

The realization that the taxi driver giving a person a ride from Chicago O'Hare Airport to Rosemont Convention Center is a taxi driver in the United States, but back home in Bulgaria he or she was a university professor or a medical physician, is difficult to comprehend for many indigenous American citizens. The life of immigrant people changes completely upon arrival to this country. Developing an understanding of people often means understanding who they were in their country of origin in order to help them in their transition process from what they were, to who they are now. While pastoring in Chicago, we had members in our church congregation who had been college professors, scientists, educators, and medical professionals who were now cleaning houses, driving limousines, driving trucks and doing other service industry jobs to survive. These were brilliant people who had held a high status in their country; but, after migrating to the United States, they found that the best jobs they were qualified for according to United States standards were labor intensive jobs.

There is a need to approach people conscious of societal requirements in their culture. However, to a great extent, people should be approached in an equitable manner regardless of their place in society. Having a consciousness of people, their cultural view of self-worth, and where they are in society, is important in building bridges of communication and relationship to them. The greatest priority for the missionary person building the bridge is to show the love of Christ to them by approaching them with respect and treating them with dignity.

Tensions regarding vulnerability

Mayers and Lingenfelter describe two characteristics in relation to vulnerability. These are the willingness to expose oneself to vulnerability and the concealment of vulnerability. Allowing oneself the opportunity to fail is a difficult part of anyone's life. In North American society, many people often settle for mediocrity in their lives in order to avoid risk. Risk of doing new things and reaching higher opens a person to the possibility of failure. Taking risks is being vulnerable. Many cultures deal harshly with failure (the inability to accomplish a task successfully), and therefore conceal their vulnerability.

Understanding how a culture views risk and vulnerability will help to know how they may maneuver within the culture. Entering into a decision making process, dealing with relationship difficulties, and strategic planning are often influenced by a people's willingness to be vulnerable or the concealment of their vulnerability.

150% Persons

Lingenfelter and Mayers discuss another key concept they developed in their writing of becoming 150% persons. Jesus Christ was all of who he was, and yet became all of who we are in order to walk in our shoes and know us. Becoming 150% persons means letting go of some of who we are and becoming some of who we are trying to reach. It means being 75% of who we are, and 75% of who we are reaching in order to truly gain as much understanding as possible about them without being them. As we build bridges from one culture group to another culture group a legitimate goal is to become 150% persons (Lingenfelter and Mayers 1986, 25).

The Assimilation Process

When a person looks at an American and asks the question, "What is an American?" there is no one specific answer in regard to the cultural attributes of an American. American people are Latino, Asian, American Indian, African American, East Indian, African, and the list continues to include just about every culture on earth. Assimilation is a process that often happens quickly in the United States. It is the process of a person or group of persons laying aside their culture and amalgamating into the culture in the society to which they have migrated. Assimilation in America can happen in as little as one, two, or three generations.

In building bridges from culture group to culture group in the United States context, it is important to understand that assimilation of cultures in a diverse community is a fact. When living in a culturally diverse community, people assimilation happens. This fact can be troublesome for the cultural purist; but, the reality of life is that people build relationships with people. They make friends with one another, marry, have children, and live in community together. Thus, assimilation takes place, to some extent, over a period of time. A person that has an understanding of the assimilation process realizes that second and third generation youth often leave the church because the church is culture bound, and they are assimilating.

Understanding that assimilation is a part of the process of life in the culturally diverse community is an important part of understanding immigrant people. This understanding to the missionary believer should be an understanding of observation and minimal participation. In other words, as people assimilate over time in the diverse community there should not be encouragement or discouragement from the missionary believer in regard to a person's or people's assimilation process. It is very easy as bearers of culture to interject in the lives of people in regard to the way they should act. Interjecting can often lead to great difficulty in their lives, and in the life of the community, and cause detrimental problems in the life of the church. The participatory role of the missionary believer is one that is often best served as a servant which deals with all of life, but minimizes altering culture out of personal feelings.

Assimilation is a process. The process of assimilation may take generations and decades. As a process, assimilation is not a journey that a culture group begins with a goal that by a certain date in a certain generation they will no longer be who they were - they will be assimilated. It is a process in which cultures evolve without any clear direction of where they are heading.

It of course is not mandatory that any culture assimilate into the main stream of society. However, there are not many groups in the United States who have not been affected by or struggled with assimilation. Perhaps only Amish people, indigenous Native American cultures living on reservations, and African American communities are examples of people groups who have experienced little assimilation over many generations in the United States. However, each of these, even in small ways, has encountered assimilation struggles in some way.

Each person working in the culturally diverse community needs an understanding of God's love for culture. God created people and, in his providence, orchestrated the development of cultures, tribes, and nations throughout the world. As missionary believers reach out to people with the gospel of Jesus Christ it is important to love people in the way that God loves people.

Loving people means loving who they are as people; and, loving who they are as people means appreciating their culture. Showing appreciation of a people's culture demonstrates the love of Christ to them. When a person is building a bridge from their culture to another culture, and they sit down and break bread together with people from the other culture, walls are often broken down through the relationship that develops. In developing multi-ethnic ministry, whether doing evangelism or building a local church congregation, it is important to appreciate people and their culture while celebrating together with many cultures. In fact, the strength of the multi-ethnic church is the unity of Christ present in the cultural diversity of people.

A Bridge from Belief System to Belief System

Belief systems are part of our existence in this world. Even when a person states he or she does not believe in God, they are making a statement of his or her belief. Their belief system is that they do not believe in anything, or do not know what they believe. People, for the most part throughout the world, worship something or someone. They have a belief. Understanding this is part of who we are as people.

Today, in America, God has been pushed to the side out of the respect of people's beliefs in their god and what is politically correct. I recently watched the news about Islam being taught in a school in California as part of a class on cultural understanding. In this post-Christian society Christians have found themselves conveniently throwing their hands in the air and saying what is the point of preaching a message that no one wants to hear? Become a silent witness and pray that people will be compelled to receive Jesus Christ by seeing Jesus Christ within the individual life. However, Christians have a responsibility to be involved in the preaching of the gospel to the world; just living life, although a part of being a witness, is not enough.

J.H. Bavinck describes this endeavor as the science of missions. Bavinck describes the mandate of preaching the gospel as the responsibility of the church. It is the Apostolic nature of the church to preach the gospel and be concerned with the conviction of sin (Bavinck 1960, 222). In this sense, evangelism is more than a ministry of the church. It is the essence of the church's ministry. The church exists ultimately to bring people into right relationship with God. Therefore, everything the church does should center on the core value of evangelism. According to Bavinck elenctics is specifically a missionary science.

> "Elenctics is at home on the mission field. There the battle must be fought and the great word said. Scientific material can be gathered and organized on the home front, but, elenctics is in its essence, a missionary science; it may never lack the call to repentance (Bavinck-1960, 223)."

Bavinck described elenctics as a missionary science that finds its place on the mission field; however, J.H. Bavink wrote his book, "An Introduction to The Science of Missions", in 1960. Today in the 21st century this missionary science approach to evangelism is very much needed in United States ministry endeavor. Our society is diverse and includes people from all over the world. They have come with their culture and they have come with their belief system. If we are to reach people, we as the church living in the world, will build bridges to them. Building bridges from belief system to belief system is imperative, and elenctics is that science associated with building these bridges. The process of convincing people of their need for relationship with God (Adonai) is the process of elenctics. Bavinck names five considerations in relation to the elenctic argument: every person is in real need of God's grace, speaking of truths that exist in Non-Christian religions must be done with great caution, the conviction factor of elenctics is accomplished through the Holy Spirit, the personhood of the preacher of the message is a starting point of elenctics, and human reason is not enough (Bavinck 1960, 229-231).

The science of missions consists of the gospel as a message going forward. In athletic terms, it is the offensive strategy of the team. Elijah (I Kings 18:30-39), Daniel (Dan 6:7-27), Shadrach, Meshack, Abednego (Dan 1:7), and Paul (Acts 17) explicitly engaged the culture of belief systems prominent in the culture in which they lived. They allowed the false gods of this world to compete with Adonai the true God. Each time in Scripture this happened God was exalted, and the false gods of the society were defeated. Believing in God is having trust that He is able to defeat the enemy in the midst of the culture. Building bridges from the Judeo-Christian belief system to other belief systems is a challenge; but, it is a necessary endeavor for the evangelizing Christian believer.

Building a bridge from our belief system to another belief system is the work of approaching people where they exist in order to understand them with the goal of presenting the gospel message with boldness to them. There is this fact of life that exists in our world that all those who do not have a relationship with God the Father through His Son Jesus Christ are on a road to an eternal destination without God. In fact, scripture speaks to us about this eternal destiny without God describing hell being a place of torment where people will live in eternal anguish for sin. However, through a relationship with Jesus Christ, sin is removed. Therefore, the body of Christ has a divine responsibility to engage people within their belief system in order to convince them by allowing scripture to convict them. Building bridges to people within their belief system successfully involves developing three natural life characteristics into specific life skills. These three characteristics are knowledge, patience, and wisdom.

1. Knowledge

Gaining knowledge about non-Christian religions is a necessary task in building a bridge to people who live believing in these non-Christian religions. Knowledge is the key that will often open the door to reaching people in order to communicate with them. It is our responsibility to go to the lost. In Mathew 28:19, Jesus said for us, his people, to go unto the world. The believer's calling is to go forward approaching people and sharing the gospel with them.

This knowledge of what people believe, how their belief system relates to their culture, and how to approach people within their belief system are areas of knowledge that help the believer in building bridges to people. Many cultures have religious belief systems which are part of their culture. The understanding of the culture and belief system are essential to convincing people of their sin, need for relationship with Jesus Christ, and developing ways in which to convince people without destroying their culture in the process.

The most basic belief systems existing in cultures are folk religions. Folk religion is an attempt by man to find God through human effort. In order to reach people who practice folk religion as part of their cultural belief system, it is important to be prepared with an understanding of general theological principles that answer the fallacies, questions, and falsehoods that exist within folk religions. In most of the world, religion affects a person's life in every way. Many cultures revolve around their religious beliefs (Hiebert, Shaw, and Tienau 1999, 31).

Evangelism of non-Christian people takes time, effort, and wisdom. People who culturally worship other gods as part of their culture, or exist in cultures wrapped in folk religion, need to be approached in a manner that will relate and connect with them (Hiebert, Shaw, and Tienau 1999, 31). Knowledge of how a people with a belief system that is non-Christian relates to their culture is an essential key to communicating the gospel to a people successfully. Belief systems are, for the most part wrapped in culture, and often form the values inherent in a culture's underlying worldview. This is a true fact. Understanding religions accompanies the understanding that religion is most often wrapped in culture.

Elenctics is the science concerned with a very special aspect of the approach: our direct attack upon non-Christian religiosity in order to call a man to repentance (Bavinck 1960, 223). Bavinck outlines four factors that determine the approach 1. to whom the message is being sent (Bavinck 1960, 82), 2. who is being sent to deliver the message (Bavinck 1960, 83), 3. when will be the time of the encounter (Bavinck 1960, 85), and 4. where will the encounter take place (Bavinck 1960, 86). Bavinck's discussion of approach theories also includes the description of the comprehensive approach and the kerygmatic approach.

The comprehensive approach

Approaching people with the message of Jesus Christ includes much more than preaching, teaching, or telling them about Christ. Approaching people includes living the Christ life before them. It is fleshing out our faith as people who are seeking to become like Jesus Christ. Christianity includes the life of the whole person living in such a way that represents Jesus Christ in all that they do. In the broadest sense the approach of the believer to the unbeliever includes all of who a person is and all of who they have become in Jesus Christ. How must the missionary live? In approaching people, it is important to understand who is being approached in order to gain their trust. The manner in which a missionary person carries himself or herself, lives, acts, walks, and talks all contribute to his or her success in building relationships with people.

Paul, the Apostle, spoke of becoming all things to all people in I Corinthians 9:19-21. Paul did not become all religions to all religions in order to reach people. In this scripture, he was speaking of cultural characteristics. More than likely when Paul approached the Jews, he ate a certain way, and when he approached the gentiles, he ate differently. In today's society a believer properly approaching a Muslim and building a relationship with the Muslim community would not take the Muslim to a pig roast for dinner. Likewise, when approaching a Japanese or Korean family, it may be important for the missionary believer to remove his or her shoes before entering the home. It is important for the missionary believer when approaching people to intentionally suppress characteristics of his or her own culture in order to be effective in building relationships with another people of another culture.

Thinking ahead is one of the greatest skills each person can develop. Thinking ahead is the skill of contemplating each step in the process of approaching people. It is the skill that includes a person's asking himself or herself how he or she will enter a room, greet the host and other guests, what will they say, how long will they listen, will they eat all of their food, and how will they leave? Thinking ahead is a key opportunity to bathe the approach of people with prayer. This prayer opportunity is a prime opportunity to ask God for cultural guidance, direction, and favor.

It is important for the missionary believer to be himself or herself at the core of how they represent themselves. Although trying to learn another person's culture is important and valuable it is equally important to understand that real people like real people. Becoming completely indigenous within a culture is dangerous and not necessary. It is also impossible. A person being themselves can not lay aside all of the characteristics of who they are in order to approach people. Doing this destroys the true picture of who they are.

Every person in the world wears their cultural clothes in some way. Being conscious of the fact that a person cannot completely separate himself or herself from their culture is important in the work of approaching people (Bavinck 1960, 110). In 1997 my wife and I traveled to a Jamaican church in Toronto, Canada, to speak at a youth convention. During the convention there was an open forum planned that we were asked to be the panel for. Some of the teenage girls immediately asked my wife one of those trap questions. The question was, "Is it okay to date?" My wife thought for a moment and responded by saying, "What do your parents say about dating?" In this situation it would have been extremely easy and natural to answer this question according to her culture. However, she realized, that as a bearer of culture, it is important to make conscious intentional efforts to leave our own culture behind in order to honor the culture we are approaching.

The kerygmatic approach

The inevitable goal to building the relationship bridge from belief system to belief system is the presentation of the gospel to the unbeliever. Simply put, in the mind of each missionary believer is the fact that he or she is working to a point of encounter. Bavinck discusses this approach as direct and indirect. The direct approach is that on the street, meet someone, and present the gospel to them. Many Christians will claim that this type of approach is not for them, but more than likely they have images of wild "John the Baptist" street preachers in their mind.

However, the direct approach is that point of contact that is often only available for brief moments in time. As an urban missionary under appointment of the Church of God (Cleveland, TN) World Missions Department in 1992, part of my responsibility was to raise my own budget. This responsibility provided great travel opportunities. It was during this period of time that God put a thought in my heart. This thought was simple, "carry a Bible everywhere you travel, and give it away." I know this is basic, and something every Christian should do anyway, but it was more than just routine for me. I went on a journey with a mission on my mind. It was during these times of travel that my path began to cross with hurting, hungry people.

While encountering these people for brief moments in time, the realization came that direct encounter evangelism may not always be on the corner of Halstead and Maxwell Streets in Chicago, but it may be sitting in seat 32C flying at 32,000 feet from Atlanta to Tampa. The direct approach opportunities a person has help him or her understand what is meant by being "instant in season, and out of season" (2 Timothy 4:2).

The indirect approach of evangelism is equally powerful and valid. It is the approach of process. Process is that place where the ground is softened, plowed, and seed is planted. Perhaps, many people in the world have a patience deficiency in the same way I do. I imagine it can be quite challenging for a farmer to wait for his/her new crop to push through the ground. However, patience in the process is what allows the farmer to harvest successful crops. The indirect process of approaching people with the gospel is the place where thought and sincere prayer lead the way to an understanding of when the time is right. It is important to lean on the presence of God in this process of knowing when it is the right time to close the deal. Both impatience and procrastination can bring poor results. Therefore, depending on the presence of God is an absolute.

Two other elements which are vital to indirect approach success are persistence and compassion. Persistence is a discipline that each person has to develop. It is the commitment to hang on to someone and not let them go. Personally, persistence to hold on to someone through the process has taken me to the courthouse to hold the hand of a crying mother, to the jail with a father to bail out a teenage son, to the hospital, and unfortunately to the funeral home. Persistence does not give up on people.

Compassion is the blood in the veins of the Christian. It is love that covers a multitude of sins, and it is love that will cover our errors in cross-cultural relationships. Compassion is the driving force of evangelism, and it is the success of the indirect approach of evangelism

2. Patience

Patience is a second characteristic that a person building bridges from belief system to belief system will need to develop into a strong life skill. The development of patience into a strong personal life skill is a necessary ingredient to successful evangelism of people who are committed in their life to a non-Christian belief system. Building bridges to people within their belief system will, most often, take time. Time may mean days, weeks, months, or even years. Understanding that evangelism is a process takes time is very difficult for people in the American culture. American people, by nature, always seem to be in a hurry. The society of people in the United States rush through drive-thru for breakfast and lunch, they drive up to the bank window, and fuss at the traffic signal because it doesn't turn green fast enough.

A person who develops patience as a life skill understands that evangelism is a process. It takes time to accomplish great things. When I pastored in Chicago I had a difficult time developing patience as a life skill. I remember pacing the floor prior to worship services and wondering where church members were because I was impatient. I wanted to see immediate growth results in the church. This anxiety led to goals that were only numbers – motivated instead of salvation oriented.

3. Wisdom

A third skill that is of vital necessity is wisdom. Wisdom is developed in the life of an individual and is that life skill that keeps an individual real. It is the ability to constantly have reality checks that alert the individual to the fact that God is in control; and, it is the Holy Spirit that is the instrument of conviction in a person's life. It takes wisdom to understand who is ultimately responsible for an individual's own recognition in their life that they need God and a relationship with God (John 16:7-10). Building bridges from belief system to belief system involves the development of specific skills in the life of the believer. These three skills will greatly help the believer in approaching people who are non-Christian with the gospel successfully.

Ministry to Muslim People

An example of this is evangelism ministry to Muslim, believers. Approaching Muslim believers takes commitment to a relationship building process. This process is accomplished by gaining knowledge, having patience, and praying for wisdom.

As the Christian believer utilizes knowledge, patience, and wisdom developing relationships with individuals who are Muslim the Christian believer will have opportunities to communicate the gospel message with meaning to the Muslim believer. These opportunities will involve more than message delivery. They will be opportunities that include the Christian believer doing the work of convincing (elenctics) the non-believer of their need for relationship with God through His Son Jesus Christ.

Knowledge

Knowledge includes gaining information about Islam, gaining knowledge about the culture of the person to whom I am building relationship with, and learning how their culture is affected by Islam. Knowledge also includes understanding how I can utilize the comprehensive approach and the kerygmatic approach.

A Basic Understanding of Islam

I will need to develop a basic understanding of Islam as I begin the relationship building process with a Muslim person. As a Christian I need to understand what the basic tenants of Islam are and where Islam came from.

Islam has grown rapidly throughout the world since its inception. It is a monotheistic religion that originated in the heart and mind of its creator Mohamed. Mohamed was born in 570 A.D. and developed the Islamic faith after experiencing what he called a "vision" in the desert. He died at the age of 62 in June of 632 (Beverly *Christian History* 2002, 12).

After Mohammed died in 632 Islam spread quickly. The spread of early Islam is marked by the Muslim military conquering Jerusalem in 638, and conquering Spain in 711. Islam has spread utilizing what some have said is the sixth pillar of Islam; the jihad. Jihad means divine struggle. According to Mateen A Elass, there are four levels of Jihad. These are the jihad of the heart, mouth, pen, and hand (Elass , Christian History, 2002, 35). Jihad is the propagation of Islam by persuasion, or force (Elass, Christian History, 2002, 35-38).

Basic Tenets of Islam

Some have called them tenets of the Islamic religion, some call them pillars of faith, and some call them principles. Regardless of what term is used to describe them the five basic principles of Islam form the foundational creed of the Islamic faith. It is within these five pillars of Islam that the religion finds its universality. Universality means that regardless of culture believers of Islamic faith practice their religion based on these basic beliefs (Carmody and Carmody 1988, 219). These five pillars of Islam are:

1. Shahadah – The Shahadah, according to Denise and John Carmody is the "heart beat" of Islam (Carmody and Carmody 1998, 219). It is the monotheistic statement of Islam. "There is no god but Allah, and Mohammed is his messenger" (Islam 101: Christian History Issue 74, 14).

2. Salat – A second pillar of Islam is prayer. Faithful Muslims pray five times a day facing Mecca (Islam 101: Christian History Issue 74, 14). I remember seeing a Muslim believer when I lived in Chicago get on his knees near the corner of Pulaski and Montrose every day and pray fulfilling one of his prayer commitments.

3. <u>Zakat</u> – The third pillar of Islam is tithing. Muslim believers must give a percentage of their wealth to help poor people (Islam 101: Christian History Issue 74, 14).

4. <u>Swam</u> – Fasting is the fourth pillar of Islam. The primary time in the year that this fasting commitment is carried out is during the month of Ramadan. (Islam 101: Christian History Issue 74, 14).

5. <u>Hajj</u> – The fifth principle of a Muslim believer's life that they are to fulfill is the Hajj. The Hajj is the journey that each Muslim is to make to Mecca to worship at the Muslim holy place once in their lifetime (Islam 101: Christian History Issue 74, 14).

The Islamic scriptures are called the Quran. The Quran is the thoughts, visions, and guidance of Mohammed written by him during his life from 610 until 632. It is finished by being completely assembled around 650 (Islam 101: Christian History Issue 74, 14). The other key text of Islam is the traditions about the prophet Mohammed called the Hadith (Islam 101: Christian History Issue 74, 14).

In learning this basic understanding of Islam, I realize at some point in the future that I will need to further develop my knowledge of Islam and develop apologetic skills regarding comparison of the Bible and Christianity to the Quran and Islam. There are many texts written about this subject which can be studied in preparation for ministry among Muslim people. One key text is the book written by Norman L. Geisler and Abdul Saleem (assumed name) titled, <u>Answering Islam: The Crescent in the Light of the Cross</u>. It is impor-tant to note that a person could study Islam for a lifetime, but the priority in studying Islam for the Christian is to know it enough to thoroughly do the work of an evangelist sharing the gospel of Jesus Christ to Muslim believers. It is therefore important to be guarded in studying Islamic beliefs. We must be *"Wise as a serpent and harm-less as a dove* (Clayton 1988, 12)".

Comprehensive Approach

A comprehensive approach is an approach where the Christian is not just speaking words but he or she is living the Christ life. People watch what we do and say. If we say we are followers of Jesus Christ we should live like Christians. Greg Livingstone tells the story of a woman who was a missionary for twenty years in Africa when she had an eye opening encounter.

"One missionary was startled when, after twenty years of service in North Africa, her Muslim friends showed amazement when they discovered that she prayed. Because she didn't pray openly and ritually (Matt. 6:6) as they did, the Muslim ladies assumed that she had no prayer life at all. They were delighted to discover that she reads a Holy Book, prays, and wants to keep God's commandments. 'We never met a Christian who believed in God,' she was told (Livingstone 1993, 123)."

It is important to live the Christ life in front of people. Allow them to see that we know God is real, and we love Him. How we live has an impact on un-believers.

Kerygmatic Approach

The goals of the kerygmatic approach include both direct evangelism and indirect evangelism goals. Approaching Muslim believers directly is probably not the most effective way of convincing them of their need to know Jesus. The direct approach is the approach of meeting someone in the street, on the bus, or on the train and sharing the gospel message right then. Although this is often an effective way of evangelism and there are times that evangelism is a now or never situation effective evangelism of Muslim believers will be accomplished through developing relationships with them. An indirect approach of evangelism is the process on which the Christian should focus their attention. Islam is a relationship based faith. David Clayton writes, "Islam is not merely a religion for the individual. It is a religion which can be enjoined fully only when one pursues it in community" (Clayton , Urban Mission, 13). Developing relationships within the community is a process that takes time and patience.

Patience

One of the most difficult life skills for people to accomplish in the modern world is patience, however it is important to understand that evangelism as a process can take years. I am probably not the exception to this rule. In fact I have to work on my patience skills. The fact is the process of evangelism takes time. Building trust takes time, and trust is what is needed to do the work of convincing people about the reality of the gospel. It takes time to truly connect with people, because it takes time to truly know them. Seeing the evangelism task of evangelizing Muslim believers as a process will help the Christian believer to become patient from the beginning of the process.

Wisdom

Developing relationships in order to communicate also takes wisdom. Wisdom is that skill that helps the Christian discern the moment and time that people are becoming receptive to the gospel presentation. Wisdom helps a person know when to press forward with a point in a conversation and when to let go and move on to another subject. In approaching Muslim people it is important to walk with wisdom. How an individual greets people, sits, stands, eats, and drinks can affect the outcome of any relationship encounter.

A Bridge from Person to Person

Building bridges from person to person is the highest challenge for an individual. It is the process that requires the highest level of life commitment of an individual. Building people bridges is the task of intentionally building relationships with strangers. Building a bridge from one person to another is not a task that Christian people should take lightly. It is an important element in living the Christ life and should be a high priority. The gospel is most effective when shared through friendship.

"The gospel must pass through a living person to reach another living person, and this involves the entire nature, life, and temperament of the person proclaiming the gospel (Bavink 1960, 84)."

Friendship evangelism is possibly the most successful method of evangelism in Christianity. It is within the confines of friendship that accountability, compassion, and forgiveness can be found. This is the area of life that real trust is developed, and trust is a foundation stone for faith.

The story of Timothy

Consider the story of Timothy. It wasn't theology, doctrine, or a church service that brought the plan of salvation to a young man named Tim: it was his friend Barry.

Tim was a young man with a young family. He grew up in a home with alcoholic parents. While growing up, his family did not attend church, or have any kind of religious tradition. They were unchurched people. His father was a career military man. One month after his father retired from the military, Tim got his first opportunity to drive a car at the age of fifteen. This first driving opportunity came suddenly and unexpectedly. Tim had to drive his father to the hospital with an emergency health need. His father never came home. After the funeral, Tim became an aspiring alcoholic just like his father.

After serving in the Air force himself, marrying and having a son, Tim was working a job during the day and going to college at night working toward a college degree. It was at this point in Tim's life that a significant life change would take place.

One night after class, Tim's college professor asked if he would join him for coffee. Tim and the professor went to have coffee; and, that night, over coffee, Tim's professor told him about his best friend. His best friend was Jesus. He asked Tim if he would like to know Jesus also. Tim said he really wasn't interested in that sort of thing. However, on the way home, Tim pulled the car over to the side of the road, and cried out, *"Jesus come into my life"*. That night his life changed forever. Through one person building a bridge to another person Tim found a relationship with Jesus Christ.

It was not long after I became pastor of the Narragansett Church of God in Chicago that I met the neighbor who lived next door to the church. His name was Pete. Pete had lived next to the church for twenty-four years, and during that twenty-four years, only one time had someone from the church talked to him. Pete was an Italian immigrant who had been living in the United States about twenty-six years. He was Catholic but seldom attended mass. Each Sunday, after service, as I was locking the doors to the church I found Pete waiting on me outside the front door. My initial reaction to Pete's friendliness was to hurriedly greet him and leave for home where my wife was preparing lunch. However, I sensed that I needed to stay and talk with Pete.

Talking with Pete, I found that he was miserable. He had retired from his job with a lump sum retirement, became bored with life, went to the river boats, and became addicted to gambling. He lost his retirement and mortgaged everything possible on his house. Pete didn't come to church and he didn't pay tithes. He became my friend though. Each Sunday we would talk, we would go to the diner and eat lunch, and sometimes when he needed a ride to Gamblers Anonymous I would give him a ride. I began to notice Pete coming around the church working on the building and picking up trash. After a year and half I invited Pete to church for the first time.

One day a pastor friend of mine called me and asked if I would allow an evangelist who had been a professional wrestler, and was now a preacher, to come on a Sunday night. I asked Pete to come that night. He was a fan of wrestling and remembered the man from television. Pete came to church that Sunday night and sat on that last row as close to the door as he could. The evangelist was new at preaching and struggled with his sermon. It didn't seem like the service was that great, but it is amazing though how God works. The evangelist gave a salvation invitation and I bowed my head in prayer along with the rest of the congregation. When I looked up Pete had walked all of the way up the aisle from the back of the sanctuary to the front and was standing with both of his arms in the air and with tears running down his cheeks. It was there that Pete committed his life to Christ.

Building bridges of friendship is being willing to be a friend to the friendless with no strings attached. It is being willing to have patience with people and to see them as more than a number that will be potentially added to a church roll. Real people have real problems and are in search of real love. Friendship is quite possibly the most powerful bridge that a person can build to another person. Building bridges of friendship takes patience, a willingness to be vulnerable, and commitment to relationship.

Building people bridges

Building people bridges is the process of developing relationships with people in the community with regard to their culture, belief system, and world view. It is getting to know them.

Building people bridges by doing evangelism will allow the local church to see people in the store, at work, at school, and in their community as people who potentially will receive salvation through direct interaction with them in relationship. People need someone who will talk to them, get to know them, and build a bridge into their world. Reaching un-reached people is an important task for the church in the United States today. As the church builds bridges to the world this task becomes a possibility.

People bridges are pathways of communication intentionally built between people. As the body of Christ builds effective people bridges to people the work of evangelism becomes a possibility. It requires continually building these five bridges:

Bridges from:

1. The Churched World to the Un-churched World
2. The Believer to the Unbeliever
3. Culture/People Group to Culture/People Group
4. Belief System to Belief System
5. Person to Person

This effort will allow the local church tremendous opportunities to begin the process of effectively communicating the gospel to their entire community. The communication process is more than speaking word. It is a process in which the message finds meaning among those to whom the message is communicated.

6

COMMUNICATING THE GOSPEL MESSAGE WITH MEANING

———∞∞∞———

Reaching the mission field of the global mobile ethnically and culturally diverse society is a great challenge. In order to meet this challenge the church will have to adjust methods of ministry without losing the integrity of the message (Sweet 1999, 51). Effective church ministry in the 21st century world calls for the church pastor to move from the role of professional pastor in the Christian world of past generations to a missionary pastor role in this post-modern, post-Christian, society of the 21st century. Becoming a missionary pastor includes learning new methods of communicating Scripture in ways that connect the message with the audience of this new world in a manner they understand. The missionary pastor role is a calling to live out faith in society every day. Being a missionary pastor is more than fulfilling a job, it is a lifestyle. It is far greater than the professional pastoral role of previous periods of time when the pastor only visited the hospital, and stayed in the office waiting for the phone to ring (Callahan 1990, 18). The missionary pastor lives among people.

The pastor walking in the role of a missionary sees the world as their ministry and has a primary goal to reach all people. Therefore, he or she will lead the local church existing in the culturally diverse community to incorporate into its ministry strategy a vision to reach multiple cultures and multiple generations with their ministry efforts. Effectively accomplishing this task is done by developing ministry efforts that are customized for each group of people present in their community. This process, according to Charles Kraft, is a communication of, *"Transculturally valid expressions of the revealed truths of God* (Kraft 1979, 293)".

The missionary pastor ministering in this post-Christian, multi-ethnic, multi-cultural, multi-generational mission field will have greater ministry success by knowing the core message of the gospel, gaining people knowledge, and contextualizing the message in order to effectively communicate the gospel with meaning to people. These leaders living in the culturally diverse community, who desire to successfully minister in the community, will come to understand the need to develop understanding and methods of how to communicate the message with meaning without losing the integrity of the message.

Eugene Nida's Three Culture Model of Missionary Communication is perhaps the simplest, and yet most effective, way of approaching our mission as Christians in communicating the message successfully. Nida deals with knowing the Bible culture, sender's culture, and respondent's culture in order to develop effective methods of missionary communication (Nida 1960, 46-47). Effective methods of communication are methods which go beyond just speaking words that may or may not be heard. Effective missionary communication is communication with understanding. Using Nida's model of missionary communication is a valid starting point for the pastor doing ministry among people in diverse communities. In simple terms the pastor will need to know his or her own culture, know the message, and know the people to whom the message is being communicated.

Sender Culture

Knowing our own culture is important when communicating to another culture. We need to understand who we are, where we come from, what our values and beliefs are, and what they mean. Understanding these areas of our lives will help us to understand why we look at the world the way we do. Our own culture is often the hardest to know because we take so much of it for granted. All people see things differently. We all have our own view of the world. Each person's world view can, and will, change throughout his or her life to reflect the way the world is seen at a particular point in life. Each person's world view is influenced by their culture.

A person's culture is part of their life. Since our culture is a part of who we are, it is important that we understand ourselves to the extent of knowing that we as people do not know it all, and our culture is not the only, or right, culture to live by in the world. Each culture is special in its own way, and knowing our own culture will allow us to respect other cultures as we build bridges to other cultures in order to understand and communicate to people.

The Message

In Christianity, the message is clear and unchangeable. It is the plan of God to redeem man in relationship through His only Son, Jesus Christ. This is the central message of Jesus Christ's life, death, and resurrection. This message is the core of the gospel; and, the mandate of sharing this message is clear in Scripture. "Go therefore into all the world...and make disciples (followers of Christ)" (Matt 28:19).

Historically, this message has been taken around the world. It has been carried down the Roman roads of the first century, to the jungles of New Guinea, to the cities of New York, Sao Paulo, Hong Kong, Manila, Moscow, and everywhere. As this message has been taken around the world, it has been sent into the world wrapped with the clothing of culture. It is because of cultural clothing that the methods of sending the gospel message throughout the world have at times leaned to extremes which have forced the sender's culture on the receiver. This has resulted in the diminishing of cultures, legitimizing governments, and at times destruction of the core message of the gospel.

Colonialism, paternalism, and ethnocentrism have hindered the effectiveness of the sender's efforts of communicating the message by destroying the culture of the receiver. Likewise, those attempting to equate the message of the gospel with indigenous belief systems of a people to the extent of placing culture over, or equal to, the message of Christianity have reduced the message of Christianity to a meaningless, marginalized story of another way to find God. This extreme compromise of the message is syncretism. Syncretism devaluates the message and destroys the integrity of the message by lowering the gospel to a level equal to all belief systems. The gospel is a clear message and Jesus Christ is clear in Scripture about the path to salvation being through Him alone (John 14:6). Syncretism happens when Christianity allows vestiges of the pre-Christian religion to remain and mix with it.

The unwrapped, uncompromised message of the gospel is the core message of the evangelical church. It is in this relentless pursuit of the true message of the historical Jesus, and the absolute unyielding stand on the integrity of Scripture, that the evangelical church, the World Council of Churches, and other theological scholars find their fork in the road.

The Evangelical church holds to a commitment to Scripture and theologically conservative doctrine that remains unchanged. This view holds to the high standards of repentance, justification, regeneration, and new birth. Pentecostals and Charismatics continue to hold as a core values Holy Spirit infilling, and holiness. The Evangelical Pentecostal Christian message is clear, concise, and unchanged. It is wrapped in the gospel, and it is this message that is carried around the world every day by Christians who share their faith with others. Communicating the message effectively will only happen through learning about the receiver's culture, life, and view of the world.

Context (Respondent Culture)

Ministry efforts will be most effective when understanding is gained of the people being reached. Understanding of people is comprehension of their life needs. Understanding the needs of people is accomplished by seeing the world through their eyes; and seeing the world through their eyes can only happen when a person walks with them, and knows them. As a person sees the world through the eyes of the people they research they can make a flesh connection and identify what their needs are. They begin to see what they see, walk where they walk, and live where they live.

Walking in another person's shoes, while they are walking in them, is of course impossible. However, it is possible to walk beside a person and do our best to see the world in some small way as they see the world. I will never know what it is like to be born in Chihuahua, Guadalupe, or Juarez. I will also never know what it is like to cross the Rio Grande River from Mexico to the United States in the hours when night turns into morning in fear of the present and with hope in my heart for the future. Likewise, no person on earth will ever fully know my life experiences, difficulties, successes, fears, and hope for the future as I do. A person's view of the world is his or her own and no one else can lay claim or fully understand it. However, we as individuals can build bridges from one life world to another. We are able to cross from our culture to another culture. We can cross from our life world to another life world with a focused effort in order to begin to understand and influence an individual or people in a positive or negative way. When we know a people, their needs, and their world view we can send a message that an individual or group of individuals will have a greater potential of receiving. (Hawthorne and Winter 1983, 384)

Research methods such as historical research and demographic research are important, however, data and information gained from this research is only the beginning to gaining the knowledge it will take to know people. In order to understand people living in a community, the missionary pastor has to walk with the people and live among the people. He or she must do the work of ethnographic research. The pastor must learn to walk in the shoes of other people and see the world through their eyes.

Walking among people in order to know them takes intentional effort because knowing people takes time. Seeing someone one day a week for one hour does not help a pastor know them. Knowing people and seeing their need is accomplished in the community people live in, and not only in the church sanctuary. For example, knowing the life of an immigrant living in the community is far more than a sanctuary relationship. An immigrant living in the United States might have a life that sounds like this:

"This is my experience, I get up at 4AM every morning, I work three jobs and I am speaking one language, but I'm trying to learn another (English). I'm in a foreign land, in fact the kind of food I like to eat, I can't find in the grocery store. My family all live, in well, (wherever) in Zimbabwe, Ghana, Bulgaria or Bombay, etc... I'm here and I'm homesick for home. I'm lonely for them, but I am here."

In order to know a people the pastor must know their history, and in order to know their history he or she must know their hopes, dreams, happiness, failures, pain, success, and life. The pastor must experience what the people experience in order to, in some small way, see what the people see and feel what they feel. Getting to the point of understanding a person's life situation is crucial to knowing who they are as people. The only way the pastor can see the life issues people have is to spend time with them and observe them.

As the pastor observes people, especially new immigrants, he or she will find changes happening in their lives. Research allows the researcher to identify changes in communities, cultures, and people. Community change, culture change, and people change are facts of life. These changes affect how people view their world, and knowing how people view their world helps those doing ministry develop methods of ministry that maximize ministry impact among people.

Communities Change

Many times, when someone different culturally than the predominate culture of the community moves into the community they are a novelty and people accept them as such. However, when many people (more than one or two families) of a different culture, race, or ethnicity move into a community, feelings of racism and ethnocentrism appear. One of the saddest statements I have heard in ministry is, "Our church is on the wrong side of town." This statement is often made as justification for moving the church to what is considered a safer more growth "potential" location. The question is, "What is the wrong side of town?" Of course, if a person were to ask this question, they would get strange looks and hear answers born out of systemic racism and ethnocentrism.

The issues of community change have traditionally been thought of in black and white terms. Steering, redlining, and white flight were the result of Caucasian people trying to keep their community Caucasian or fleeing their community when the community changed. We find today though that these issues are no longer just black-white issues as they once appeared but are culture, as well as racial. Today, the issues of cultural difference are greater than white black issues, or white brown issues. Today community change may include African American communities becoming Haitian, Puerto Rican communities becoming Mexican, and Korean communities becoming Vietnamese. Class issues within culture groups also exist. Middle class African American people may attempt to distance themselves from poor African American people, and Anglo-American people may do the same regarding poor Anglo-American people.

Cultures Change

Cultures change as they are influenced by other societies, cultures, and their environment. When working with a geographically remote people group in Indonesia, or on the African continent, cultural changes may be much more difficult to identify than cultural change happening in New York City, Chicago, Dallas, or Los Angeles. Changes happen in cultures over time, and change is inevitable.

The traditional anthropologist may cringe at the thought of cultural change, but the reality of history is that any culture present in a given period of time is the culmination of the inheritance of what that culture group's ancestors learned and passed down through generations. Simple life practices passed down through generations become sacred traditions. Many times people do not understand their cultural traditions but practice them because they are the traditions that they believe and know.

It is imperative in the North American context to understand that culture groups are in a state of transition. They begin the assimilation process as a people group the day they step into American society. The assimilation process in the American society brings people groups together and these groups change in the process. People groups in America work together, go to school together, live in communities together, and should have the opportunity to worship together. Worship opportunities are best accomplished through a church ministry intentionally bringing people together in community. These worship opportunities affirm the power of Christ to redeem people while maintaining who they are as individuals made in the image of God. It is this type of worship experience that destroys ethnocentrism and racism in the church in America. People arriving in the United States are beginning the process of cultural change. As they change and assimilation happens the church has a responsibility to understand, love, embrace their culture, and help them if they do not have a salvation experience to find salvation in Jesus Christ.

People Change

People change as they grow, gain knowledge, and experience life. They become experienced, gain wisdom, and view the world in new ways. The fact that people can change and very often do change is the hope of the gospel. Because there is potential for a life to change regardless of the age or background of a person, there is hope for all living people on earth to receive Jesus Christ as personal Savior.

It is important to examine in particular the spiritual life changes in a foreign born person's life prior to or after arriving in the United States. Knowing when, if, and how they received Christ will help to identify the type of ministry planning that needs to take place in order to meet their needs. Foreign-born people can be separated into at least one of six categories in a questioning/ data collection process regarding their spiritual experience. There are four questions that will help the researcher to develop a view of when, where, what, and how a person received salvation. Answering these questions will give the researcher the needed knowledge to ascertain which category a person immigrating to the United States is in spiritually. These descriptions of categories describe the spiritual category a person is in, their probable perspective of church ministry, and strategic thoughts for the researcher to consider in contextualizing ministry to them. It is important to understand these questions, and categories are not absolutes, but serve only as guides to assist the researcher to approach people in a way that considers that they come from different perspectives and have different views of God and the church. Knowledge of where a person is at in their spiritual life will help the pastor to understand how to approach people, and how to disciple them. A person who was a Christian prior to arriving in the United States has different life needs than a person who received Christ after their arrival. The following pages provide additional detail and insight into the six categories of spiritual experience and the four questions of spirituality, and how a leader can use them to better understand another person's spiritual outlook.

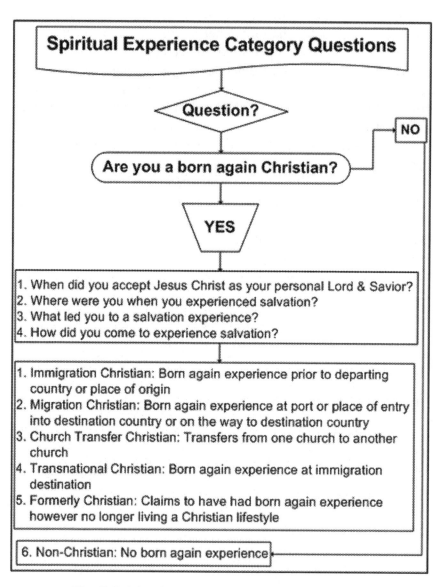

Fig. 5 Spiritual Experience Category Questions

Spiritual Experience Category

Category 2
Migration Christian: Born again experience at port or place of entry into destination country or on the way to destination country

Perspective of Church Ministry
Have little or no understanding of what it means to be a church member. Church attendance, rules, doctrine, and tithing have no significance. Open to new ideas as they assimilate into the new culture of their destination country

Strategic Thinking
- **Vulnerable to false doctrines and cult religious groups**
- **Interested in hearing their own language and being with other people from their own ethnic/ culture group**
- **Open to various worship styles**

Fig. 6 Spiritual Experience Category 1

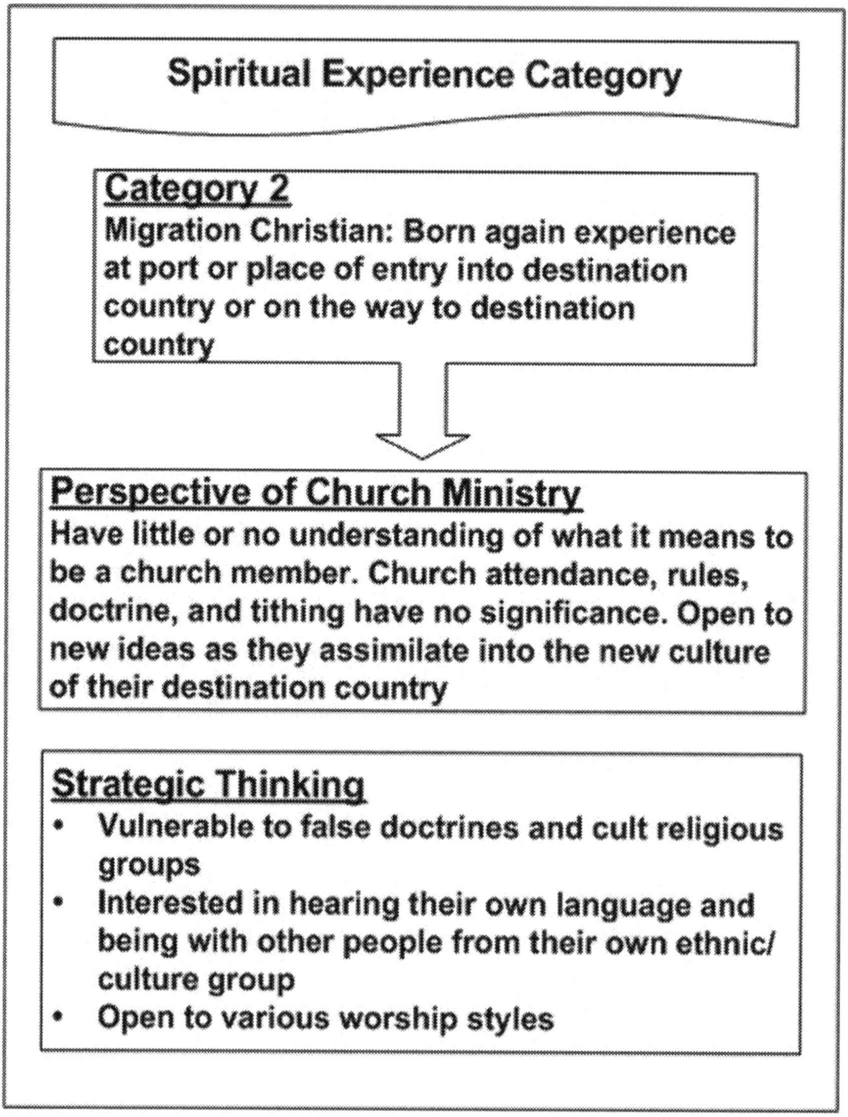

Spiritual Experience Category

Category 2
Migration Christian: Born again experience at port or place of entry into destination country or on the way to destination country

Perspective of Church Ministry
Have little or no understanding of what it means to be a church member. Church attendance, rules, doctrine, and tithing have no significance. Open to new ideas as they assimilate into the new culture of their destination country

Strategic Thinking
- Vulnerable to false doctrines and cult religious groups
- Interested in hearing their own language and being with other people from their own ethnic/culture group
- Open to various worship styles

Fig. 7 Spiritual Experience Category 2

Spiritual Experience Category

Category 3
Church Transfer Christian: Transfers from one church to another church in country of residence in the same city / area to another church in the same city / area

Perspective of Church Ministry
Church transfer Christians are often 1st generation children who are in the assimilation process, or are 2nd and 3rd generation looking for a worship experience that is different their parents

Strategic Thinking
- May have been hurt. May be lonely, have low self esteem, and may need pastoral care
- Open to new styles for worship
- Probably bi-lingual or multi-lingual (speak more than two languages)
- Comfortable with other culture/ethnic groups

Fig. 8 Spiritual Experience Category 3

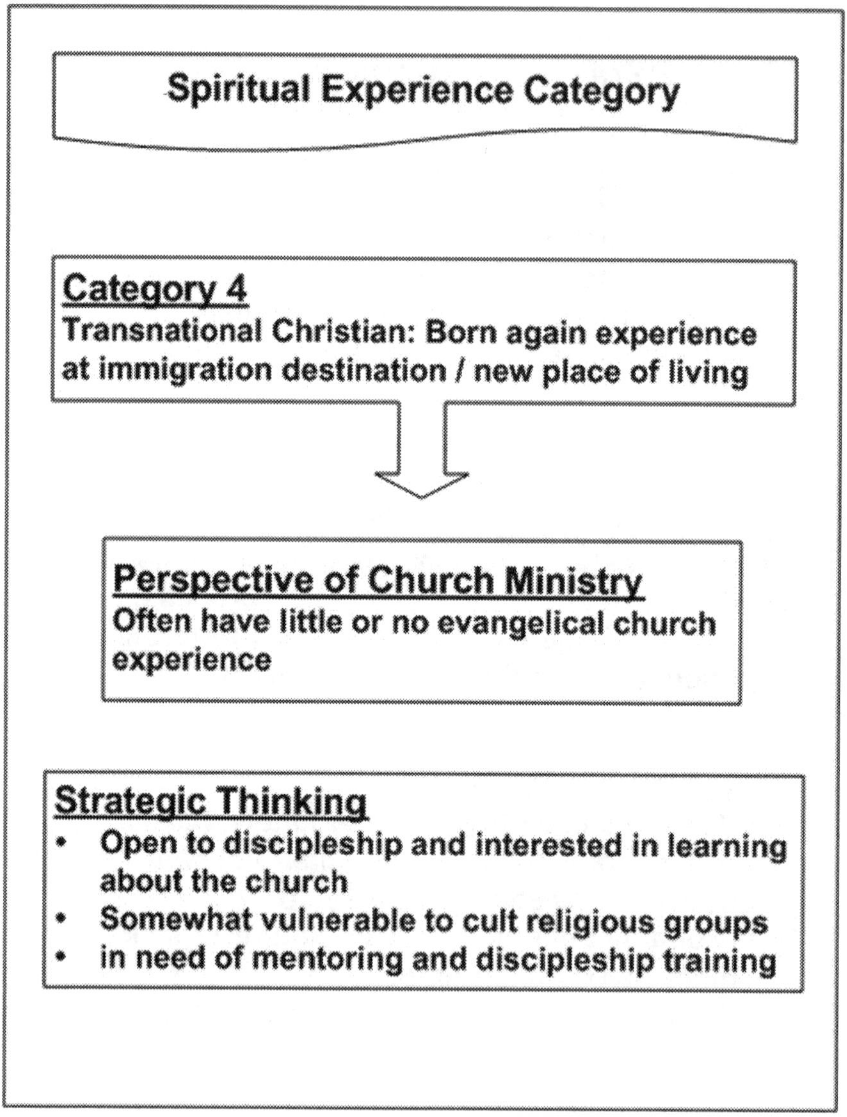

Spiritual Experience Category

Category 4
Transnational Christian: Born again experience at immigration destination / new place of living

Perspective of Church Ministry
Often have little or no evangelical church experience

Strategic Thinking
- Open to discipleship and interested in learning about the church
- Somewhat vulnerable to cult religious groups
- in need of mentoring and discipleship training

Fig. 9 Spiritual Experience Category 4

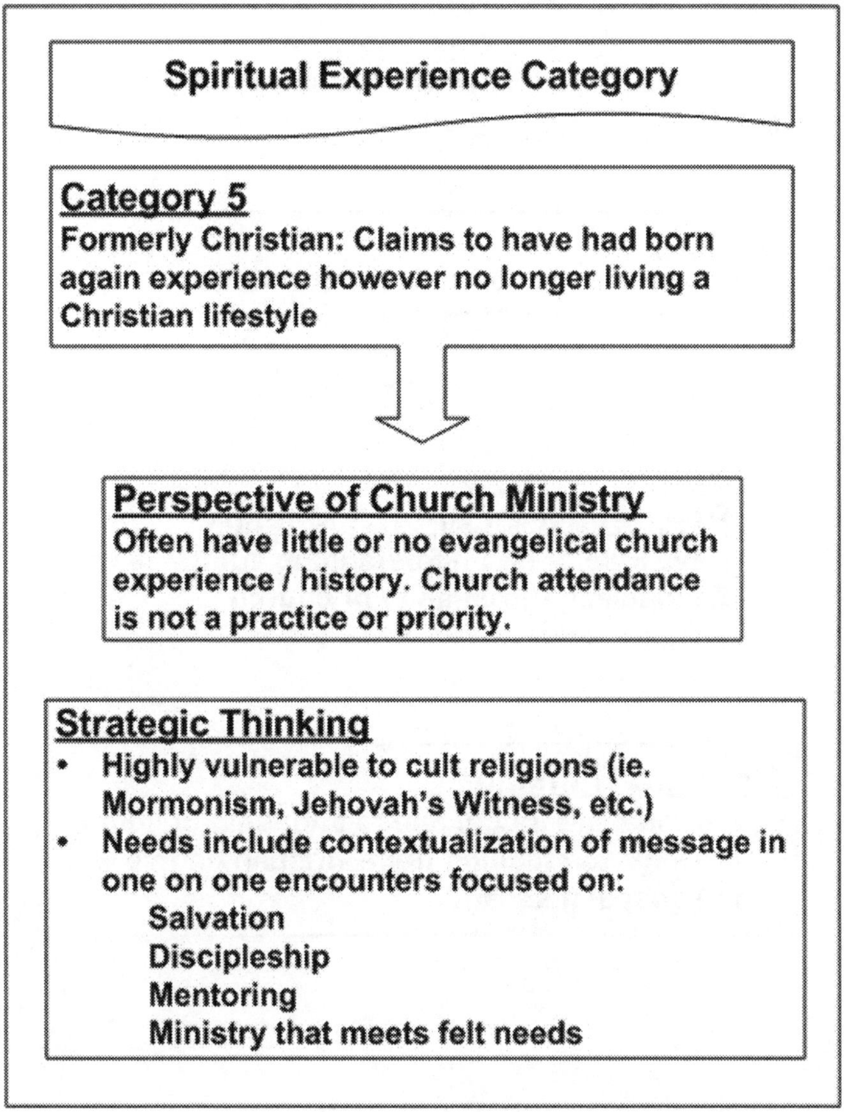

Spiritual Experience Category

Category 5
Formerly Christian: Claims to have had born again experience however no longer living a Christian lifestyle

Perspective of Church Ministry
Often have little or no evangelical church experience / history. Church attendance is not a practice or priority.

Strategic Thinking
- Highly vulnerable to cult religions (ie. Mormonism, Jehovah's Witness, etc.)
- Needs include contextualization of message in one on one encounters focused on:
    Salvation
    Discipleship
    Mentoring
    Ministry that meets felt needs

Fig. 10 Spiritual Experience Category 5

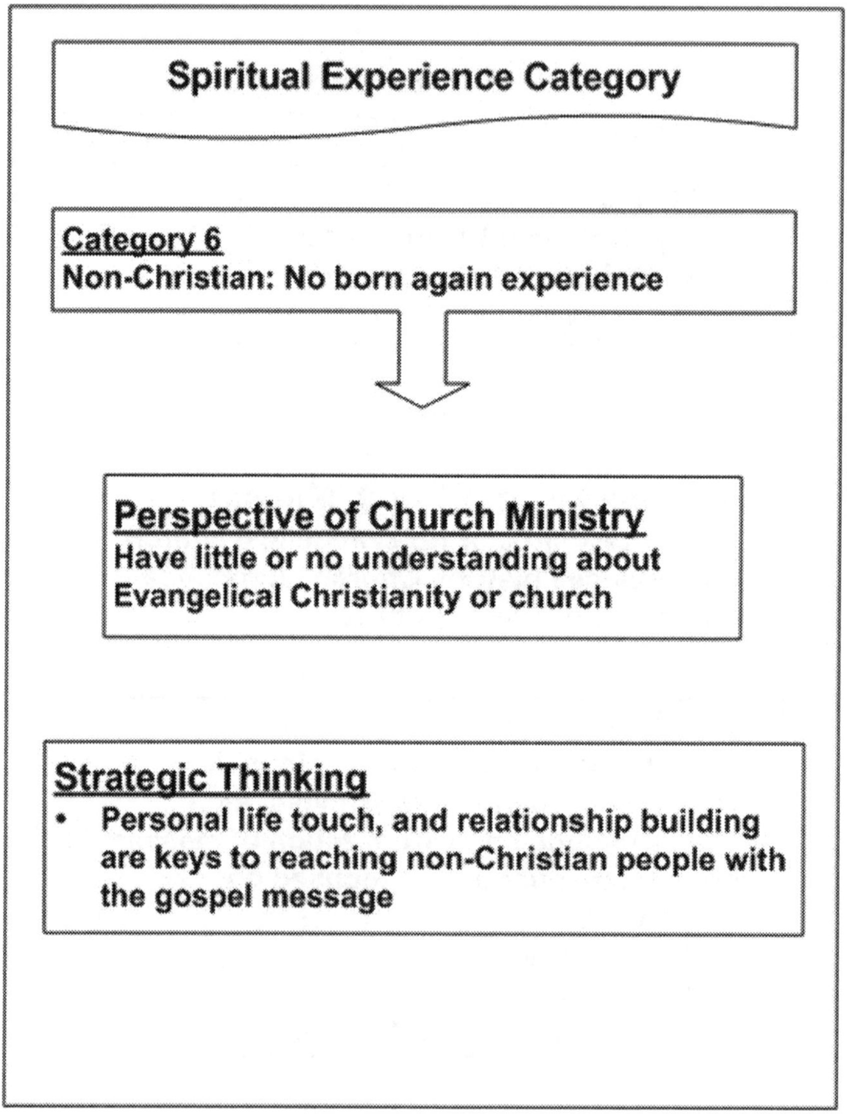

Spiritual Experience Category

Category 6
Non-Christian: No born again experience

Perspective of Church Ministry
Have little or no understanding about
Evangelical Christianity or church

Strategic Thinking
- Personal life touch, and relationship building
  are keys to reaching non-Christian people with
  the gospel message

Fig. 11 Spiritual Experience Category 6

People Research

Understanding people is accomplished through people research. In order to gain knowledge that leads to understanding people groups living in the United States the researcher will gain knowledge of what is happening in the fabric of American society, and do research of people groups within their life community. Researching people within their life community will be best accomplished through techniques of applied anthropology research. Applied anthropology research includes ethnography and the research tool of participant observation.

Anthropology is the science that focuses on people research. It is research that is best accomplished by being with people, observing people, and experiencing their cultural behavior within their life world. Anthropology in its simplest definable form is the study of humanity, and it deals with this study of human beings within their life world (Howard [1983] 1986, 17).

Anthropology as a ministry tool in the multi-cultural context will be accomplished specifically with applied anthropology, and more specifically with an understanding of missionary or urban anthropology. Engaging a people group in researching them with a purposed outcome is the proactive step for the researcher to take in this modern world. In other words, as change is inevitable for every culture group present in the world today, being proactive with goal oriented research will help to bring the best possible outcome within a people group as they change. Missionary anthropology has as its primary goal accomplishing this task.

Missionary anthropology is applied anthropology and as such it seeks to approach the whole person within their life world in order that they may be researched, and their lives impacted with a gospel that touches their whole life. Goal oriented research for the missionary pastor and church leader has a primary core value of bringing people into right relationship with God through his only Son Jesus Christ. This primary core-value is centered on the historical Jesus of Scripture, not a Christ dressed in western or for that matter any culture. Applied missionary anthropology is where the missionary pastor and church ministry leader need to focus his or her attention. In the environment of the city applied missionary anthropology may be specifically described as urban anthropology. Urban anthropology is applied anthropology dealing with the study of people and groups of people living in the urban context.

Urban anthropology helps a person who is doing ministry in a culturally-diverse community begin to understand people living in their culturally diverse context. Urban Anthropology is accomplished by intentionally seeking to accomplish two goals: 1.Understand people through ethnographic research in order to present the message of Christ with meaning that will be effective. 2. Seek to present a Scriptural message devoid as much as possible of the messenger's cultural baggage (i.e. ethnocentrism) thus, preventing the ethnocide of a people's culture as a result of the messenger being among people as the people assimilate into the primary culture within which they exist. Assimilation may be a great possibility when cultures intermingle with other groups. However, assimilation should not be accelerated or encouraged in any way by Christianity, the church, or the gospel except where the cultural norms of people are inherently opposed to Scripture.

In order to accomplish these two tasks a pastor will need to become a missionary pastor. This is true for anyone anywhere in ministry today. Whether a person is pastoring in Sebree, Kentucky, and their community has transitioned overnight into a community that is 25% Mexican immigrant populated, or they are in the middle of the largest most diverse city in the United States, their life calling as a Christian, and especially as a minister, is to reach people with the gospel of Jesus Christ. Suppose they have lived their entire life in Sebree, Kentucky. If this area now has a 25% population of people who are Mexican immigrants and a great percentage of them need to hear the gospel of Jesus Christ in a way they understand, it is vital for the pastor to begin to see his or her world as a missionary would. The pastor will have to develop methods and strategies that will effectively reach people living in the community. In order to accomplish this task he or she will need to become an anthropologist researcher so they may understand and know the people who are there.

In a sense the missionary pastor becomes an anthropologist. This does not mean that a pastor must have a PhD. in cultural anthropology and become a professional anthropologist. However, having an understanding of what cultural anthropology is, and how to utilize applied anthropology will equip the pastor with the ability to gather data in order to accomplish ministry at the optimum level in today's culturally diverse world. Urban anthropology research is accomplished by doing ethnographic research and writing an ethnographic report of each people group being studied.

Ethnographic Research

Ethnographic research "Is the work of describing a culture". This research is best accomplished through observing people within their context (Spradley 1980, 3). Defined by Michael Howard, ethnography is the process of describing cultures, largely through fieldwork (Howard [1983] 1986, 17). Ethnographic research is a fundamental research endeavor of successfully ministering the gospel in the multi-cultural, multi-ethnic community.

This level of research is a key aspect of ethnographic research. Understanding how a culture behaves, what they know, and what items they cherish is important to knowing who a culture is as a people.

"When ethnographers study other cultures, they must deal with three fundamental aspects of human experience: what people do, what people know, and the things people make and use. When each of these are learned and shared by members of some group, we speak of them as cultural behavior, cultural knowledge, and cultural artifacts. Whenever you do ethnographic fieldwork, you will want to distinguish among these three, although in most situations they are usually mixed together. Let's try to... (Spradley 1980, 5)."

These three aspects of human experience are depicted below.

Cultural Behavior   What People Do
Cultural Knowledge   What People Know
Cultural Artifacts   The Things People
                           Make & Use

The critical observations can be made at either macro or micro level. At the macro level the researcher looks at the "big picture," noting common characteristics across the whole group. At the micro level, the researcher makes personal connections with individuals in the group.

Macro Level Research

Research conducted at a macro level is abstract cultural anthropology research. It is called abstract because the research is of a general nature, often from indirect resources. For example in doing macro level research I might get history books about that culture, find maps of their country, search Webster's Dictionary and news sources to get a feel for their political and social situation (including the situation in their country of origin). It is important to go to the community prepared with a high level of knowledge of their current situation and home country.

Macro level "Big Picture" research can be obtained through:
- History books about the culture and the country people come from
- Maps of their country of origin, including historical atlases
- Internet and news sources (will help the researcher to better understand the political and social situation of their country of origin today)
- Gross National Product (GNP) of the country

Micro Level Research

This level of research is where the pastor will gain the understanding of what the life situation of a family is today and how they see the world. The goal of this research is not focused on knowing how a family would have seen the world from their home in Varna, Bulgaria or Gonaives, Haïti. The goal of micro level research is to understand how people see the world from where they are at the present time. How does Mr. Curescu, a Romanian immigrant living in Chicago, see his world? Answering this question is the level of life learning that the pastor needs to grab hold of, and this level of life learning comes from spending time with people.

Prior to undertaking the research task ministry leadership in a church must decide who will do research of people groups existing in the ministry context of the church. Will this research be accomplished by the pastor, a committee appointed by the pastor, or a team recruited by the pastor? Regardless of who does the research the pastor as visionary point leader of the church should always be involved in the research process. Delegation of ministry tasks is vital in the growth of any church or ministry, but the task of researching people groups in the community is so imperative and directly related to ministry vision that this research effort is a priority task for the pastor of a growth motivated church.

Culture Research Teams

The most successful research effort in the culturally diverse community undertaken by a church ministry will be accomplished by the efforts of a Culture Research Team (C.R.T). A Culture Research Team is recruited, trained, and commissioned to research people groups living within the targeted community of the church. A Culture Research Team should consist of at least three members and no more than five members with the pastor of the church serving as a member of the team. Forming one or more Culture Research Teams will also help accomplish the task of research in a fast, efficient, and comprehensive manner. This team approach will accomplish more effective research in a shorter amount of time.

The journey of studying a culture is never ending because cultures are continually changing. Studying culture is an open book study, because the last chapter of any culture being studied is always yet to be written. Each ethnography report the team prepares will later be added to because of further research. Accomplishing the task of studying cultures involves learning and implementing practical, usable research tools including foundational research and participant observation as primary factors of doing ethnography research in order to accomplish the ministry of the gospel through the church located in the culturally diverse community.

There are seven steps of effectively doing people group research in the culturally diverse community. These seven steps include people group identification, people group selection, foundational research, participant observation, data analysis, ethnography writing, and ethnography presentation.

1. People Group Identification

The first step of effectively researching people groups in the culturally diverse ministry context is to identify what people groups are living or working in the community. This identification process is done by doing history, and demographic research of the community. This research must be detailed in order to identify each people group living in the community.

This detail breaks down demographic data from broad categories of ethnicity to specific categories of culture group identification. An example of this is demographic data that shows groups of ethnicity living in the community like 20% Black, 30% Latino, 15% Asian, and 35% Caucasian, but these broad categories only identify shades of color and not specific cultures. Cultural identification is done by visibly walking neighborhoods, interviewing school personnel, hospital personnel, police officers, and others in the community in order to determine what people groups make up the broad designations of Latino, Asian, Black, and Caucasian. For example 30% Hispanic may be 10% Mexican, 10% Cuban, and 10% Puerto Rican. Thirty-five percent Caucasian may be 20% Romanian, 10% Polish, and 5% assimilated Anglo-American. Each people group is different, has different characteristics, belief systems, and felt needs. Each group needs to identified and researched individually.

1. Step One – Demographic research - Available data will include demographic and historical data. Demographic data of the community, people groups in the community, and economics show who is in the community, their economic status (how much money they make), and how the community has changed as people have moved into and out of the community.

2. Step Two – Historical research - Research the history of the community, and the people living in the community. When, why, and how did they arrive in the community? Who came to the community first, why did they leave, and where did they go?

3. Step Three-Analysis of Demographic Groupings - Identifying the diversity of major demographic groupings is vital to laying a foundation for research. Demographic data is broken down into broad categories in regard to ethnicity and race. These broad categories include Caucasian, Latino, Black, Asian, etc. This data may help a restaurant business to know what language to make their menu, or what type of foods might be preferred by customers living in the community, but these broad categories fall short of identifying who is living in a culturally diverse community.

An example of this might be a Chicago neighborhood that is 40% Caucasian, 10% Asian, 20% Black, and 30% Latino. This is considered a diverse community but it may be a community which the data does not represent accurately. At first glance the community may be made up of a 40% white Anglo population. However, when examined closer the community may have an Anglo population that looks like this: 10% Romanian, 10% Latino, 10% Bulgarian, 5% Russian, and 5% assimilated Anglo-American.

Therefore, in a neighborhood with a representation of diversity similar to this, census data does not tell the whole story. The people of a Caucasian grouping like this are not just Anglo. They are from groups who have their own specific cultures, language, foods, and needs. This diversity of major demographic groupings can be true among all categories. A 10% Asian community may include 8% Korean, and 2% Chinese. A 30% Black population may include 8% American Black, 12% Haitian, and 10% African born. Likewise, a 30% Latino grouping may be 20% Mexican, 5% Puerto Rican, and 5% Dominican. Each people group exhibits different cultural attributes. These attributes are shaped by where they were born, where they grew up, and what culture they are from.

Detailed community information is vital knowledge to be gained in the research process. This knowledge will help a ministry to strategically plan their vision for a community. Many church ministries begin planning ministry to culture groups living within their community with little or no cultural understanding. If they see that the demographic data for their community shows a population which has transitioned to become 20% Latino they may make plans to begin a Spanish ministry. However, without detailed community research of what people groups make up the 20%, the ministry may not succeed.

The identification of people groups living in the community can be accomplished by doing community research. Community research includes walking, talking, working, and living in the community. There is no substitute that can take the place of the personal touch, and seeing people face to face. It is important to identify each people group living in the community. This process begins with gathering and analyzing demographic data. The following People Group Demographic Data Worksheet can help the researcher begin this process.

People Group Demographic Data Worksheet

1. Designated Ministry Community Area (Boundaries)
   North   Street-highway-community etc._____

   South   Street-highway-community etc._____

   East   Street-highway-community etc._____

   West   Street-highway-community etc._____

   Zipcode(s) of designated ministry area _____, _____

2. Demographic data of designated area:
   Population Amount:

   Population Ethnicity Demographic Description (major groupings) and % of population:

3. Identified People Groups within each ethnicity grouping % of population if available:

Fig. 12 People Group Demographic Data Worksheet

Once community research has been accomplished to the extent of identifying the demographic breakdown of ethnicity present in the community, research will need to be focused on each particular group.

2. People Group Selection

Once the people groups existing in the ministry community have been identified the task of research project selection must be accomplished. Which people group will be researched first? This selection of a research project is not a task that focuses on a broad field of research choices. The selection process is focused specifically on researching the culture groups who are living in the community. This selection process should be approached both practically and prayerfully. This process must include fixed research goals that include a begin date, and report date for each people group researched.

Selecting which group to research first is done in a practical manner by assessing the group with the greatest needs, and greatest accessibility. Accessibility often may be determined by relationships the Culture Research Team, Pastor, or people in the church already have with a particular people group. Groups with which the church already has relationship connection should be the first groups the research team selects to do research among.

Selecting the research project should be finalized after doing some preliminary research of people groups living in the community. This analysis includes gathering data about the demographics of each particular group. This data is facilitated by utilizing a worksheet like the People Group Description Worksheet on the following page.

People Group Description Worksheet

Date:_____
People Group:_____

Percentage of Population:

_____ %

_____ not identified

Average Age % of population:
_____ 0-10yrs
_____ 11-19yrs
_____ 20-30yrs
_____ 30-40yrs
_____ 40-50yrs
_____ 50-60yrs
_____ 60-70yrs
_____ above 70
_____ not identified

Apparent Religious Heritage:
_____ Roman Catholicism
_____ Evangelical Christianity
_____ Islam
_____ Buddhism
_____ Hinduism
_____ Atheism
_____ None Evident
_____ Animism
_____ Voodoism
_____ Not identifiable
_____ other (designate-
)

Approximate immigration period:
_____ beginning date
_____ ending date
_____ continuing to immigrate
_____ not identified

Average Age % of population:
_____ 0-10yrs
_____ 11-19yrs
_____ 20-30yrs
_____ 30-40yrs
_____ 40-50yrs
_____ 50-60yrs
_____ 60-70yrs
_____ above 70
_____ not identified

Apparent Economic Status:
_____ high % poverty level
_____ medium % poverty level
_____ low % poverty level
_____ high % middle income
_____ medium % middle income
_____ low % middle income
_____ high % high income
_____ medium % high income
_____ low % high income
_____ not identifiable

Apparent Education Level % of group:
_____ little or no formal education
_____ highschool level education
_____ university level education
_____ graduate level education
_____ post graduate level education
_____ technical / trade school education
_____ not identifiable

Level of Assimilation:
_____ no assimilation evident
_____ some assimilation evident
_____ high level of assimilation evident
_____ not identifiable

Primary language:
_____ Spanish
_____ French
_____ Italian
_____ French-Creole
_____ Korean
_____ Tagalog
_____ Chinese
_____ Vietnamese
_____ Thai
_____ Russian
_____ Polish
_____ Romanian
_____ Bulgarian
_____ Swahili
_____ Other (designate-
_____)

Fig. 13 People group Description Worksheet

3. Foundational Research

Research always begins somewhere, and good research begins with exploring available data. Ethnographic research begins with foundational research that lays the groundwork for researching people within their context. It is research that includes existing data, and moves on to observe people in their context. Existing data provides a picture drawn as a result of observations made by previous researchers, of a particular area, society, or culture during a period in time. Because communities, cultures, and people change this information is valuable and un-duplicatable (it can not ever be reproduced). This information provides a picture of how a culture or cultures lived within a given community during a certain time. This allows the researcher to compare how the community, culture, and people have changed since the research was done.

4. Participant Observation

Participant observation is the primary tool of ethnographic research. Participant observation research of a people group will take time. Learning about, relating to, and building relationships with people of a particular culture group does not happen overnight. Understanding that it will take time to do ethnographic research is crucial to developing long term thinking in bringing people to Christ. This is not to say that there will not be short term successes, but the long term goal of bringing people into relationship with Jesus Christ is the ultimate goal.

According to James Spradley we are all, or we all live as, ordinary participants. We know what to expect and we live without much effort in doing those things which come natural to us. The ordinary participant exists with the sole purpose of living life without a second thought. The participant observer on the other hand approaches the world with an agenda (Spradley 1980, 51).

"Ethnographers do not merely make observations, they also participate. Participation allows you to experience activities directly, you get the feel of what events are like, and to record your own perceptions. At the same time, the ethnographer can hardly ever became a complete participant in a social situation (Spradley 1980, 51)."

A participant observer is aware of the obvious. This simply means that they make a conscious effort to notice those things we usually tune out, or take for granted. I can not tell you how many times I have driven down the street, and thought to myself, "Did I remember to lock the door?" As an ordinary participant I often do not think about things like how I shut the door, was there a loud noise, did it slam, and even did I remember to lock the door. The participant observer works to consciously become aware of everything that happens.

Participant observation is accomplished by observing the lives of people. Observing people allows a picture to be drawn by the observer of people living in their community. In the North American context it is important to get as close to where people live as possible in doing participant observation. When the researcher goes among the people, speaks their language, eats their food, and listens to their heart, smiles with them, laughs with them, and cries with them, a connection is made.

Many people who live in the culturally diverse area are new immigrants and it is important to understand most immigrant people live challenging lives. Immigrant people have challenging lives. Their lives often include waking up at 4am or 5am, working all day, coming home, eating dinner, going to bed for a few hours, and getting up and starting the process all over again. In fact they often work more than one job, and work six days a week. They deal with issues of their children learning English, wanting to eat McDonalds, Burger King, and Pizza Hut. Their children want to date in this country when, if they were in their country, they would not date.

Observing immigrant people is not only observation of how they are changing in the immigration process, but it is also observing their children and the issues they are dealing with. What will it mean for a family who is Haitian if their son marries a person who is Jamaican, or a Romanian daughter marries a Mexican young man.

Demographic research and historical research draw a picture of the community. Participant observation puts a face on the data of demographics and historical research. Participant observation is where a picture is drawn of who people are, and relationships are developed that help the observer to know people. Knowing people will help the researcher make a connection with them in a manner that allows them to discover their needs.

It is important to understand the need to maximize the research effort of the research team by separating the team so that each member of the team does participant observation of a different family within the people group being researched. This will maximize the research effort by allowing three to five families to be researched simultaneously thus providing more research data for the team to analyze in the search for cultural themes in preparation to write ethnography and present the ethnography report to church leadership.

According to James Spradley there are six features of participant observation that distinguish it as a research tool from ordinary participants. In life we as people are all ordinary participants. We live life and participate in life as people who tune into what is important to us. This, of course, is both how we were developed to live and the necessity of our lives. If we were to tune into everything around us all of the time we would experience information overload, and probably get very little accomplished in life. The six features that distinguish participant observation from ordinary participation are 1. dual purpose, 2. explicit awareness, 3. wide angle lens, 4.insider-outsider perspective, 5. introspection, and 6. record keeping.

Six Features of Participant Observation
1. Dual Purpose

Participant observation has a dual purpose whereas ordinary participation has a single purpose. An ordinary participant may observe activities happening around them but the participant observer both observes activities happening and asks questions to find out what is happening, why things are happening, and take notes of what is taking place (Spradley 1980, 54).

2. Explicit Awareness

Every day we all tune out to the world in an effort to focus on the tasks we are in doing at a particular point in time. The participant observer intentionally forces themselves to pay attention to the details of the context they are observing. They force themselves to tune in to what is going on around them with an explicit awareness intentionally noting everything going on around them (Spradley 1980, 55).

3. Wide Angle Lens

The researcher who is utilizing the tool of participant observation also looks at each situation with a wide angle lens. Again this is giving attention to detail. It is not just seeing what food is being served at dinner, but noticing what people are wearing, who is serving the food, the manner in which the food is served, and how the participants act (Spradley 1980, 56).

4. Insider-Outsider Perspective

As people we are most often insider participants in the activities in which we are involved. However, the participant observer walks in a role that is both insider as a participant and outside as an observer looking on at the activity (Spradley 1980, 56).

5. Introspection

Introspection happens when the participant observer looks at a situation he or she has just experienced and reflects on their feelings about what they observed and experienced. Introspection is an intentional time of the researcher debriefing themselves. Spradley describes introspection as the researcher learning to use themselves as a research instrument (Spradley 1980, 57).

6. Record Keeping

Participant observation researchers will keep records of what they experience and observe. Record keeping separates the participant observer from the ordinary participant. Keeping records might include taking notes during the observation process, or taking notes immediately following a research experience. Note taking is crucial to participant observation research and will help the researcher analyze, and describe those being studied in an accurate manner (Spradley 1980, 58).

Types of participation

According to Spradley there are five types of participation including non-participation, moderate participation, active participation, and complete participation. These descriptions of participation types describe levels of participation. The lowest level of participation is non-participation and the highest level is complete participation.

In order to accomplish the task of researching a family or household with in a specific people group in a pre-determined amount of time it will be beneficial to set a goal of accomplishing moderate participation or active participation (Spradley 1980, 58).

Moderate Participation

Moderate participation according to Spradley happens when the researcher balances between insider and outsider experience within the group of people being studied. However, moderate participation is at a level that does not include becoming a regular participant who is involved in activities that are taking place. Moderate participation involves observation rather than participation (Spradley 1980, 60).

Active Participation

Active participation begins with observation but involves the researcher moving to a high level of participation in an effort to experience what those being researched experience. It is active participation that enables the researcher to begin to see what people see. It is at this level of participant observation that the researcher borrows the shoes of those being researched and walks seeing as much as possible the world through their eyes and recording what they see.

Active participation can only be surpassed by complete participation in gaining the fullest view of life from another person's perspective. However, doing complete participation is research that is done over a period of months or years while being immersed in the culture of the people being researched. This amount of research time involvement is not expedient to accomplishing the task of studying all of the people groups living in the culturally diverse ministry context in a reasonable amount of time. Therefore, the goal of the researcher doing participant observation in this context is to achieve the level of moderate or active participation during their research (Spradley 1980, 60 and 61).

Asking Ethnographic Questions

Good questions are the key that unlocks the door to good information when doing ethnographic research. Observations of people begin the data collection process, but ethnographic questions open the flood gate of information. Ethnographic questions, in fact, are often questions that the researcher asks and answers through making observations. According to James Spradley there are three major kinds of ethnography questions. These are descriptive, structured, and contrast questions.

Descriptive questions are those broad questions like, who is in the community, why are they there, what do they do, etc. (Appendix 3). Structural questions are used to make focused observations and contrast questions help identify differences of things between categories of data. Asking questions helps the researcher move from gathering broad data to gathering specific data. It is this data, broad and specific that allows the researcher to begin the work of describing the culture being studied (Spradley 1980, 76).

Questions are the pathways to information. However, many times it is more important to listen to people, observe them, and intentionally focus attention on being among them than it is to constantly ask questions. Effective questions are well thought out, appropriately asked, and well timed. No one is perfect and no time may seem like the right time. The key is to do the best that an individual can do by developing cultural sensitivity. Questions are also many times not audibly asked, but are questions the observer asks themselves while making observations. These are self-directed questions in which the researcher acts as an informant in the research context, and asks themselves questions which help to describe in detail everything that is observed.

Questions and observations are the key to participant observation. The participant observer asks questions of themselves continually as they do research. They also ask questions of others. These questions are the pathways to making observations, and obtaining good research data. Asking others questions involves both informal and formal interviews (Spradley 1980, 123).

Informal interviews involve asking people questions in the process of observing them and the activities around them. An informal interview is an interview that happens in the process of observation. It is simply asking questions during normal conversation. These questions can be self directed or directed toward others.

A formal interview involves interviewing someone with their prior knowledge. A formal interview often happens at a pre-determined time at a pre-determined place. It is helpful to video tape, or tape record formal interviews in order to later write down exactly what the informant said and how the said what they said (Spradley 1980, 124).

Well done ethnographic research is built on the foundation of good record keeping. Making ethnographic records takes time and focused effort. According to Spradley the ethnographic record includes recordings, pictures, fieldnotes, artifacts, and other materials that will help the researcher write clear, concise, and accurate ethnography of the people being researched (Spradley 1980, 63).

Field notes are the major portion of ethnography writing, and the language used to make fieldnotes is a key to the writing of good ethnography. Spradley identifies three principles regarding language to keep in mind when doing ethnography research. These three principles are the language identification principle, the verbatim principle, and the concrete principle. These principles focus on how language is used in writing ethnography.

The language identity principle is simply identifying each person who speaks when making fieldnotes. This identification will help the researcher know who said what and identify the difference between those who are speaking (Spradley 1980, 66).

The verbatim principle is simply keeping an exact or verbatim record of what people say. It is natural for people to want to summarize and restate what is being said, however, ethnographic writing will better reflect what is happening when verbatim fieldnotes are taken as much as possible. Spradley recommends using terms like "observer" and "native" to describe language use (Spradley 1980, 67). It may be necessary to use other terms to describe the participants in a research setting. An example of this is using terms like observer, participant 1 (p-1), participant 2 (p-2), participant 3, (p-3) etc.

It is also necessary to utilize the concrete language principle. The few times in my life that I have been involved in situations of dealing with real estate agents, the agents seem to always quote the three most important words in real estate as being "location, location, location". Like real estate, ethnography also has three important words detail, detail, and detail. The concrete language principle that Spradley describes focuses on detailed writing. Concrete language is the detailed language of describing a situation. For example, it is the difference of describing a meal event as 1. *"we met around 7pm, ate a delicious dinner, talked, and socialized", or 2. "we arrived at the home at 6:50pm, climbed the steps and rang the doorbell. While we waited for the door to open we stood on the porch looking around the neighborhood. There were some teenagers hanging out around a car across the street. The door opened. Our host was wearing a green tuxedo with a pink shirt and pink shoes. He welcomed us, took our coats, and we entered the house...etc. (Spradley 1980, 68-69)."* Fieldnotes utilizing these language principles will provide a great deal of material for writing ethnography. When taking fieldnotes, there are three types of fieldnotes that will be taken. These are condensed account notes, expanded account notes, and a fieldwork journal.

Condensed Account Fieldnotes

Condensed account fieldnotes are done on the spot. These notes include making quick notes of words, phrases, and observations that describe what is happening. If someone was to go through my files they would find gum wrappers, napkins, business cards, and scraps of paper with notes scribbled on them. These notes are notes that were taken in restaurants, churches, in people's homes, on airplanes, trains, and buses. These are condensed account fieldnotes taken in the observation process. It is advisable for every researcher to carry a small notepad for making condensed account notes rather than using gum wrappers. Regardless of what is used to write the notes on, taking condensed account fieldnotes is an important part of the research task. (Spradley 1980, 69).

Expanded Account Fieldnotes

Expanded accountant fieldnotes are best done immediately following observation opportunities. These notes need to be as detailed as possible using the condensed account notes to help recall everything that took place during observation. These notes also need to differentiate between all of the participants observed designating who they each are and try to write notes using the language each person spoke as much as possible (Spradley 1980, 70).

Fieldwork Journal

The fieldwork journal is the place for written reflection. It is where the researcher writes their thoughts of interspection, comments on what they have seen, and records their analytical thoughts. Journal entries should be done as often as possible. Although journal notes may be done every day as a normal process of research, at times during research there will be days when entries are made throughout the day, and times when entries are made every other day. It is important to be vigilant with journal entries, but not bound to the thinking that journal entries can only be done at a specific time and place.

Each journal entry should include six information items. These are date, time, place, people, observation thoughts, and analytical thoughts. Including these information items in each entry will help the researcher when they prepare to analyze their data and write their ethnography (Spradley 1980, 71).

5. Analysis

Analysis is the point in the ethnography research process that the culture research team (C.R.T.) reassembles and share the data they have gathered through participant observation with the team members. After sharing information the team then works together to analyze the data. Through analysis of the research data the team has a goal of identifying and describing at least five areas of the participant observation research. These are listed as follows:

1. Family history of families researched
   a. History in country of origin
   b. Immigration process
   c. Life today in the United States

d. Identified felt needs
2. Cultural themes of people group studied
3. Identified felt needs of people group
4. View of God of the people group studied
5. Needs of children and youth among the people group researched

This identification and description process will generate analysis thoughts of the people group researched. This analysis will help the Culture Research Team to make recommendations and strategy suggestions in their ethnography report.

6. Writing Ethnography

The people group research process is an open ended adventure of learning about the life and culture of a people group. This process is cyclical in the sense that there is no end to researching a group of people, or a particular situation. Because cultures change and people change, researching people is always ongoing (Spradley 1980, 160-161).

The ethnography report is done by taking all of the information gathered up to a determined point in time and compiling, analyzing, and writing in a manner that accomplishes: 1. the reporting of research data, 2. description of the big picture of the people group, 3. a focus on the individual / people researched, and 4. Analysis and recommendations for delivery for developing a plan of contextualization of the of gospel message for that people group.

The Culture Research Team ethnography has as its primary goal the presentation of a useful tool for church members and leaders. The Culture Research Team should give creative thought to the manner in which the material will be presented, and develop a uniform standard for their ethnography reports. This way their audience will have an easier time of following them from one report to the next. The ethnography report should include the following information:

• Demographics data of the community
• Description of people group researched
• History of people group researched
• Broad observations of people group

- Focused observations of family life within their culture
- Their view of God, the church, and religion
- Their felt needs
- Analysis
- Strategic plan for communicating the message of the gospel with meaning

7. Making an Ethnographic Presentation

When the Culture Research Team (C.R.T.) completes ethnographic research and writing it needs to be shared with the church leadership, and then with the congregation. This is vital to the development and implementation of strategies of contextualization aimed at reaching the people within the culture group researched. Presentation can make a crucial difference in communicating the findings of the research process. If a presentation is poorly done people may not hear or understand the information being presented. However, if the presentation is sharp, organized, and clearly articulated, people will listen. It is important to accomplish the task in a manner that people will hear and understand.

Preparation of the presentation is done by delegating each area of the presentation to a member of the Culture Research Team. Team members may have a preference of which area they would like to present. Presentation areas may include:

- Introduction
- History of people
- Language spoken
- Why they came here
- What the issues are
- What their needs are
- View of God, church, and religion
- Their felt needs
- Analysis
- Recommendations
- Conclusion

The presentation needs to be alive. This is accomplished when the presenters approach their subject with passion. Other key elements to the presentation are a good introduction, a great conclusion, the utilization of media, drama, and visuals.

The anthropology research process is a powerful experience accomplished by building relationships with people. Building relationships with people can be very exciting and fun.

I have found that many people from various cultures enjoy the experience of sitting down and having coffee together. As our ministry began to involve working among different cultures, I learned to drink coffee. I have had coffee with Romanian people, Hungarian people, Bulgarian people, Haitian, Puerto Rican, and other people from many culture groups. Sharing in the coffee drinking experience is not about the coffee. It is about relationship. Likewise sharing a meal together is also one of the greatest methods of building relationships with people. There is great significance to the shared experience of eating food together, and drinking coffee together. This is especially true among immigrant people groups.

Sitting down together with a Romanian family and eating chicken soup, bread, and cabbage rolls that mom made from scratch is a powerful way to make connection. Likewise, joining a Haitian family for rice with black mushrooms and fried goat, or with a Jamaican family for breakfast enjoying Salt-fish and Ackie will not only help you to make great people connections, but leave you with memories and friendship that may last forever.

Contextualization

Contextualization is the effective communication of the gospel to people that is evidenced by dramatic life change and the growth of the indigenous church. Ministry must be strategically planned in order to be effective in affecting life change in people living in this post-Christian society. In order for a people to accept Jesus Christ they need an opportunity to hear the message of Jesus Christ in a way they understand. Just because the church is preaching does not mean anyone is listening, or hearing what is being said. Like the example from philosophy class, "If a tree falls in the forest and no one hears it fall, did the tree really fall?" If the church preaches the message and no one hears the message was the message really preached? In other words a message that does not understand the needs people have where they live may be preached, but may never be heard. Likewise, a message that communicates to people will be spoken in language they understand.

This example of a message miss-communicating with a people group was printed in Campus Life Magazine in the spring of 2001,

"When Coca-Cola first started marketing its soda in China, it was translated to 'ke-kou-ke-la'. Thousands of signs were printed before Coke found out that phrase really means, 'bite the wax tadpole' or 'female horse stuffed with wax,' depending on the dialect. Oops! After doing a little more research, Coke settled on 'ko-kou-ko-le,' which can be translated, 'happiness in the mouth.' Sure beats a wax tadpole! (Campus Life, May/June 2001, 63)."

Accomplishing the task of a particular message finding meaning among the intended audience is often a challenging task. Governments, businesses, educators, anthropologists, and missionaries very often struggle with their message finding meaning. Culture, and language continue to be great barriers to effective communication (communication in which a message is received and understood) even in today's global, and technologically advanced society.

The church like any other organization has the need to communicate effectively. This communication need includes understanding the language people speak, and how messages translate across cultures. This is vividly shown by the Coca-Cola situation in China. Although language is one aspect of communication, it is important to understand that merely translating a message does not necessarily guarantee effective communication of the message. Thus in order for a message to find meaning the message must be culturally customized in a way that the message does not deviate or lose its intended meaning, but finds comprehensive understanding with the intended receiver of the message.

This process in the course of ministry endeavor has come to be known as contextualization. Contextualization as a process has developed over a number of years, and today continues to be defined in various ways depending upon which author, expert, or group is describing contextualization. As an endeavor of communication process regarding the gospel message being sent from sender to receiver, contextualization finds its origins in another term known as indigenization.

> Indigenization – "Contextualization is not simply a fad or catch-word but a theological necessity demanded by the incarnational nature of the word. What does the term imply? It means all that is implied in the familiar term 'indigenization' and yet seeks to press beyond. Contextualization has to do with how we assess the peculiarity of Third World contexts. Indigenization tends to be used in the sense of responding to the gospel in terms of a traditional culture (Hesselgrave and Rommen 2000, 31)."

The men who originally most influenced the development of indigenization were Rufus Anderson, and Henry Venn. In 1860 Anderson and Venn developed the Three Self Model in regard to effectively communicating the gospel to other cultures. Effective communication has taken place when the gospel has helped a people become 1.self-funded, 2.self-governed, 3.self-propagating.

The process of accomplishing these goals among an indigenous group of people has become known as contextualization. Contextualization as a term was first used by the Theological Education Fund in their publication, Ministry in Context: the Third Mandate Programme of the Theological Education Fund (1970-1977) (Hesselgrave and Rommen 2000, 28).

Contextualization is not a process that can be approached or accomplished from a sterile non-interactive approach. The days of the walled missionary compound are long past as an effective way to bring the gospel to people. Whether ministering in the North American City or in a third world country to be effective in the contextualization process the missionary pastor must be among the people.

The Apostle Paul was keenly aware of the need of gospel presentation to be culturally relevant. He moved into communities, lived among people, and preached to them with language and action that was relevant to them in their life world. Paul became all things to all people as he writes about in I Corinthians 9:19-23. This simply meant he related to people within their life world. For instance, at the Acropolis he spoke to the people about the unknown god, directly connecting with them in language they understood. He was an educated man yet while in Ephesus he repaired and made tents. He was a humble man that could communicate to aristocrats.

Paul was a tremendous contextualizer. He related to people by knowing His message, learning the culture to which he was communicating, and knowing himself as he went among people. He saw what they saw; lived like they lived, and ate the food they ate. We as leaders can become effective at doing what Paul did in relating to people, and communicating the message to them (Keener 1993, 472)."

One of the greatest testimonies of contextualization ever written about is the story of Don Richardson among the Sawi people of New Guinea. Richardson entered the life world of the Sawi people prior to many culture changes happening. The Sawi were an indigenous people group living as their ancestors had lived for generations. Richardson made friends with the Sawi, learned their language, learned their culture, developed relationships, and lived among the people. When he felt the timing was appropriate he shared the gospel story with them. Their response to the gospel discouraged Richardson greatly. Upon hearing the gospel the Sawi people were thrilled by the betrayal of Jesus by Judas. In fact they saw Judas as the hero in the story. Richardson learned that in Sawi culture betrayal is celebrated and admired (Richardson 1976, 177 and 178).

The Sawi had a tradition called "tuwi asonai man" which means fatten your friend for the harvest. The Sawi people and surrounding tribes would develop friendships between each other for the purpose of betraying one another. The goal of the relationship was to gain the trust of a friend until they let their guard down, and then kill them, and eat them (Richardson 1976, 34).

Richardson was quite discouraged. Imagine trying to present the message of Jesus the Savior to a people who saw Judas the betrayer as the hero in the story. Richardson alludes to his frustration in his writing (Richardson 1976, 182 and 183). The question lingered, how does a person communicate the gospel message to the Sawi people in a way they will understand? (Richardson 1976, 183).

Richardson begins his book "Peace Child" with the story of "tuwi asonai man", fattening your friend for the harvest. His account of the work among the Sawi includes the struggles of his family, struggles between the Sawi villages living along the Kronkel River, and the challenges he faced in bringing the gospel to the Sawi.

After months of witnessing the Sawi people of the Haenam and Kamur villages fighting and killing each other Don Richardson told the Sawi he would leave. This prompted the people of Kamur, and Haenam to make "cool water" which means peace (Richardson 1976, 192).

The Kamur and Haenam villages met in a special ceremony that would bring peace. In this ceremony Kaiyo of the Kamur Village gave his son to Mahor of the Haenam village. "Mahor shouted 'eehaa!' 'It is enough! (Richardson 1976, 199)." Then Mahaen of the Haenam Village gave his son to Kaiyo. They exchanged commitments of peace, after exchanging the "tarop tim". The "tarop tim" was the "peace child". This peace child was the only possible way to bring peace between the villages. The peace child sealed the covenant between Kamur and Haenam (Richardson 1976, 200 and 201).

As Richardson witnessed this powerful sacrificial event he realized this was the answer to bringing the gospel to the Sawi. Richardson met with the people and spoke of the peace child named Jesus. He contextualized the gospel message and communicated to the Sawi. The betrayer in the Sawi culture could only be surpassed by the peace child (Richardson 1976, 211-214).

The most powerful example of contextualization that I have personally witnessed was in the Philippines. Contextualization of the gospel was accomplished through a ministry called Word for the World Fellowship. Word for the World Fellowship emerged from the heart of a missionary living in Manila desiring to accomplish effective ministry among Filipino people.

In the summer of 1988 I lived among the Filipino people for a few months learning about their culture. The Philippines is a beautiful country, and the Filipino people are wonderful people. They, like many other cultures, have a religious history that involves superstition and animism. Their animism belief system includes worship of a far off supreme-being, lower gods, ancestral spirits, lesser spirit beings and objects with power. Little is known about how this animism worship was practiced and the religious experience of the Filipino people prior to Catholicism entering the country in 1521 (Henry 1986, 6).

It was in 1521 that Ferdinand Magellan arrived in the Philippines, and as it was the goal of Spanish explorers to claim territory for Spain, and Christianize the world, Magellan wasted no time doing either (Henry 1986, 6). Magellan claimed the Philippines for Spain, Catholicism became the official national religion, and the people were baptized. The result of this according to Rodney Henry was the establishment and coexistence of two religions, Roman Catholicism and folk Catholicism (animism) (Henry 1986, 11). This is an example of syncretism.

This can be seen in the church of the Black Nazarene of Quiapo. People stand in line for hours to touch the Black Nazarene statue, or the feet of a statue of Jesus lying in a glass coffin. It is believed that these statues have power to heal, and protect from evil spirits. Thus Catholicism becomes the fulfillment in the life of the individual of their higher concerns, and their superstitious practices help them with every day life.

> "It is not difficult to see the animistic elements in the above beliefs and observances. In these areas where Roman Catholicism overlaps with animism, there is no apparent inconsistency seen by the individual or the church. Roman Catholicism and animism can coexist quite nicely together as long as each is fulfilling its separate functions. Roman Catholicism is the religion of ultimate concerns, while animism is the religion of everyday concerns, and together, they are called "Folk Catholicism" (Henry 1986, 13-14)."

Fig. 14 The Black Nazarene of Quiapo

In 1902 the Roman Catholicism ceased to be the official religion of the Philippines. This allowed Protestantism to enter the Philippines. Although protestant missionaries did not advocate the practice of animism for those receiving salvation like Catholicism had done, Protestantism remained a religion of higher concern that took place outside of the home in the church. Because of this, many people who became protestant practiced animism in their home while practicing Protestant Christianity in the church (Henry 1986, 14).

The practice of living in a world where Catholicism, Protestantism and animism are integrated and worshipped simultaneously is not exclusive to the Philippines. The Dominican Republic, Haiti, Jamaica, and other culture groups in other countries of the world practice this same type of religious experience. Each of these result from failed contextualization of the gospel. Failed contextualization leads to syncretism. Syncretism is the diminishing of Jesus Christ as the savior of humanity and way of salvation and blending of

Christianity with animism which creates false religion that leads to spiritual bondage.

> "'Syncretism was said' to occur when critical and basic elements of the Gospel are lost in the process of contextualization and are replaced by religious elements from the receiving culture; there is a synthesis with this partial Gospel (Conn 1984, 176)."

In 1985 during a trip to Haiti I visited an old fort at Cap Haitien north of Gonaives with our mission team. A little boy volunteered to be our paid tour guide as we went to the fort. On our way up the mountain I asked the boy if he went to church. He said yes. He then explained that he and his mother attended mass at the Catholic church one night of the week, and the voodoo ceremony another night of the week. He was very proud of this religious experience that he and his family lived, and he celebrated his pride with a little dance.

> "In the long run, when pagan customs are practiced in secret, they combine with public Christian teachings to form Christopaganism – a syncretistic mix of Christian and non-Christian beliefs. For example, African slaves in Latin American homes taught the children of their masters the worship of African spirits. When the children grew up and joined the Roman Catholic church, they combined the Catholic veneration of saints and the tribal religion into new forms of spirit worship that had a Christian veneer (Hiebert 1985, 185)."

Winning people to Jesus Christ and helping them to cease the religious practice of their ancestors is challenging and difficult. Well accomplished contextualization should be the goal of each missionary pastor. In 1988 when I visited the Philippines I learned about the culture, people, and the failed contextualization of the Catholic Church, and Protestant Churches. I visited places like the church of the Black Nazarene of Quiapo and wondered if there was a way to start over and truly bring a contextualized gospel message to the Philippine people that would free them from the religious bondage they were experiencing.

Then I met a man named Gerald Holloway. Holloway was a missionary who had served in Asia in a traditional missionary role (educator, administrator, etc.) However, after gaining a great deal of knowledge about the Philippine people and building relationships with them, Holloway did something non-traditional for most evangelical missionaries. Holloway resigned his responsibilities and started an evening fellowship meeting in his home. In essence this meeting was a Bible study. The meeting grew during the first two years, and soon they moved the meeting to the Hotel Intercontinental in Makati. This fellowship meeting became a powerful worship celebration meeting.

By 1988 the ministry had already reached thousands of people, was duplicated in barrios, other islands, and other countries. Today the ministry has sent hundreds of missionaries throughout the world and has established many churches in the United States and Canada. They have accomplished the three goals of the three self model; self-led, self-funded, and self-propagating (Hesselgrave1991, 605).

What did they do differently to reach the Filipino people? Pastor Holloway focused ministry efforts on building relationships. They named the ministry Word for the World Fellowship and did not require membership. This allowed Catholic, Protestant, and unchurched persons to attend the fellowship and find personal relationship with Jesus Christ, without the barriers of coming to a church different from their own.

Holloway was able to accomplish contextualization of the gospel by presenting Jesus Christ as being the Lord of ultimate concerns as well as the Lord of every day living. This presentation allowed the Filipino people to see Jesus Christ as their Savior and not a far away remote supreme god. It was this true gospel message that met the Filipino people within their life-world and culture, and connected with them (Holloway 1992).

Developing contextualization strategy for local church ministry existing in the culturally diverse community begins with self analysis. The self analysis of contextualization is self reflection that includes seeking the presence of God to reveal to the person those things which are cultural as compared to those things which are scriptural in relation to their own theology. Self-analysis is the exercise of de-contextualizing oneself for the purpose of removing one's culture from the manner in which they serve and worship God as much as possible in order to understand scripture without the baggage of one's culture. (Hesselgrave and Rommen 2000, 43).

Scripture analysis is a second step in the contextualization process. It is scripture analysis that helps a leader see scripture in the context in which it was written. It is seeing the gospel as it should be understood. The third step is to understand the culture to which the message sender is taking the message. This understanding begins with studying the culture, and is further gained by doing ethnography research.

Contextualization strategy developed for implementation by the local church ministry existing in the culturally diverse community in North America is more challenging than contextualization utilized by the missionary going to another culture within that culture's home country. Contextualization strategy in the culturally diverse North American community utilizes the same principles as those utilized overseas, but understands the unique issues inherent to the culturally diverse community in the North American context. These include the fact of cultural assimilation, generational differences, the need for culture groups to evangelize inside and outside of their culture, and their need to see the future of their group before it takes place. A contextualization strategy in the church that is committed to reaching the culturally diverse community will follow a pattern similar to this flow chart:

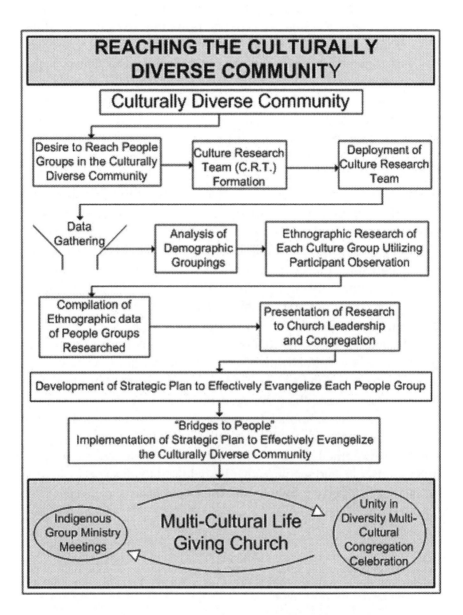

Fig. 15 Reaching the Culturally Diverse Community Flow Chart

Implementation of contextualization strategy is accomplished by developing effective Indigenous Group Ministry Meetings among each people group being reached, and providing worship opportunities within the greater community of those people groups who desire to come together and experience unity through Jesus Christ within the diverse community worship experience. Unity in diversity is a key to multi-cultural church growth, and is only possible through the presence and reconciliation power of Jesus Christ, because it is in Jesus Christ that we are one (Eph 2:14-17).

Indigenous Group Ministry Meetings target each people group being reached by the church ministry. These meetings can be accomplished in many ways including Bible studies, fellowship meetings, and cell group ministries. Indigenous Group Ministry Meetings are implemented with the focus of achieving two goal areas: development of Christian community (koinonia), and contextualization (communicating the gospel message with meaning). The area of Christian community development focuses on building relationships among people. These relationships are centered on the love of Christ between Christian brothers and sisters (John 14 12:17).

The goal area of contextualization specifically targets the accomplishment of contextualization of the gospel within the lives of the group by focusing on five areas of life development. These five areas are leadership, evangelism, mission, theology, and personal worship. These five areas accomplish the goals of contextualization described by the three-self movement, include the accomplishment of what has been described as the fourth self (self theologizing) (Heibert 1985, 210-211), and include what I would call the fifth self, (self-led worshipper). This is shown by the following chart:

Five Goal Areas of Contextualization			
1.	Leadership	Self-Led	Development of Three-World Conscious Leaders
2.	Evangelism	Self-Propagating	Development of Mission Mandate Motivation
3.	Resource Investment	Self-Funded	Development of Mission Mandate Commitment
4.	Theology	Self-Theologizing	Development of Self-Learning Abilities
5.	Personal Spiritual Experience	Self-Led Worshipper	Development of Personal Worship Ability

Fig. 16 Five Goal Areas of Contextualization

1. Leadership: Developing Three-World Conscious Leaders

Developing national leaders is the priority of missionary contextualization effort within the boundaries of the country where a missionary serves. Developing national leaders is a challenging task necessary to accomplishing contextualization of the gospel successfully. Hiebert writes, "It is essential that we train leaders who can wrestle with the theological issues that emerge within their cultural context (2 Timothy 2:2) (Heibert 1985, 215)." A national leader may also be called an indigenous leader. (Indigenous simply means from within their own culture group).

Developing indigenous leaders living in the culturally diverse context is an endeavor that is possibly more challenging than training a national leader (indigenous) within their own country. The indigenous leadership person being developed in their country of immigration destination must be trained to become a leader with three world thinking. Three world thinking leaders seek to understand the old world of the first generation, the new world in which they now live, and the coming world of new generations. Three world thinking leaders indigenous to their culture group will best understand where they have come from, where they are now, and what is happening to their children as they assimilate into a new culture and their culture evolves. Three world thinking indigenous leaders are more effective at bridging from the old word to the new, and across generations than are those who only think in one world terms.

205

One world thinking people are people who are focused on their life world experience and do not have enough natural leadership vision or skill to connect with the future or the past. They only see one life world and that is the life world where they exist. Many people groups have established churches in the new world of America after their migration with one world thinking leadership. These churches often worship the way they did in the old country. They speak their indigenous language, practice their customs and culture, and often close themselves off from the rest of the community. They maintain their cultural purity; however cultural purity in the diverse community is a short journey.

I have personally observed Hispanic, Romanian, Hungarian, Italian, and Yugoslavian churches live the cycle of the first world thinking church ministry. Some of these were early in their journey and the church had many people. However, there are some which are no longer in existence today. When immigration of their people group ended in their community, the church began its journey to the end.

2. Self-Propagating: Evangelism

Three world thinking leaders will motivate people to fulfill the mission mandate of scripture. Many immigrant churches and culture group based churches focus on reaching those who speak their language best, and they do not move very far beyond the walls of the sanctuary to accomplish this task. In Mathew 28:19 "Jesus said go into all of the world and make disciples". Three world thinking leaders will develop strategies of evangelism to bring the gospel to their own people group, and inspire the desire within them to reach all people from all groups living in their community. Motivating people to fulfill God's mission mandate is helping people to come to the realization that *"God sent us here for a purpose."*

3. Self-Funded: Resource Investment

Fulfilling the American dream is the goal of many immigrant people. This dream is only second to survival. It is for these reasons that people from many culture groups work two and three jobs, many times six and seven days a week. This lifestyle along with little, or no understanding of the scriptural concept of tithing equal limited financial commitment to the church ministry. New converts need training in the financial area. People who were church members in their country of origin often gave little to the church because little was expected from them. In many places throughout the world the mission boards have funded and continue to fund ministry, and people do not learn how to be self-funded.

The primary way to train new converts, and retrain old ones is to develop leaders who will inspire commitment from people to the mission of God. Mission commitment includes time, effort, and finance. Scripture states, "Where a person's treasure is you will find their heart also (Matt 6:19-21)." Inspiring mission commitment is plowing the ground of the heart with scripture to a place that the Holy Spirit inspires the individual to faithfully bless God's ministry.

4. Theology: Develop Self Learning Abilities

Helping people to learn how to study the Bible and search scripture for themselves is empowering them to find answers about the things of God on their own. Finding answers about the things of God is the foundation to forming theology within a people group's worldview.

> "It is the responsibility of the missionary not only to teach the people Scriptures, but also how to study the Scriptures for themselves, and to apply them to their own lives. (Heibert 1985, 215)."

Developing theological understanding is a primary goal of contextualization. When a people group begins to self-theologize, they have moved from believing in God because of what the missionary said to a place where they can prove God, who He is, and how to live for Him for themselves. Self-theologizing is the key to knowing God in personal relationship and growing to the point of seeking and worshipping God as individuals.

5. Personal Spiritual Experience: Self-Led Worshipper

The opportunity of praying, worshiping, and knowing God for oneself is the highest privilege of a Christian's life. There are two primary things that separate Christianity from other religions.

1. The fact that Christianity is the worship of the one, true, living, creator God, His Son Jesus Christ, and the Holy Spirit.
2. The personal experience of knowing creator God (Adonai) in personal relationship through His Son Jesus Christ.

The ability of a person to enter into worship as an individual is a fundamental of Christianity that must be emphasized in developing people. Often in history the church has seen itself as the only place for access to God. However, it is through Jesus Christ that worship is personal, and possible. In Him the worship experience of prayer, meditation, and singing become a daily experience in the life of the believer. It is through these personal worship experiences that a believer's spiritual life lives.

Many cultures influenced by the church over thousands of years have been trained that the only place an individual can know and experience God is in the sanctuary by way of the priest or pastor. However, Jesus never spoke in creeds, declarations, bylaws, or constitutions, he simply said in John 14, "I am the way" (John 14:6). Although creeds, theological statements, and doctrinal declarations are necessary to lead us and guide us as people as we walk the Christ life, they are not necessary in order for us as people to know and serve God. Developing people to become self-led worshippers of God who will seek God for themselves is the powerful ingredient that gives life to contextualization.

Communication of the gospel to people is not a task that is accomplished with little effort or thought. People have life needs and as Christians we can not help them with their life needs if we do not know or understand them. It is imperative that interaction with the community, observation of people in the community, and relationship building with them be established as core values in our lives, and the life of our churches.

Principles of urban anthropology and the tools of participant observation research are available to any person. These tools of ministry along with the process of contextualization will help the local church reach its community more effectively with the gospel of Jesus Christ. These tools are especially beneficial for the church which exists in the culturally diverse community.

7

DEVELOPING VISION STRATEGY

———⊶⊷———

Churches face three fundamental dilemmas in their endeavor to grow: a lack of mission focus, a lack of visionary thinking, and geometric deficiency. 1. A lack of mission focus - The reality of many churches is that they often do not understand what they believe (their mission in this world). 2. Lack of visionary thinking – many churches who understand what they believe do not know what to do about what they believe (they have a lack of vision and cannot see the future). 3. Geometric deficiency – geometry states that the shortest distance between two points is a straight line. When churches figure out what they believe and what they want to do with what they believe, they often lack the ingenuity and fortitude to go "there". Going "there" is that point in the church organization's existence that the leader strikes the water with his or her staff like Moses did when the children of Israel stood at the shore of the Red Sea. Going "there" is the action that enables vision to be accomplished. It is seeing the line between the point of where the church is and where the church wants to go. When the church identifies what they believe based on Scripture truth, where they want to go based on what they believe, and act, they can move beyond the limits of ordinary thinking.

A vision strategy includes an organization's mission statement, vision statement, glossary of terms, core values, strategic implementation plan, evaluation process, and vision revision strategy. These seven elements form a dynamic vision strategy plan that will take the organization from mediocrity to excellence (Wall, Bob, Robert S. Solum, and Mark R. Sobol 1992). A vision strategy is more than just a road map showing the destination of the organization. It is the global positioning system that shows where an organization is today, where it will be tomorrow, and how it plans to get there. It is the key to helping the organization fulfill its destiny. There are three critical variables to developing an effective vision strategy. These three critical variables are:

1. shared purpose - People working together, their sights elevated to the goal, sharing a mutual commitment to the goal – the vision – of the organization, and have the ability to individually articulate that vision (Wall, Bob, Robert S. Solum, and Mark R. Sobol 1992, 32).
2. shared values - Shared values should be easier to come by in a church organization. Scripture should guide us in this area. Shared values effect the way each member treats their ministry task as well as other people (Wall, Bob, Robert S. Solum, and Mark R. Sobol 1992, 32).
3. Presence of Leadership - Leaders are the keystone to the quality of the organization's environment. Without enlightened leadership, vision collapses (Wall, Bob, Robert S. Solum, and Mark R. Sobol 1992, 33).

The Mission Statement

Peter Drucker writes, *"What matters most is not the leader's charisma. What matters is the leader's mission. Therefore, the first job of the leader is to think through and define the mission of the institution (Drucker 1990, 3)."* Peter Drucker is an exceptional writer and strategist. I love to read Drucker's books. They are filled with great leadership and management tools. However, this statement regarding a leader's mission is a dangerous statement for the local church leader, although Drucker's book is about non-profit management and does not deal directly with the church organization. Therefore the principles are not directly related to what should happen in the church.

It is important to understand that the mission of the church is directed and set forth by God in Scripture. The leader who goes it alone in defining the mission of the church organization will end up a lonely leader. Too often church leaders attempt to mandate a mission in the church without including anyone in the process. Sometimes they do not even include God. The mission statement in the local church should identify God's mandate for His church. Mission statement development needs to include people from the organization. Including the people in the process gives them ownership. The mission statement is a summary statement that captures the scripturally based theological mission of the church. The mission of the church is scripturally mandated and it is non-negotiable. It does not change.

The Vision Statement

The vision statement is the description of the church's future successful outcome. In a nutshell, the vision statement of a ministry is a clearly stated definition of what the ministry seeks to accomplish. It defines the goals and purpose that drive the ministry, and generally serves as the foundation of all that the ministry hopes to accomplish. It should be clear, concise and memorable. Vision based in the mission mandate of God has the strength and authority of God's presence in it, through it, and behind it.

Writing a vision statement is quite challenging and fulfilling. However, effectively working by the standards of a well written vision statement can make the difference between excellence and mediocrity for an organization. A vision statement should challenge the church to do the undoable, and strive to go where few dare to go. This sentiment was expressed by Theodore Roosevelt who once said:

"Far better is it to dare mighty things,
to win glorious triumphs even though checkered by failure,
than to rank with those poor spirits
who neither enjoy nor suffer much because they live
in the gray twilight that knows neither victory nor defeat."

In this spirit, it is vitally important that church ministries take careful, yet bold and faith-filled steps toward meeting the tremendous needs in the culturally diverse community. The best means to do this in a systematic way is to develop a vision statement that embodies what their objectives are. By doing so, a ministry can move from a day - to - day reactionary posture to a carefully designed direct action agenda. Thus the church will become a vision driven ministry. The vision statement should be definable, doable, and daring. Definable – the vision can be captured. It is big enough to dream, but small enough to barely get our arms around. Doable – it is possible to accomplish. Daring – it is daring enough that very few try to go there.

Glossary of Terms

The glossary of terms describes the terms in the vision statement. It defines what the organization's intent is for the key words used within their vision statement. A vision statement will utilize words that have contextual meaning. Contextual meaning is based upon the context. These words need to be defined in order to provide understanding for people who read the vision statement and are not a part of the church's context (Wall, Bob, Robert S. Solum, and Mark R. Sobol 1992, 33).

Core Values

Core values are the guiding principles that help the church to maintain focus upon the fulfillment of their vision. Core values are the ditches on the sides of the road that keep the organization on track. As such, core values should be reviewed often by members of the church, emphasized by the pastor in preaching, and visibly obvious in the life of the church (Wall, Bob, Robert S. Solum, and Mark R. Sobol 1992, 34).

Strategic Plan of Implementation

Plans written on paper but never put into action have as little long term value as a sand castle constructed on the beach in low tide. Paper plans with no life create excitement for a moment that fades into disappointment. A key aspect of developing the vision strategy is the strategic plan of implementation (Wall, Bob, Robert S. Solum, and Mark R. Sobol 1992, 126). Regardless of how well intentioned a ministry might be, well written their mission statement, and well designed their vision statement, a church that does not have an effective strategy of implementing their vision strategy will ultimately be unsuccessful.

A strategic plan of implementation includes determined action points and determined points in time. Determined action points are key starting points in the process of implementing the vision. It is important to establish a determined action point that moves the church into action immediately following the completion of the vision strategy. Each determined action point needs to be implemented at a determined point in time. Determined points in time cause the church to work toward the goal of beginning or completing a process by a fixed deadline.

The strategic plan of implementation will establish how the vision strategy will be accomplished. Like the vision statement the plan of implementation may be changed, and revised. In fact the strategic plan of implementation will need to be revised more often than the vision statement as the vision is accomplished. This plan will always include targeted goals with projected dates.

Evaluation Process

In life it seems there is always room for improvement. Everything can be improved, and adjusted. Another fact in life is things change over time. Change in an organization is inevitable. It is in the knowledge of these two facts that the evaluation process happens. Evaluation is the point in time when looking back is essential. It is necessary to evaluate the church's progress in accomplishing its vision strategy. An evaluation is an analysis of where the congregation is in this process. When evaluating the effectiveness of vision strategy implementation two things are important.

1. Being real with reality - The organization needs to be real with reality. In other words, it is important to be honest with how the church is doing. Honesty allows the organization to make the right adjustments based on right decisions drawn from real facts.

2. Celebrate victories often – Victories are not as fulfilling when no one is there to celebrate. I remember a story I heard about a pastor who skipped Sunday morning worship by playing sick so he could sneak to a golf course and play golf. The pastor went to the golf course and played golf by himself. During the golf round the pastor hit a hole in one. He was extremely excited until he figured out that he couldn't tell anyone. He had to celebrate all alone. Celebrating victories together and often will keep the energy level of the congregation at a high level, and fulfilling great vision takes energy.

Measuring growth success is more than taking surveys, and looking at statistical data. Measuring growth success is accomplished by looking at and evaluating the vision strategy of the organization and asking the question, is the vision being accomplished? This question can be answered by asking and answering three similar questions. Does the church's desire correlate to its direction? Does the church's purpose correlate to its performance, and is the church's vision seen in its efforts of action? (Shenk 1983, 104).

If the vision of the church is not being accomplished at an acceptable level, something must change. Determining the results, action and direction will be accomplished using numerical data, surveys, interviews, and observations. This evaluation process should be done one year, three years, seven years, and ten years after the implementation of the vision strategy in the church.

Growth Measurement - Growth measurement is important to the evaluation process of the church's vision strategy. Growth measurement asks the questions, is the church experiencing growth?, and in what areas is the church growing? Growth measurement takes into account numerical, organic, conceptual, and diaconal growth by utilizing interviews, surveys, observation, and numerical analysis.

Interviews - should be conducted with the pastoral staff, Sunday School teachers, general church members, youth ministry members, church neighbors, and businesses in the community. Interviewing those who are in the church will help gain information about internal factors, and interviewing those outside of the church will help gain information about the contextual perspective of the church.

Surveys - are a viable tool for data collection. Surveying can be done randomly or within a defined group such as a Sunday School class, or cell group. Data gathered from surveying people can focus on particular areas of growth.

Observation - allows those participating in the evaluation process to visualize the effectiveness of the church in successfully living out their vision strategy. Church members involved in this process need to take a two week break from their normal church activities, and attempt to become an outside observer as much as possible. Doing this allows them to be objective with their observations, and see the picture of the church more clearly. Another possibility to do excellent observation analysis is to invite someone in to observe the church who is not a normal part of the church. The outside observer will be the most objective and will see the church with the freedom of not knowing what things in the church are assumed. Assumed things are those things church members know but others have no clue about.

Growth Rate Analysis - Peter Wagner writes about how to find the composite membership of a congregation in his book, Your Church Can Grow. The process Wagner describes was developed by Charles Mylander according to Wagner. The composite membership analysis is a number arrived at by using a formula that adds the membership, Sunday worship attendance, and Sunday School attendance together dividing by three. In the traditional Sunday school, Sunday worship, membership conscious church this is probably a valid formula to gain a number of about how many people are involved in the life of the church. However, in today's North American society there is less emphasis placed on church membership in many churches than what was once considered the normal process for a church. Also, many churches no longer do Sunday School and worship may be done on Sunday but may also be done on Friday, Saturday, or another day (Wagner 1984, 69 and 70).

Another factor to consider in measuring numerical growth is the fact of life mobility. A church existing in the culturally diverse community that is reaching people living in the community will feel the shifting of the community as in-migration, and out-migration happen. A church of one hundred could grow numerically but then subsequently decline due to out-migration of people. There is an obvious question that must be asked about this type of church. Is this church a growing church? The answer has to be yes, even though the numerical data does not reflect this growth accurately. Think about the church in Jerusalem that stayed in Jerusalem until Stephen was stoned, but after the martyrdom of Stephen the church scattered. It is the scattering of the church throughout the area that grew the church (Acts 8:1).

Numerical analysis is important. In fact the greater the detail the more powerful numerical data becomes. In other words reporting numerical data by showing that fifty people were added to a church in a year is the minimum amount of numerical data needed. If detail describing where each of the fifty came from can be given (25 converted, 20 transferred, and 5 biological) the numeric data is more powerful. Detail gives numeric growth validity.

Vision Revision

Vision revision is an exercise that should not be attempted often. However, there will be points in a ministry's life when vision revision is necessary. The primary reason vision revision may be needed is the community demographic changes. This may lead the church after an evaluation process to realize that they are no longer fulfilling the mission of God in the community because their vision has not grown in the direction of the community.

"Since vision involves the future, once it is reached it is no longer vision. Before the vision becomes reality, it is altered to include new factors, such as growth and changed context (Neumann 1999, 47)."

Practical Steps for Developing Vision Strategy

Step 1 – Leadership Reflection

The first step in developing the vision strategy in the local church is pastor centered. The pastor as the visionary point leader of the church must spend focused time in prayer. This focused time in prayer means both talking, and listening to God. Too often we as ministry leaders go to a conference or read a book and come home to our congregation like superman. We want to change the church in a phone booth in the twinkle of an eye and fly faster than a speeding bullet. Even if it was possible to fly and fly this fast it is meaningless if we don't know where we are flying. It is dangerous and the results birth confusion in the congregation.

Finding a place and the time to get away with Jesus is the key to beginning solid vision strategy development in ministry. Everything is meaningless without God directed passion. The leader alone with God in prayer will find guidance, renewal and power. He or she will be challenged and changed. This is where personal God-passion and powerful visionary leadership is born.

Step 2 – Identify Vision Strategy Development Team

In order to receive as much input as possible from the congregation, a vision strategy development team should be identified and appointed to develop the church's vision strategy. It is important as the visionary point leader of the church to lay a foundation for ministry vision strategy by consistently preaching about vision, and mission. In other words pulpit ministry should affirm the vision strategy development team.

This team may include elders, board members, young people, senior adults, and other identified leaders. We must be conscious of the fact that our pastoral tendency is often to have our church board do anything and everything that pertains to the business of the church. In fact very often vision strategy development is seen as a business tool; and therefore, we want our business people to develop our vision strategy. However, it is vital to our success in developing vision strategy that we see vision strategy development as more than a business tool. We need to see vision strategy development as a dynamic ministry tool that will transform the church ministry in a power and effective way.

Therefore, as a ministry tool, vision strategy development will be best accomplished by a team of people who represent the ministries of the whole church. When developing the vision strategy plan for a culturally diverse congregation, culture groups represented in the church should also be represented on the team. Utilizing people who represent the cultural diversity of the church will help the entire church to gain ownership of the vision strategy. The goal of implementing a vision strategy development team is to develop the vision strategy through a solid representation of the congregation. This will help the church to accomplish a high level of commitment to the vision because the church has ownership of the vision.

Step 3 – Beginning the Process

In its initial meeting, the vision strategy planning team should set a goal of accomplishing two tasks:

Make a prayer connection - Spend time together in prayer asking for God's wisdom and guidance throughout the vision strategy development process. (An ideal situation will be to have a prayer summit or retreat with the vision strategy planning team at this beginning stage of the process).

Explanation of the Process - Explain the dynamics of the vision strategy process and what the vision strategy looks like.

Step 4 – Develop the Mission Statement

Set a goal of developing the mission statement of the church by a certain date. This goal is not concrete, but is a target in time to finish the mission statement in order to move the team through the process. The mission statement is the biblical mandate of the church body in the community. Writing a mission statement will be centered on what God has instructed us in scripture. This mission statement is the church's contextualized creed of what they believe scripture is saying to them within their community.

After examining scripture together, reflecting on the doctrine of the church, and prayer, the team should enter into discussion and begin to form a mission statement that will explain what the congregation believes is its mandate from scripture.

- <u>Doctrinal Reflection</u> - A church congregation should follow a process that includes prayer, Bible study and doctrinal reflection in developing its mission statement. This vision strategy development process is an ideal opportunity for the vision strategy development Team to review and reflect on the doctrinal standing of the church: what we believe and why we believe what we believe as a Church congregation. The team may begin the reflection by looking to the church's doctrinal statement, and the Bible.
- <u>Prayer</u> focused on the community and what God says in scripture about the responsibility of Christians in the community.
- <u>Biblical Study</u> – Reading Old and New Testament passages and researching their context in order to better understand the church's responsibility in the world and the mission mandate from God to the church.
- <u>Refining Process</u> – The process of refining the mission statement will take time and effort. When roadblocks arise, frustrations build or people conflict begins to happen, stop the process and pray specifically asking God's guidance in the process.
- <u>Mission Statement Presentation</u> - A mission statement may be presented to the congregation in a number of ways. The more the congregation is able to participate the greater the level of ownership will be possible in the congregation. However, the danger of a high level of participation in the process is the process may never get anywhere. A great way to present the mission statement portion of the vision strategy to the congregation is for the vision strategy development team to perfect the statement, share with the congregation the process, and a copy of the newly revised mission statement for a vote of confirmation. Help them to understand that this is the first part of the vision strategy for the church and report the vision strategy development team's progress to the congregation on a regular basis.

Step 5 – Develop the Vision Statement

Once the mission statement is complete, bring the vision strategy development team back together and begin work on the vision statement. Remember the mission statement is what the church believes. The vision statement is what the church intends to do about what they believe. It is a congregational plan of action for accomplishing the mission mandate of God for the church. The vision statement will need to be revisited, revised, and updated periodically in the future. Set a goal of developing the vision statement of the church by a certain date. This goal is not concrete, but is a target in time to finish the vision statement in order to move the team through the process.

- <u>Prayer</u> is the primary tool in finding God's direction for the church. Prayer should focus on the community and what God says in scripture about the responsibility of Christians in the community, how God will work through the congregational ministries of the church to accomplish His will.

- <u>Vision statement research</u> can be accomplished through doing basic research. Basic research is research that seeks to understand the institutional and contextual factors affecting the church.

- <u>Institutional factors</u> are the internal factors of the church. Institutional factors include the age groupings, ethnicity, culture, primary language, history, income level, education, worship style, and traditions of congregation members. These are the factors that influence what the church may or may not be willing to do with the gospel mandate. The congregation is where ownership of vision must be sensed. Without a sense of ownership of the vision within the congregation the vision will never be accomplished by the congregation. Therefore, it is important to not only gain data about the congregation but to include the congregation in the vision statement development process. Involvement in the process can be accomplished through open forum discussions, surveying the congregation, and progress reports presented to the congregation often.

- <u>Contextual factors</u> are those factors which are external to the church. Contextual factors include demographic data, historical data, and anthropological data collected through ethnographic research and participant observation. Contextual data will help the vision strategy team to sense the felt needs of the community in seeking vision from God of what the church should be doing in the community.

- <u>Vision statement development</u> - Vision statement development should include a focus on the core values of becoming a wholistic church growth driven church. Wholistic church growth – The wholistic, growth model includes numerical, conceptual, organic, and diaconal growth goals.

- <u>Refining Process</u> – The process of refining the vision statement will take time and effort. When roadblocks arise, frustrations build or people conflict begins to happen, stop the process and pray asking God's guidance in the process.
    1. Writing the vision statement
    2. Writing glossary of terms
    3. Writing core values

- <u>Vision statement presentation</u> - A vision statement may be presented to the congregation in a number of ways. The more the congregation is able to participate the greater the level of ownership there will be in the congregation. As with the mission statement, a great way to present the Vision statement portion of the vision strategy to the congregation is for the vision strategy development team to perfect the statement, share with the congregation the process including the needs of the community and congregation, and present a copy of the new vision strategy for a vote of confirmation.

Step 6 – Develop the Plan of Implementation

One of the most important responsibilities of the vision strategy development team is to develop a legitimate doable plan of implementation that will guide the church in putting their vision strategy into practice. Implementation will more than likely take time and require patience. However, it is important for the team to lift the vision strategy from the paper it is written on and give it life.

Writing a vision strategy is a process that is challenging and rewarding. A vision statement established in a solid mission statement will help the church get from point A to point B by seeing the future. There is a great need for churches in culturally diverse communities to have a vision strategy for ministry that reaches all people.

8

LIVING ON THE EDGE

DEVELOPING MINISTRY LEADERS IN A
CHANGING WORLD

L eadership is the single most effective important factor of effective church ministry in culturally diverse communities. Ministry can not function without leaders, and successful ministry does not happen without good leaders. Successful ministry leaders in the culturally diverse communities are leaders who understand the issues of the culturally diverse community. These leaders are often difficult to locate. In fact it is probably more feasible to develop leaders from within the community than find leaders outside of the community.

Indigenous Leadership Development
    In doing Christian ministry churches are most often inclined to hire new leaders for new ministries in the church who are not

from the church community. Most churches search diligently to find leaders that can be imported into their ministry context. These churches often become frustrated in this process. It is difficult to find leaders who are affordable, qualified, compatible, importable and who are willing to come to a church. This is especially true in the culturally diverse context. A powerful solution available to churches is the utilization of their own untapped leadership resource. Like the prophet Elisha said to the widow who cried out to him, "What do you have in the house?" (2 Kings 4:2). Churches need to look in their own house, and develop leaders indigenous to their ministry context. God has many leaders in waiting within the church who are often overlooked. They are seen as unqualified and unprepared. It is important to note that Jesus didn't go to the seminary to recruit His team. He went around the community and found unlikely, untrained potential leaders. He recruited, trained, prepared, and sent them into ministry.

The leaders Jesus called and developed were everyday people who experienced God in a real way and shared their experience with the people in their communities, and later other communities.

> "According to Paul, a primary task of the urban pastor is to discover and call forth those in the congregation to whom God has given these gifts of leadership. Every church has in it those who have been placed there by God who can exercise authority, call the church to accountability, proclaim the gospel, nurture the people, and instruct in the faith. The pastor's job is to discover those people, call them forth, and train them to do that work even more effectively. A sign that a congregation is, indeed, the legitimate church of Jesus Christ is the presence in it of people functioning as apostles, prophets, evangelists, pastors, and teachers (Linthicum 1991, 189)."

There are church denominations ad mission organizations that have expanded with exponential growth throughout the world by developing indigenous leaders. Developing indigenous leaders is practical and powerful. People indigenous to a community understand the context, possibly know the language of a people group living in the community, live among, and work with people in the community.

Potential Leader Identification

Identifying potential leaders is challenging. Think about how Samuel felt when he made his way to Jesse's house, commissioned by God to anoint the future King of Israel (I Sam 16:1). On his way he probably thought to himself, "This is an easy task; I'll anoint the eldest son of Jesse and be on my way." However, God had a little shepherd boy in mind to be king who was out tending sheep. What about Peter? Who would have ever thought a rough, uneducated fisherman, would become one of the greatest leaders of the early church. Then there is Paul (a.k.a. Saul of Tarsus the terminator of Christians). No Christian in their right mind would have ever recruited Saul for Christian leadership. In fact, many Christians would not have been too upset if he met some untimely demise. Even later when he was a great leader in the church we have come to know that he was not much to look at, and perhaps not the most elegant in speech. However, Paul is known as the greatest missionary in the New Testament Church.

Think about it, who would you anoint as king? Would you pick Saul the tall handsome guy or David the shepherd boy who is small young and smells like sheep. Would you anoint Abraham to lead the nations who traveled to Egypt three times and caused great turmoil through deception while there, had no children, and gave the best land available to his nephew? There are numerous examples in history recorded in scripture and elsewhere of God choosing the least likely to succeed for great leadership. It is important to understand that the best choice is not always the most obvious or likely choice. Things are not always what they seem. Looking for potential leaders is a process that must not focus on picking only the most likely choices. Identifying potential leaders is a serious endeavor that should be approached with the greatest level of care. Leadership is often difficult, and choices leaders make are challenging. Therefore, identification of potential leaders should focus heavily on seeking the heart of God in the process.

Potential leadership identification must be approached in prayer. It is important to understand and always remember that God sees people in a much more complete manner than we see them. Our human tendency is to look for the best looking, most educated, most elegant speaking people for leadership, however, God sees people as they are and as they will become. The reality is that there are not many churches who would hire the leaders God commissioned in the Bible as their pastor. Before the flood they would probably see Noah as delusional, Abraham as unstable (no permanent address), Joseph as an ex-convict, Moses too old, David too young, Peter uneducated and too expressive, John the Baptist too loud and Jesus as a homeless man. God must be involved in the leadership development process. He chooses leaders who are committing their lives to Him as a result of the ministry of the gospel taking place in their lives, and it is our responsibility to develop the leadership ability within them. Developing the leader within people in our community is the most powerful method of fulfilling the mandate of the gospel in our community and throughout the world. Developing leaders includes real life involvement, teaching moments, motivation, prayer, accountability, expectation without expiration, and prodigal love.

Real Life Involvement

The Jesus teaching model includes modeling, mentoring, and coaching. Modeling, mentoring, and coaching are only effective when the teacher is involved in the real life of the student. Jesus was involved in the lives of those He recruited as His students. He wasn't only involved in their lives on the Sabbath day. He was involved in their lives every day. Jesus was with them during their real everyday lives.

Modeling

Modeling is vital to real life involvement. It includes being among leaders so they may see you the leader-teacher in prime time moments and when you are just living life. Seeing the leader-teacher in the non prime time moments of life reveals the reality of life. If the only time potential leaders see their leader-teacher is in the pulpit when people are clapping for him or her, the potential leaders will become infatuated with the fame of ministry. They will not understand the reality of leadership. The reality of leadership is that the majority of leadership labor is unseen by masses of people. Leadership labor is often doing the thankless unseen tasks of life.

An important part of modeling for the leader-teacher to always keep in mind is that they have boundaries or limits that should not be crossed. The temptation may be present at times to compromise character in order to connect with potential leaders. By this I do not mean avoiding contextualization. However, a leader must be careful where he or she walks, how he or she talks, and acts. Leader-teachers have to be, *"Wise as serpents and harmless as doves"* (Matt 10:16).

Mentoring and Coaching

Mentoring and coaching are terms that have become extensively popular throughout the business world in the past few years. Corporate leaders have paid large amounts of money for corporate coaches to coach them to become better leaders. Many corporations and businesses have hired consulting firms to teach their managers mentoring principles with a goal of creating a better organization by creating better employees. Mentoring and coaching as principles, tools, and techniques utilized to create better people and leaders are valid principles. These principles can be utilized to develop tremendous leaders who are indigenous to their community and culture. Mentoring and coaching begin in personal relationship built on openness and honesty.

Mentoring is the process of helping an individual with his or her life journey through a friendship relationship in which the leader-teacher mentors the potential leader. Those who are mentored eventually become mentors themselves. This leadership development tool is powerful, and can be seen throughout scripture in Moses and Joshua, Eli and Samuel, Elijah and Elisha, Jesus and his disciples, Paul and Timothy, and others.

"...mentoring as a form of ministry is open to all. It is one of the most basic forms of love relationship, and we not only need mentors in our lives at various stages and life transitions, but we need to be mentors to others, particularly when we enter mid-life (Sellner 1990, 35)."

Coaching is mentoring at a different level. In sports, as athletes develop, their coaches are many times older, wiser, and more knowledgeable than they. However, when an athlete is involved in professional sports, the athlete often surpasses the coach in knowledge and ability. Therefore the coach must take on a different role than that of mentor. Think about Phil Jackson showing Shaquille O'Neal how to slam dunk a basketball. It is not a likely scenario. The coach takes on a different role in the life of the developing leader. The coach stands on the outside of the photograph of a developing leader's life at any given moment able to see behind the developing leader, and in front of them. A good coach can help someone who is at a higher leadership level than they are. Coaching does not involve the ability to play the game as well as the one being coached. Coaching is the skill to help that person play their game better by seeing them from a distance and pointing to their weaknesses, strengths, and potential possibilities for greater success. Coaches do not only encourage improvement, they expect improvement, and help guide leaders to excellence.

Teaching Moments

Leadership development also includes the implementation of teaching moments. Teaching moments can include structured times of training and instruction. However, the most valid and powerful teaching moments are found in the everyday process of living life. It is important for the leader-teacher to recognize these moments in time and seize them as the greatest opportunities to develop leaders. Jesus utilized teaching moments often in His ministry. His teaching moments are visible throughout the gospels in the account of Peter walking on and then sinking into water, the woman at the well, the feeding of the multitude, the last supper, the garden experience, and others. Jesus used life moments as his classroom material for leadership training.

Motivation

Sometimes in life it is difficult to motivate one-self and at these times motivating others can even be more difficult. Therefore it is important for leader-teachers to develop motivation as a discipline in their lives. Motivation as a discipline is that focused effort that rises within an individual when he or she is working to finish a project in the early morning hours with little or no sleep and does not give up. It is motivation that inspires people to become greater than they themselves are and to do what it takes to accomplish their dreams. Instilling motivation within potential leaders is part of the leadership development journey. Motivated leaders accomplish great success, and leaders who motivate those whose success is seen in the people whom they have motivated.

Prayer

Praying together connects people in ways that no other exercise or bonding can. Prayer is the most powerful relationship experience any person can have with God. It is therefore the place of the greatest relational friendship opportunity between people. Jesus prayed with the twelve. Throughout history people who pray with God connect with God in a manner that cannot be duplicated with any other deity anywhere. Speaking together to the living God connects people together in a God relationship. Prayer is important and vital in the process of developing leaders.

Accountability

Accountability is an important word that is sometimes over-looked, and many times in the church overused. Being accountable is a good thing. Often in this new century people have promoted accountability to the point at times that the concept is a turn off to some individuals. However, it is important to understand that without some structured accountability built into the leadership development process it will be difficult to develop leaders. Accountability is the agreement between a leader-teacher and potential leader in which the leader-teacher helps the potential leader by checking with him or her as they accomplish tasks, develop skills, and work to meet their goals in their leadership development process. Good growth can be accomplished quicker when there is an accountability process in place. Accountability should be presented in a positive manner that affirms potential leaders in their development process and does not chastise them when they fail.

Expectation without Expiration

Developing leaders is a process that takes patience. Many leader-teachers who develop leaders focus a great deal of effort on the importance of accountability. Accountability is important and vital to the successful development of leaders. However, account-ability without patience causes leader-teachers who are developing potential leaders to give up on them too soon.

Leader-teachers who are developing leaders will be more successful in the leadership development process as they learn to have expectations without expiration. An expectation without expi-ration simply means that the leader who is developing leaders has expectations for them, but does not place a mental expiration date on their expectations. As leaders we have a tendency to give up on people too soon. Often we mentally fix points in time that we expect people we are developing into leaders to accomplish certain levels in their lives. If they do not meet our mentally fixed unwritten expectations we give up on them and move on. In other words we put expiration on our expectations.

A commitment to develop leaders must be a commitment that puts no expiration on our expectations. It should be a commitment that holds onto potential leaders throughout the leadership develop-ment process. Holding onto potential leaders through the process takes patience. Think about Jesus walking the earth pouring himself into twelve men for 3 ½ years. He never gave up on any of them. He didn't even give up on Peter, or even Judas. Jesus expected them to change, grow, and live a life patterned after His teaching. Jesus had expectations without expiration. He loved them unconditionally.

Prodigal Love

Have you ever wondered why Jesus shared the parable of the prodigal son. Many have preached about the prodigal son by focusing on the rebellion of the son, and the results of wild lifestyle.

However, the greatest aspect of the prodigal's story is His Father's love. His Father loved him when he left, while he was gone, and when he returned. He never stopped loving his son. Developing potential leaders is best accomplished when the leader-teacher has prodigal love in his or her heart. Prodigal love is the compassion in a person's heart that exists regardless of the outcome. Perhaps Jesus spoke this parable as a foreshadowing of His love for humankind. Prodigal love is willing to walk where few will walk in order to help people become the person that God desires for them to become.

Developing leaders is a process that takes time and patience. It is a process that is worth the effort. Leaders who are developed from within a community can be powerful leaders in the kingdom of God. They are people who know their world and love their world like no one from outside their world can. These people often do not have higher education, experience in ministry, and great financial resource, but they are people whom God can utilize in fulfilling His mission. They are people that we, those foreigners from outside their world, can move among, live among, and pour our lives into in the same manner that Jesus poured His life into the twelve in order that they could accomplish His work.

Leadership development takes time and effort. It is important that potential leaders be empowered in their process of learning to become an effective leader that they grasp basic concepts of leadership. These basic concepts include the understanding that leadership development is a journey, critical life moments shape and reveal leadership ability, and leadership is an achievement of persistence.

The Leadership Journey

Leaders understand the importance of critical life moments, but they also come to understand that true life success is not based on one event or even on a series of events. Success is not found in one moment or a series of moments. True life success is about the journey. Understanding that becoming the leader God intends us to become is to understand that the leadership journey is a process. The process begins as the leader senses a passion to become something more than they are.

Leaders come to understand life success is about meeting the challenges of the journey of life every day with a winning attitude. Most people do not know who built the Sears Tower, Empire State Building, or St. Louis Arch. They know where the buildings are and perhaps they have visited them at some point in their life, but they don't know who designed the structures or built them. Isn't it amazing, three of the greatest structures constructed in the history of humankind and most people do not know who built these buildings. In contrast Jesus Christ took twelve men on the journey of life for 3 ½ years and poured himself into them. Eleven of these twelve men turned the world upside down. Jesus knew the journey was an important element of success. Success is absolutely about the journey.

So where do leaders come from?

Leaders are not just born, although there is an element of leadership that exists in the fiber of a potential leader's life. Leaders are also not made. They are not made in the sense of being appointed or selected. An individual can not wave a magic wand and say, poof, you are a leader. On the other hand managers are made. They are made in the sense that they are appointed to a management position. They are typically assigned to the task based primarily on previous performance. Just because a person is placed in a position of management in an organization, it does not necessarily make them a leader by default. In other words, leadership is not something that can be assigned, but management can be assigned.

Leaders very often are mavericks, entrepreneurial, eccentric, and on the edge of what is considered, safe thinking. They are the ones who are willing to take risks and try something new in order to accomplish a greater goal or vision. Leaders realize that the job does not make the individual. The position does not make the person. Leaders to a great extent are developed. Leadership is birthed, nurtured, and developed in the life of the leader. Every day of a leader's life is a preparation day for the future fulfillment of their purpose. The purpose of their life is the foundation of their vision and their dreams, dreams which can only be dreamed by a leader and visions which are only seen by a visionary. Leadership skills that exist within a potential leader's life must be developed in order to be effectively harnessed for the greatest success.

Every leadership person in a church organization which is in transition must understand the need to personally develop along with, but ahead of, the congregation. Once evaluation of the church has been made, the leader must stop and take a moment in time to do self reflection. Once an analysis of the organization is in process, those who are in leadership must actively do self-analysis. This is most true for the visionary point leader than any other member of the leadership team.

The ability to lead is an absolute for the pastor and those in positions of leadership in any church organization. This ability to lead is especially important in the church congregation that is in transition. Whether the congregation is striving to stay in their community, moving to a new community is intentionally crossing racial and cultural barriers, or intentionally doing ministry in a way the congregation has never done before, leadership will make the difference between an organization existing in mediocrity, facing death, or being continually successful.

Each person in a leadership position must personally look into the mirror. After analyzing the church and gaining an understanding of where the church has been, where the church is today, and where the church desires to go in the future, the leader must pause for a moment and ask three specific questions in light of each new revelation of the church's desire for the future.

1. **Direction** – As the leader of the organization, is the organization going in the same direction as I am? Are we on the same page?
2. **Level** – At what point of leadership level or trust am I currently on? Am I the pastor or just the preacher? Will they walk through the heat of hell with me?
3. **Commitment** – Am I here for the long haul? As we develop a vision statement, core values, and strategic plan of implementation, I have to ask myself, am I willing to make the commitment it will take to see this vision become reality?

It has been said, as the leader goes, the organization goes. The church, of course, is our organization and we are the leaders. It is vital to the present and the future of the church for the pastor to be the leader. *As the leader - the pastor must lead.*

The pastor is the primary visionary point leader of the church. He or she will make the difference in the church being what it has been or becoming what it should become. Becoming the leader means we are willing, in the words of Robert Quinn, *"to build the bridge as we walk on it"* (emphasis mine) (Quinn 1996, 83). Leaders are the people who chart the course. The old science fiction television drama Star Trek always began with the words,

"These are the voyages of the starship enterprise, to seek out new life, new civilizations, to boldly go where no man has gone before." Captain James T. Kirk. (Crawford 1991).

A leader is in fact the captain, the point leader, the one forging the way through the darkest night, deepest valley, and over the highest mountain. Visionary leadership can be a lonely place at times. *It is a place of living on the edge.* Leadership is a place of hard work and tough decisions, and a steady hand is needed that will stay the course. Leaders have qualities deep inside that will develop as they develop. These qualities include, but certainly are not limited to:

Humility	Strength
Meekness	Confidence
Forgiveness	Compassion
Mercy	Mentor
Delegator	Motivator
longsuffering	Visionary

Critical Life Moments

Every person who lives will experience critical life moments in their lives. A critical life moment is that moment in time when life offers us as people an opportunity to seize our destiny. Critical life moments come during tragedy situations, triumph situations, or in the process of everyday life. Most often critical life moments include some level of risk, and the possibility of failure. These moments are defining moments for leaders. People who are not leaders generally let their critical life moments pass them by. They do not change their life course or allow anything else to change their life course. However, potential leaders grab opportunities to change the world when these opportunities happen. They not only grab hold of their critical life moments, but they look forward to these moments in time that may catapult them to places of more influence and greater leadership opportunities. One of the greatest critical life moments in history happened during Israel's battle with the Philistines recorded in I Samuel 17. As the army of Israel watched while Goliath the giant mocked them and God a teenage boy named David was running an errand for His father. David didn't know when he woke up that morning that he would become the hero of Israel in a few hours. However, when his moment came he did not hesitate. Leaders respond to critical life moments regardless of the outcome. When the result is not positive, leaders learn from their experience and move forward. When the result is positive, true leaders are humbled by the outcome, learn from the process and move forward.

Creating Stuff

People may say a person is either born with it, or they aren't. A person either has it, or they do not have "it". That "it" a person either does or does not have is that elusive stuff inside a person that distinguishes mediocrity from greatness. Those who are average are willing to accept what life gives, and those who are excellent are willing to go beyond what life offers to that level of life where few dare to step, and even fewer stride.

Yes there may possibly be some who have the right doors open, the wrong ones close, don't get cavities, and never gain weight. There may indeed be some who get all of the breaks. However, most people only struggle to live out an existence, paying bills, and trying to save money until the car breaks down and drains the savings. People are often struggling in life trying to buy a home, or figuring out how to pay the rent. People for the most part just get by. Many start life with great visions and dreams, but somehow, somewhere along the way they hit cruise control, forget the dreams, and ease through life.

Most lose their dreams. Their dreams slide from their fingers and aspirations dissipate like cold breath on a winter's morning.

A few hold on to dreams with a tight grip. No thing and no one can pry their goals and dreams out of their grasp. ***These people, the ones who persist, they are the people who have "it".*** They have the fire, the grit, the fortitude. They have the stuff it takes to climb mountains. They are the people in this world who can swing through hell on a rotten rope. They are the people who, when the rope breaks, they will find another way. They have the stuff. They are people like Paul the Apostle who preached the gospel until his death, John Calvin, who through physical difficulties of failing health pursued God until his last breath, Horatio Spafford, who kept serving God even after losing his children at sea, and Tom Newton, who hung onto the word of God that his mother instilled in his life as a boy even in the turmoil of near death. Newton, later in reflecting on his experience, penned the words of the song "Amazing Grace".

Seven Principles of Successful Leadership
Along with understanding these concepts every leader needs to learn seven principles of successful leadership.

1. The Purpose Principle
Purpose is a determined view of future outcome. It is knowing somewhere deep within that you are destined for something great in life. Purpose is the foundation that vision is built upon. Without purpose vision is meaningless. Likewise, without purpose a vision statement in an organization is no more than words formed into sentences on a page. When an individual can say, "I have purpose", it is powerful. My life is meant to be for a divine reason. God has destined me to accomplish great things in His kingdom. When a person can say these things, things will happen around him or her. Excitement will be generated. Vision will be born, and leadership nurtured.

Leadership and vision walk hand in hand. Joseph had a sense of purpose in his life from a very young age. He dreamed dreams God gave him, and upon this purpose in his life vision was built. That vision was inside his being for a long time. God prepared him along the way for the fulfillment of the dream. Joseph kept the vision of God alive within him even through the pit experience, even through the slave experience, while in prison, and in the palace. Joseph never quit. He stayed the course. He held onto his sense of purpose for his life. God brought him through every situation, and the vision was fulfilled. Andy Stanley writes,

"If God has birthed a vision in your heart, the day will come when you will be called upon to make a sacrifice to achieve it. And you will have to make the sacrifice with no guarantee of success" (Stanley 1999, 129).

A leader sees his or her life as vital to the plan of God being fulfilled in this world. This sense of being, of destiny is the purpose that drives them to dream dreams, see visions, and fulfill the visions. A leader will allow the vision to form and grow. The purpose principle is a leader knowing this is my destiny. This is my purpose.

2. The Patience Principle
Leaders will hang on to their vision, and allow the vision to nurture and grow. You see, it is important to understand that a vision cast too soon is destined to be defeated or at least delayed. Developing a vision takes effort, energy, and great patience. Casting the vision at the appropriate time is crucial to success. Joseph had not yet learned the patience principal when he first shared his dreams with his brothers. I can just picture them saying to him, "What do you know? You're just a snot nosed kid." It is important to not despise our youth when they are young, as Paul encouraged Timothy. However, it is equally important to understand that very often in life we learn more in our silence, than in our speech.

3. The Pain Principle
When Jesus was on his way to imminent fulfillment of destiny, he stopped by the garden Gethsemane to pray. It is evident that the disciples (especially Peter) were ready to go all the way with Jesus, the Messiah, their friend. If he would fight to the death, they were

with him. Jesus exemplified true leadership power. He understood the pain principle.

The pain principle simply put is, a leader will not expect their followers to endure any greater pain than they themselves are willing to endure. Whether it is the pain of criticism, undeserved or deserved, the pain of sacrificed potential income, lifestyle comfort, schedule, or sleep. Followers generally will not be willing to give more than the leader. Andy Stanley says it like this,

"Don't expect others to take greater risks or make greater sacrifices than you have. One thing about Nehemiah, he was committed. Both flippers were in the water. He wasn't asking anyone to do something he had not demonstrated a willing-ness to do himself (Stanley 1999, 32)."

4. The Plow Principle

Elisha the prophet was a servant to Elijah his Prophet Mentor. Elisha's life is interesting. In fact, I have always been especially intrigued by the way he entered ministry. Elijah, under direction from God, found Elisha plowing in the field. Here in this field while Elisha is plowing, Elijah walks by and throws his mantle (robe) on him. Elisha runs after Elijah and asks him to wait while he goes and says good-bye to his parents. Elijah's reply is simply, you don't need to talk to me, you need to talk with God. Elisha then goes back to the field pulls his oxen from the field, slaughters the oxen, breaks the plow, and burns the plow. It is clear at this point that something significant and supernatural has taken place (1 Kings 19:19-21).

Whether it was tradition at this point in history to recruit young men for ministry in this manner, or perhaps God had placed a vision in Elisha's heart, Elisha kept the vision inside allowing it to be nurtured and grow until an appointed time when he would assume the leadership role from Elijah. It is clear that when the time came for Elisha to move from the farm field to the ministry field, it came immediately. Immediately Elisha's life changed.

Elisha takes his livelihood, his plow, and breaks it in pieces. The plow principle is that point in our lives that we are able to face forward with the energy to not look back. It is being able to let go of everything in order to see God's vision within us come to pass, regardless of the sacrifice. Elisha didn't lease out his plow, he didn't store it for use later, just in case ministry didn't bring in enough resource. He in fact destroyed the plow. He stepped out of the boat, never looked back, and didn't give himself anything to fall back to. He totally jumped into the arms of God. Andy Stanley writes,

> "Visions don't become reality until somebody is willing to jump in. Launching a vision always involves committing wholeheartedly to what could be. Goliath never would have been defeated had David not stepped out from the ranks of the Israelites to challenge the giant. Peter never would have known the thrill of coming to Jesus on the water had he not swung both legs over the side of the boat and stepped out into the deep. And the Apostle Paul never would have known the joy of taking the gospel to the Gentile nations had he not packed his bags that first time and headed off into the unknown (Stanley1999, 127)."

5. The Persistence Principle

A few years ago the commercial on television about Dunkin Doughnuts showed the doughnut man waking up really, really early in the morning. In the commercial it was evident that the man really did not want to get out of bed. However, he would repeat over and over, "It's time to make the doughnuts."

Making the doughnuts is one of the greatest keys to successful leadership. We have to understand that the day in day out difficulty of life work is not the aim of our lives, but is part of our process.

I imagine there may have been many times David, or even Moses, grew tired of tending sheep, but tending the sheep was part of their process of fulfilling the vision. The persistence principle is the understanding that we have to be persistent about our vision in order to see the vision become reality. We may make doughnuts, tend sheep, paint houses, wash cars, counsel, visit, fellowship, mow the church lawn a thousand times, or sell pencils on the street, but persistence means we will keep doing what we have to do in order to accomplish what we are called to do. Zig Ziglar writes,

"Failure has been correctly identified as the line of least persistence, whereas success is often a question of simply sticking to the job and working and believing while you are sticking. If your particular job is harder than you might wish, just remember you can't sharpen a razor on a piece of velvet and you can't sharpen a man by spoon feeding him. Success occurs when opportunity meets preparation. Many times it is just over the hill or around the corner. Sometimes it takes that extra push to climb that hill or round that curve. The wit was right when he said, 'If you have enough push you don't have to worry about pull.' President Calvin Coolidge wrote, 'Nothing in the world can take the place of persistence. Talent will not. Nothing is more common than unsuccessful men with talent. Genius will not. Unrewarded genius is almost a proverb. Education will not. The world is full of educated derelicts. Persistence, determination and hard work makes the difference" (Ziglar [1975] 1977, 319).

6. The Potential Principle

The old song goes, *"Little is Much When God Is In It"*. Potential wasted is often the most identifiable potential in the world. In high school I had a friend who received a full four-year scholarship offer to play football for the University of Michigan. He was a great athlete, and one of the best linebackers in high-school football that year in the state of Florida. My friend wasted his giftedness though. Every day of our senior year he smoked grass (marijuana) and got high during lunch. His football abilities remained steady and strong. However, his grades reflected his inebriated state during school. He failed our senior year, lost all the scholarship offers, and last I heard he was working at a carwash; potential lost.

A few years ago I met a homeless man on the streets of Chicago. That night we were on lower Wacker Drive ministering among familiar faces, but there was a new man there who began to talk with us. After talking with him for a while he began to share his story. He had lived in New York City and lost his wife and child in an accident. Since losing his family, he gave up on life and ended up on the streets. We found out that he was fluent in five languages and well educated. Yet, he was on the street: *A man with great potential; yet his potential was unrealized.* The potential principle is the realization of an individual that they have the stuff it will take to fulfill God's plan. They have what it takes to be the leader that will accomplish the dream and vision God has given them.

"Wherever you look, you can find smart, talented, successful people who are able to go only so far because of the limitations of their leadership (Maxwell 1998, 9)."

7. The Principle of Perceived Future Outcome
Futuring – Cultivating memories of the future. Futuring is the ability to take a picture of where we will be before we get there. It is beyond our vision, and more than a goal. Perceived future outcome is seeing the vision, becoming the vision, and by faith, confident in the fact that when we commit to God and submit to God, he will bring it to pass: we can see it when it is accomplished. We can take a picture mentally of the future of our church's impact in the community (Sweet 1999, 24).

Somewhere in the world today there are those few individuals in Christian ministry who expect nothing and sacrifice everything in order to accomplish the mission of God in the world. They are people who are so convinced by what they believe that their passion for their belief drives them to create destiny without regard to their own life status, personal health, wealth or public recognition. These people who are believers in Jesus Christ not only accept Him as Lord and Savior, but give their life to Him without thought to "what is in it for me". These people are leaders with the passion of Paul the Apostle, the patience of Joseph the dreamer, the boldness of Peter the fisherman and most of all the compassion of Jesus the Messiah. Leaders are those who will dare to speak truth when speaking truth is not popular.

When the Apostle Paul stood at the Acropolis on Mars Hill, he was not worried about what people would think about him personally. Paul contextualized the gospel message and spoke it with boldness. Paul did not begin his life as a Christian leader, but was transformed in the resurrection power of Jesus Christ. Like Paul,

Christian leaders perhaps are not born but created from their personal desire to become what few are willing to become for God. They are in fact, so committed to the passion of Jesus Christ' compassion and commission that they give all they have to accomplish his mission.

If in fact leaders are created, how can we create them? Is it possible to take any person and develop him or her into a leader? The answer to these questions is yes and no. No, it is not possible to develop every person into a great leader. Some people do not have the stuff in them to become a great leader, and some never have opportunities to uncover that leadership stuff buried in them somewhere. There are some who begin the process of leadership development only to break their neck on the leadership lid of their environment or their lack of ability. A developing leader confined under a lid may become frustrated to the point that his or her frustration imprisons their passion and births the acceptance of mediocrity within them. John Maxwell in his book, *The 21 Irrefutable Laws of Leadership,* defines the law of the lid as, *"Leadership Ability Determines a Person's level of Effectiveness (Maxwell 1998, 1)".* It is viable to add to this definition that leadership opportunity is an important ingredient to a person's effectiveness. Every leader-teacher and potential leader person should be aware of the scripture where Jesus says he who is faithful in the small things I will make lord over many. There have been many times in my personal leadership journey what I did not desire to do a particular task, but the task had to be done. It is in these moments that leaders mature. Leaders are strengthened by doing the small things faithfully.

Although some people do not have the stuff inside them to become great leaders, there are those who have great passion inside to do whatever it takes to become great leaders. This is the yes to the question. Yes it is possible to develop ordinary people into extraordinary leaders. Extraordinary leaders are these few who sense destiny and reach for it. They know that there is an untapped well of potential within them to do great things in life, and they reach forward to forge their destiny. These people are people who may work in many occupations. They may drive nails, drive cars or drive a delivery truck. They may be physicians, educators, factory workers or computer programmers. They live each day of their life hungry for more, willing to pay the price to achieve it and intentional in becoming what they have not yet become. They are ordinary people with extraordinary dreams.

9

RESURRECTION

—∞∞∞—

"Awake, sleeper, and arise from the dead, and Christ will shine on you" Ephesians 5:14"

People continue to search for peace, and in their search move from place to place migrating throughout the world. It is the responsibility of the body of Christ, the people of God, (the church) to emerge in society proclaiming the gospel of Jesus Christ in word and through life. The challenges faced by people who are hungry to see a movement of God's presence in the world are staggering and too often have been debilitating. The book of Ezekiel documents the account of Ezekiel's experience with God in the valley of the dry bones (Ezekiel 37). God asks Ezekiel, *"Ezekiel, can these bones live?"* Today the impossibilities facing the church are as challenging as that question posed to Ezekiel. We must in some way ask ourselves the questions, *"Can these bones live?" "Can the dead come to life?"* It is only in asking these questions that we can truly say within ourselves that what strength, energy, and wisdom we have is no where near enough. We are in need of God's miraculous resurrection power to accomplish what can only be accomplished through Him.

Tensions of race, culture, ethnic identity, class, and status continue to be issues on the visual screen of our society. Perhaps these are issues that will always prevail and we as people should maintain the ambivalent attitude of many who have walked before us in history. After all, it is much easier to live life minding our own business, acting as if there is nothing broken in our society, church, or community than get involved and become a world changer. However, we as Christian believers have a divine directive to go to the whole world and preach the gospel. This preaching of the gospel is more than proclamation but includes the participation of engaging culture, society, and life with the goal of becoming a catalyst for redemption and lift of individuals living in the community. The gospel communicates to us that ambivalence is not the answer. We are to be proactive with our proclamation of the message through the power of Jesus Christ.

Therefore, our preaching should and must be done with strategic, concise effort in the power of Christ. Tools, training, and guidance are needed for the church to become equipped to reach the world. However, the most important ingredient in our recipe for ministry success is the powerful presence of God doing His work both in plain view and behind the scenes. As we come to the realization that there is more to life than the satisfaction with the way things appear to be, we begin new journeys exploring and realizing the full potential of life lived with the guiding presence of the Holy Spirit.

"So the captain approached him and said, 'How is it that you are sleeping? Get up, call on your god. Perhaps your god will be concerned about us so that we will not perish'. Jonah 1:6"

The age of reason has ended and as the embers of modern society burn their last; postmodern thought has led to the emergence of post-modern culture. In the midst of this societal culture shift the modern church continues to struggle in its effort to keep the institution of church alive. In fact many people in the church desire for what they call the good old days, oblivious to those who know little or nothing about the gospel who are living lives with no eternal hope and little present hope. People in our world continually search for life while the church sleeps. It is this awareness that causes people who are hungry to fulfill the passion of God to develop internal struggle – a divine prophetic tension – if you will – between the way things are and the way things can become.

This tension happens in the life of individuals who experience an awakening moment or event in their lives. Awakening moments are those stirring passionate moments in life that can be caused by an experience, happen through prayer, or may be stirred in the heart by gaining knowledge. The scriptures highlight the account of many individuals experiencing awakening moments in their lives.

Think of the Prophet Elisha in the valley surrounded by the armies of the enemy. Elisha's servant, in fear says to Elisha, "What shall we do?" (2 Kings 6:15). Elisha then prays for his servant and asks God to open the eyes of his servant so he may see. When God opens the eyes of Elisha's servant the servant has an awakening experience. He sees with spiritual eyes and knows the presence and power of God.

"O Lord, I pray, open his eyes that he may see."
2 Kings 6:17

We as people have a divine moment opportunity before us to experience the mission passion of God and pray that our eyes be opened to the realization that through the presence and power of Jesus Christ the dead can have life. Our journey begins when we truly follow God through fulfilling His mission in the world. As we experience tension between what is and what can happen we know that God has the power to awaken the dead. His power can awaken a dead church to give life in the community. His power can create awaken moments in the lives of people. His power can bring life to the world and light in darkness.

God alone exclusively has the power and authority to raise the dead. A dead church, dead community, and dead life can be resurrected in His supernatural creation power. Through His power we can live and give people life.

"I am the resurrection and the life; he who believes in Me shall live even if he dies." John 11:25

A church existing in the changing community has three options. They can stay and change, stay and remain the same, or move out of the community. If the congregation existing in a transitioning community that is evolving from a mono-cultural community to a multi-cultural / multi-ethnic community decides to stay, they must change in order to thrive, and live. It is important to consider the reality that church ministry is more than theology, preaching, teaching, praying, visiting the hospital, marrying, and burying people. All of these tasks are part of ministry, but ministry is greater than the total of all of these tasks together. Developing a local church ministry into a growing healthy church is a process that takes time, energy, effort, and faith. This is true for the church planter, or the pastor who assumes the leadership of an existing church. Tools for developing the church into a living healthy organism are needed for successful ministry endeavor in any context. There are no quick fixes, and churches do not grow by just adding water. However, leaders who learn how to utilize fundamental ministry tools, commit themselves to continued self-improvement that includes their whole person, and consecrate their lives in prayer to knowing Jesus personally in daily relationship. He or she will have the necessary ingredients for making a difference in church ministry, and seizing the opportunities that lie before him or her in today's culturally ethnically diverse society.

There is of course a difference in seeing the opportunity and seizing the opportunity of building bridges of relationship between people of different ethnicities existing in culturally diverse America. Seizing this opportunity includes developing ministries within diverse communities that bring people together in Christian relationships through the reconciliation power of the gospel of Jesus

Christ. This type of ministry effort in the diverse community is not only possible it is ministry effort that is theologically imperative to the mission of God being fulfilled by the church in the world.

Congregations located in culturally diverse communities, and communities in the process of becoming culturally diverse often struggle with the dilemma of how to minister to all people. These congregations face challenges of not knowing how to communicate faith or build relationships with people who do not look like them, speak their language, or eat the type of cooking they are accustomed to eating. People who face a lack of cultural understanding often find it much easier to live their lives in the comfortable place of a worship experience in which one does not attempt to move beyond his or her life world into the life world of another. Inability or lack of desire to adapt and transition ministry has limited the ability of the local church to grow in multi-ethnic culturally diverse communities, and often has been the cause of churches closing or relocating outside of their community leaving a vacuum of hope in many cities and communities.

Momentum

Although this has often been the journey for many congregations there is great potential for churches to move beyond this method of operation and be different. Yes, being different will mean being intentional, focused, and willing to sometimes make hard choices. The fortitude (GUTS) needed to be intentional is the ingredient planted into the soil of an organization that yields movement and momentum as its fruit. Focused fortitude fosters and environment for momentum. Momentum is the energy resulting from moving forward. It is real, inspirational and contagious. Momentum has fueled revolution, inspired businesses, and transformed dying organizations from death to life. There are those who have pushed, pulled, worked to inspire and at times pounded their head against the wall to cause momentum to happen.

Momentum does not take place without movement. Movement is the fuel of momentum. Momentum can begin with one little step, breath of prayer, or glancing thought. Momentum is contagious. When one person gets excited and other people are presented with the opportunity to get excited momentum finds the fertile soil to grow from one person to another and then another, and another, and so on; and soon.

> *"Moses My servant is dead; now therefore arise, cross this Jordan, you and all this people, to the land which I am giving to them..." Joshua 1:2*

Divine Time

When Joseph was going to see his brothers in the fields where they were tending sheep he possibly walked along day dreaming and contemplating how God would bring him into the position that he had dreamed about. Joseph walked into the unexpected. He did not plan to be in a pit, a prison, or a palace. Sometimes in our lives we walk into the unexpected. It is quite important that we understand that God keeps divine time. Esther, Joshua, Elisha, John the Baptist, Peter, and even Paul could all tell us their stories of divine time. We may have our own schedule based upon our view of how things should be for our future, but God has a divine time for our lives that He designed for us with us in mind.

As we wonder about the future, our role in the plan of God and how we can best accomplish the intentional building of relationships in our community we can experience the human tendency to feel like there is no possible way to succeed in our mission task. We can look at all of the seeming impossibilities and say that people who are Buddhist, Muslim, Hindu, Jehovah's Witness, will never accept Christ or people in a pluralistic postmodern culture will never listen to someone who speaks only about Jesus. Maybe the issues of poverty, pain, and hopelessness seem impossible to overcome or perhaps cultural diversity may seem like an impossible place to plant church, build relationships and share Jesus Christ with people. The fact is we walk in a dead world that is in need of life and we who know Christ have life and are life givers. Alone in our humanity we have no power to give life. However, through the presence of the Holy Spirit in us God gives life.

Mission

Mission has been a primary objective of the church throughout the history of the church. Yet there is little doubt to the reality that the institutionalization of the church and continued compartmentalization of Christianity have led the church down a path of being a form of Godliness with no power. Oh yes, there are many today who are jumping onto the latest fad using all the language, all of the words, trying to re-fashion the church into relevance by cramming, stuffing, and putting cultural relevance and missional ministry focus into the modern construction of institutional church. There in fact are people who use the words, the labels, read the books, blog, email, shouting to the Christian church, *"We are relevant – we are post-modern – you aren't – ha,ha,ha..."*. All the while 300 million people live in this country 85% of whom are un-churched. Many of these on a road leading to an eternity without a relationship with God.

Reggie McNeal, writes in his book, "The Present Future Church" that the institutional modern construction of the church continues to ask the wrong questions. One primary question that McNeal writes about is, *"How can we do church better?"* Which for the cool, hip generation means, *"How can we do church different?"*, and our answer in the North American Context has been to un-tuck our shirts turns the lights down, brew coffee, and do worship with a guitar.

So here we are, we call ourselves postmodern, emergent, missional, whatever pick the name that is most popular at the moment. The challenge is that in the journey to be relevant nothing often changes because the authentic reality is we are like hamsters running on the wheel in the cage. We painted the wheel, its cooler now, but we are still running as fast as we can trying to make the institutional church thing work in a pre-Christian world.

God through His mapquest gives us the plan. It is His plan and it involves all people. He desires for us to be whole, and as whole people we are commissioned to help other people become whole. Becoming missional people means that we will see the world filled with people as our field of service and build relationships among them.

Building relationships with all people in a culturally diverse society is accomplished by being intentional, dealing with our issues and challenging ourselves and our church to be authentic. Authenticity will be evident as we live out what we say and what the Bible speaks through its words.

This book has embraced a vision for people to live their faith in the world being authentic, intentional and compassion inspired through relationship with God found in relationship with Jesus Christ. As we follow the teachings of Jesus Christ and the ways of scripture we will become people through whom the fabric of society may be changed. We are inspired by the words of Jesus to *"Go into all of the world..."* (Mt. 28:19) and empowered by the experience of the Holy Spirit on the day of Pentecost at the upper room in Jerusalem, ten days following the ascension of Christ. Our mission is the vision that continues to drive the way forward for those who desire to fulfill the cause of Christ in the world. The compassion of Christ births in us compassion for people and passion for the cause of Christ – *"The Mission"*. Passion often compels people to do what they must do in terms of work, education, and life in order to accomplish what God calls His people to accomplish. Christ's compassion, passion, and mission are the key ingredients in our DNA as people who believe in, have relationship with, and follow Jesus. We can accomplish building relationships, sharing faith, and develop churches that will reflect our population in that these churches will be multi-ethnic, reflect socio-economic diversity, empower people causing redemption and lift opportunities in their lives. We are commissioned to build bridges to people and connect them with God.

APPENDIX 1

―――∞∞∞―――

Development of the American Urban Context

The original American City was not a strategically thought out creation. It was a small settlement that grew into a town, and eventually a city. Spontaneously evolving cities soon appeared throughout the early North American Continent. Many formed as business and population centers without any vision for what they would become in the future. The development of the first large modern American cities can be traced to the colonization of European people on the Continent. Colonial outposts are as close to a city as the first Anglo European settlers would get. John Palen writes in his book, *The Urban World*,

> "Five communities spearheaded the urbanization of the seventeenth – century English colonies. The northernmost was Boston on New England's 'stern and rockbound coast'; the southernmost was the newer and much smaller settlement of Charles Town in South Carolina.(5) Barely making an indentation in the 1,100 miles of wilderness separating these two were Newport, in the Providence Plantations of Rhode Island; New Amsterdam, which in 1664 became New York; and William Penn's Philadelphia on the Delaware River at the mouth of the Schuykill. (Palen [1975] [1981] 1987, 60-61)."

Jamestown was the first of the Anglo-European outposts. Along with Jamestown there were other cities unknown to early Anglo-European settlers. Although less mentioned in history, they were just as significant in their own right. Two cities of historical significance are Santa Fe, New Mexico, and St. Augustine, Florida (Ortiz 1993, 42-43). Jamestown barely survived and today stands only as a tourist attraction of what once was. Soon after Europeans began exploring and settling in the new extension of Europe, the North American wilderness, people began to migrate to inland areas. However, these areas were all close to water which were either connected with or on the Atlantic Ocean.

These five urban centers were the first real cities in the new world. They were accessible by ship, and received both goods and people on a regular basis into their ports. These areas grew beyond any vision their founders may have ever dreamed. In fact, of these five areas, three are still prominent today as major urban areas in the United States. They are Philadelphia, Boston, and New York City.

"The census of 1790 showed that the largest city in the young nation was New York, with 33,000 inhabitants. Philadelphia was the second largest city, with a population of 28,000. Twenty years later New York had over 100,000 persons (Palen [1975] [1981] 1987, 65)."

Very early these population centers became diverse because they were points of entry for new immigrants. Today, anyone traveling to these cities will quickly notice that roads, city planning, and population were after-thoughts forced upon them by growth. In fact, Boston continues to be one of the most difficult cities to get into and out of by car because of the unplanned rapid growth it has experienced throughout its history. To date, the United States government has spent millions of dollars trying to fix the problems in Boston without any real success.

Soon these original five cities were no longer in a category of their own as the largest cities. They shared their largest city distinction with other cities. Today, in 2001, there are nine cities in the United States with a population over 1 million. They are:

Largest Cities In The United States 2001
(The World Gazetteer, November 2002)

New York	8,143,197
Los Angeles	3,844,829
Chicago	2,842,518
Houston	2, 016,582
Philadelphia	1,463,281
Phoenix	1 461,575
San Antonio	1,256,540
San Diego	1,255,540
Dallas	1,213,825,

Cities grew and eventually exploded into large urban areas. These metropolitan areas often connected one city to another, and cover many miles with a large population density.

Today, in 2002, there are forty-five metropolitan areas within the United States or straddling the borders of the United States with a population of more than 1 million. The ten largest of these are:

New York	29 936.9
Los Angeles	16 615.6
Chicago	10 914.4
Washington-Baltimor	7 624.7
San Francisco	7 121.8
Boston	7 038.1
Detroit-Windsor, Canada	5 970.1
Dallas	5 086.8
Miami	4 932.4
Houston	4 656.0

(The World Gazetteer, accessed November, 2002)

The modern city as we know it today finds its roots in modernity and industrialization. The construction of the railroad, modernization, and industrialization helped cities to rapidly expand. People were able to travel in more efficient ways than ever before. Factories, assembly lines, railroads, and technology all contributed to society's ability to conquer time and space. This changed the face of the nation.

Industry blossomed in the city, thus drawing even more people, who came to find work in the factories and mills. The city was where the jobs were located. Mass out-migration would begin in places like Kentucky, West Virginia, and Tennessee, finding its destination in burgeoning cities such as Chicago, Cleveland Ohio, Pittsburgh, New York, and St. Louis.

In general urbanization in the past century has tended to follow industrialization and economic development. Factories, government agencies, and distribution centers tend to be located in the cities; and if the jobs provided by these major employers did not exist, there would be little reason for rural residents to migrate, because of this situation, the less developed nations of the world have also tended to be less urbanized (Hadaway and Rose 1984, 22).

By the turn of the 20th century, as cities grew in population, and land grew scarce, they began to build in the only direction they could. They began to build up. Steel became the primary material for this new construction. Utilizing steel building material, buildings were constructed taller than previously thought possible.

"It wasn't Carnegie's money alone that was building America towns and cities. His steel (and steel supplied by others) made possible a new kind of architecture, a style of building uniquely suited to the new American city. The use of steel to create a structural cage made possible buildings that could be much taller than any masonry structure. The steel supports, not the walls, bore the load of the building (Axelrod 1999, 77)."

Chicago would become home to the first of the tall buildings that came to be known as the skyscraper. The skyscraper became a symbol of American strength and ingenuity. Cities competed to build the tallest buildings (Axelrod 1999, 77-78). Chicago would finalize this competition with the construction of the 110 story Sears Tower Building located 233 South Wacker Drive in downtown Chicago.

The Sears Tower was constructed between 1970 and 1974. When it opened in 1974 it was the tallest building in the world. It retained this distinction for 23 years, until the Petronas Towers opened in Kuala Lumpur, Malaysia. Incidentally, the Sears Tower is 1,454 ft, and the Petronas is 1,483ft (Columbia Electronic Encyclopedia, sixth edition. Copyright 2000, Columbia University Press, Columbia, S.C.). The influence of builders, bankers, and the steel industry all contributed to the rapid expansion and population growth of the American city in the late 19th and early 20th centuries. All of these influences were great contributors to the growth of cities. However, one of the greatest influences to this growth was that of a man born on a Michigan farm: Henry Ford.

Ford was born on July 30, 1863 in Dearborn, Michigan. Ford was a mechanically inclined man who became a machinery repairman at a young age. He would build his first automobile in 1896, and later built a racecar called the 999. The 999 ran at a top speed of more than one mile a minute. Later Ford started his own custom car-making company. The Ford Motor Company opened for business in 1903. Ford soon realized the key to being successful in his new business venture was to cut production time, since labor was the highest cost of production. The desire to further lower production costs led Ford to develop the assembly line. Of course the development of the assembly line changed industry production forever (Axelrod 1999, 110).

The 21st Century

When we look at many cities today it appears that the city experienced an exodus into the suburbs. Suburbs and edge cities formed, and today it seems that the central city, suburbs and edge cities are becoming massive urban areas co-existing and co-dependent. In other words they exist by depending on one another at many different levels. These metropolitan masses of population are connected together as metropolitan areas (Garreau [1991] 1992).

When our family lived and worked in Chicago in the early 90s our son was about 3 years old. One day we had traveled somewhere out of state, and we were talking with someone who asked our son what state do you live in? He replied, "Chicago". Of course he was 3 years old and didn't yet understand what he was saying, but perhaps his view of the city wasn't far from the truth. Perhaps Chicago is more than a city. Looking at Chicago a person sees a city with a population of 2.9 million people. Add to this number possibly as many as 500,000, or more undocumented residents. Add to this number 6 million people living in suburbs and edge city areas from Northern Indiana to Southern Wisconsin. The Chicago area is more than a city. It is in fact a large Metropolitan Area, or megalopolis. This megalopolis includes the city, suburbs, and edge cities; all with a large culturally diverse population.

Commuting from suburban home to center city high-rise office became a 20th century American ritual. This ritual was a fiber of our new fast paced, "successful", seeking the "American Dream" life-style. While growing up, I remember my father leaving our suburban Brandon, Florida three bedroom ranch home for his commute to work in a downtown Tampa high rise before I woke up for school. He would then arrive home in the evening about 6pm or a little after. This process of life was one of occupation in the city, long commute, and the pursuit of the utopia relaxation that was thought to come with living in the suburb. This type of suburban-urban lifestyle is still functioning in many metropolitan areas today. However, something new has evolved around us, affecting how we live, how we work, and where we work. In or actually around two hundred metro-politan "Urban" areas in the United States something has emerged: called the edge city.

Edge city is defined and described by Joel Garreau in great detail in his book, *Edge Cities: Life on the New Frontier*. Garreau gives great explanation and detailed description of the Edge City. Garreau describes the edge city as becoming our new city center.

"Our new city centers are tied together not by locomotives and subways, but by jetways, freeways, and roof top satellite dishes thirty feet across" (Garreau [1991] 1992, 4).

Garreau is describing the shift of the city center from the urban downtown, high rise to being that point somewhere between the old downtown and the suburb which, in many places, has a workforce population larger than the old downtown. Garreau writes,

"I have come to call these new urban centers Edge Cities. Cities, because they contain all the functions a city ever has, albeit in a spread-out form that few have come to recognize for what it is. Edge, because they are a vigorous world of pioneers and immigrants, rising far from the old downtowns, where little save villages or farmland lay only thirty years before (Garreau [1991] 1992, 4)."

In September of 2000 I visited the Dunwoody area of Atlanta. Dunwoody is an Edge City area. The campus was beautiful. There was light rail service nearby, a beautiful mall, hotels, health clubs, condominiums, and many corporate office complexes intermingled with trees all around the area. I walked outside of the hotel where business meetings were in progress. Outside there were jogging paths, a lake with fountains, people sitting on the lawn eating lunch, and people walking during their lunch break for exercise. The population was culturally diverse. I walked to the front of the hotel, and the taxi drivers asked if I needed a ride. I politely declined, but noticing their language was Haitian Creole, I asked *"Como Ye?"* or how are you? They looked at me with great surprise. I was speaking their language. After conversing with them for a few moments I learned that two of them were Church of God (Cleveland, TN) Members from the Haitian Church of God congregation in Atlanta. The Edge City clearly has many characteristics of the center city including cultural diversity (Garreau [1991] 1992, 5).

Edge Cities are not like major metropolitan areas as we have known them. Their size, composition, look, layout, and design in essence do not resemble the old downtown in anyway. However, these Edge Cities have become major centers of business in the late 20th century, and into the 21st century. This new phenomena of Edge Cities has not, and may not completely disassemble the major cities in the United States such as New York, Chicago, and

Los Angeles. However, Edge Cities have clearly had an impact on cities like Tampa, St. Louis, Atlanta Philadelphia, and others. Their emergence has transitioned the flow of business and people in the American society. It is important to understand this in order to identify an Edge City area, as well as contemplate the potential ministry impact and opportunity which exists in and around the Edge City. Garreau defines the Edge City with a five part definition:

"Edge City is any place that:
- *Has five million square feet or more of leasable office space – the workplace of the information age.* Five million square feet is more than downtown Memphis. The Edge City called the Galleria area west of downtown Houston – crowned by the sixty-four story Transco Tower, the tallest building in the world outside an old downtown – is bigger than downtown Minneapolis.
- *Has 600,000 square feet or more of leasable retail space.* That is the equivalent of a fair – sized mall. That mall, remember, probably has at least three nationally famous department stores, and eighty to a hundred shops and boutiques full of merchandise that used to be available only on the finest boulevards of Europe. Even in their heyday there were not many downtowns with that boast.
- *Has more jobs than bedrooms.* When the workday starts, people head toward this place, not away from it. Like all urban places the population increases at 9AM
- *Is perceived by the population as one place.* It is a regional end destination for mixed-use not a starting point – that 'has it all' from jobs, to shopping, to entertainment.
- *Was nothing like 'city'* as recently as thirty years ago. Then, it was just bedrooms, if not cow pastures. This incarnation is brand new" (Garreau [1991] 1992, 6-7).

These areas are co-dependent on one another. People live in the city and commute to the suburbs for employment and likewise people living in the suburbs commute to the city for work. This edge city area is multi-cultural, hi-tech, densely populated, busy, and often fast paced. These edge city areas in the United States are very similar to one another. Many are growing together and connecting cities to each other. The Tampa to Orlando I-4 corridor is continuously growing together. The New York Metropolitan Area is continually growing, and expanding its perimeter. Traveling from Hartford, Connecticut to Washington, D.C. by car is a continuous flow of dense traffic.

Other areas include Miami, Dade County, Dallas, Houston, Los Angeles, San Francisco, and Atlanta. There are many others perhaps on a smaller scale which are only beginning to explode with great growth. Dr. Harvie Conn writes, *"The symbol of the new city is not a skyline of skyscrapers but a network of superhighways as seen from the air. The new city is a 'growth corridor' stretching 50 to 100 miles. The streetcar created the first suburbs. Highway construction and the automobile have created the new cities* (Harvie M. Conn 1994, 135)."

Although Edge Cities are new in our society, the movement of people around the world is not a new phenomena. Throughout history people have moved from place to place. They have moved in search of work, a hope for the future, and a better way of life. Some have moved as they ran from their oppression becoming refugees. Some were taken by force as captives and moved from one place to another. Whatever the case, historically people have crossed country borders, language barriers, and cultural barriers.

APPENDIX 2

Policy for the Hispanic Church of God Mission
(Indiana Church of God)

Be it known that the Mother Church _____
_____ is entering into a joint venture with the
Hispanic Community of our city and county to establish an Hispanic
Congregation that will eventually become an Hispanic Mission of
God. The congregation will be Pentecostal in its belief and teach
and adhere to the doctrine set forth by the of Cleveland Tennessee
Assembly. Given the sensitivity of the differences of the Anglo
Community and the Hispanic Community, we find it necessary to
create a policy which all can abide in the unity of the Holy Spirit.
Ultimately, the Hispanic Congregation will fall under the authority of
the Indiana Church of God Hispanic Board. Be it further known that
it is not the intention of this policy to hinder the Hispanic Mission
in any way but to allow a greater understanding of both cultures
and to make the transition from a Mission Church to an Organized
Hispanic Church of God.

1. **The Mother Church will appoint a member of the congregation to be the Liaison to the Hispanic Congregation.**
   The duties of the Liaison will include, but not be limited to:

   a. Coordinate all issues, events, and opportunities that will
      impact the two congregations.

b. Be a mediator should any difficulties arise that may cause hardship or hard feelings between the two congregations.

c. Work closely with the Ladies' Ministry, Men's Ministry, Youth Ministry, Children's Ministry or any other ministries, to coordinate the use of the mother church's facilities.

2. **It is important that the two cultures have an open line of communication. This will be accomplished through:**
   a. The Mother Church will receive a monthly report from the Liaison relative to the progress of the Hispanic Mission. Such report will include, but not be limited to:
      i. Finances
      ii. Attendance
      iii. Conversions
      iv. Baptisms
      v. Membership

   b. All issues of concern between congregations will be addressed in a quick and orderly manner.

   c. The use of the Mother Church's facilities will be scheduled between the two congregations utilizing a master twelve-month calendar.

   d. The Mother Church Advisory Board will meet with the Hispanic Pastor and spouse to review all financial reports and plan future events.

   e. The Mother Church will commit to assisting the Hispanic Mission in providing a parsonage for the pastor and his family for a period of six (6) months in the amount of $___ _____ per month. At the completion of the first six (6) months a progress review will be done. If it is deemed appropriate this commitment will be renewed for an additional six (6) month period or unless the Holy Spirit directs otherwise.

f. The Indiana Church of God State Office has committed to $_____ per month. Said amount will be sent to the Mother Church for disbursement to the Hispanic Mission as deemed appropriate.

g. The financial commitment is for a one (1) year period for both the Mother Church and the Indiana Church of God State Offices.

4. **In order to avoid any conflict of facilities use, the continuously scheduled days and times that the Hispanic Mission will use the facilities of the Mother Church are:**
    a. Weekly Sunday Service (or its equivalent)
    Facility _____
    Day _____
    Time _____
    b. Weekly Mid-Week Service
    Facility _____
    Day _____
    Time _____
    c. Other Service
    Facility _____
    Day _____
    Time _____

5. **In order to maintain the integrity of the Mother Church's facilities security, access to the facilities will be managed as follows:**
    a. For the first six (6) months, the pastor of the Hispanic Mission will receive a key. The pastor will be the only person of the Hispanic Mission allowed using this key.
    b. After the completion of the six (6) months, if deemed appropriate by the Liaison and Mother Church's Advisory Board, the Hispanic Pastor may present a list of designees (*no more than 3*) to receive additional keys.

6. **Both congregations will maintain respect for the Mother Church's facilities and property. The willful destruction of facilities and/or property will not be tolerated.**

Said facilities and property will include, but not be limited to, all buildings, furniture, appliances, equipment, grounds, flowers, shrubs, and trees.

If damage should occur, the party and/or parties responsible will be required to pay for the repair(s) and/or replacement(s).

7. **If the Mother Church maintains a Nursery Facility, the following guidelines for said Nursery will include, but not be limited to:**
   a. All toys and/or equipment will be placed into their proper place after each service and/or use.
   b. All trash will be emptied.
   c. The entire floor will be vacuumed.
   d. The Nursery will be cleaned completely at the close of the service and/or use.

8. Use of any additional room(s) and/or facility, other than scheduled as agreed in Item #4 above, shall be at the discretion of the Senior Pastor of the Mother Church. At the conclusion of said usage, the room(s) will be completely cleaned and left in order.

9. To maintain the integrity and performance of the Mother Church's Sound Equipment, only trained Sound Technicians from the Mother Church will be allowed to operate said equipment. Any exceptions to this item will be at the discretion of the Senior Pastor of the Mother Church.

10. In keeping with the spirit of cooperation and unity, it is requested that the Hispanic Mission assist the Mother Church with any increase of utilities (i.e. electricity, gas, and

water). While this is NOT mandatory, it would be greatly appreciated.

11. The use of the Mother Church's vehicle(s) is solely at the discretion of the Senior Pastor of the Mother Church. There are NO exceptions to this item.

12. The Hispanic Mission will be asked to contribute $_____ _____ each month for the custodial supplies. If the Mother Church does not have a custodian on staff, the Hispanic Mission will provide members of its congregation to assist with cleaning the Mother Church.

13. Until the Hispanic Mission is organized as a Church of God, all monies will be kept separate, but financial reports will be prepared monthly that will reflect all receipts, expenses, and balances.

14. A separate checking account will be established for the Hispanic Mission with two signatures required on said account and disbursements. The pastor of the Hispanic Mission MUST be one of the authorized endorsers.

15. Until the Hispanic Mission is organized as a Church of God, it will not be required to obtain a Federal ID Number.

16. The pastor of the Hispanic Mission will be considered a staff member of the Mother Church; therefore, a valid Form W-4 will be on file and proper taxation will be handled in accordance with IRS regulations.

17. Until the Hispanic Mission is organized as a Church of God, it will be under the coverage of the Mother Church's Insurance Policies.

18. At no time will the Mother Church be a part to, nor tolerate assisting illegal aliens into the United States. The Mother Church will insist upon and promote the guidelines and regulations of the United States Department of Immigration and Naturalization Service (INS).

Should any incident that contradicts this policy arise, said incident could result in the discontinuance of the relationship between the Mother Church and the Hispanic Mission.

18. Additional Items:

It is our desire that God would use our church and its facilities to promote the evangelization and discipleship of the Hispanic Community. While this shall not be an easy process, I believe it will be an educational and rewarding experience. It is with much spiritual anticipation and joy that we enter into this partnership and area of faith.

Date _____

Mother Church of God_____
Address _____
Mother Church Pastor Signature   _____
Hispanic Pastor Signature   _____

(This policy was written and developed by the Indiana Church of God Hispanic Ministries Board)

APPENDIX 3

Descriptive Questions = Descriptive Observations:

Family Values

Marriage
Do children marry?
inside of culture
inside of culture and within religion
outside or inside of culture but within religion
outside or inside of culture and religion
Do children date or court prior to marriage?
How do children get engaged and what kind of activities are involved in becoming engaged?
What activities take place during a wedding?

Death
How does the family deal with death?
What kind of activities take place at a funeral?

Language
What is the primary language of the family?
What is the primary language spoken in the home?
Are children encouraged to learn and speak English?

Family Leadership
Who directs-leads the family?

Matriarch	Patriarchal
__mother	__father
__Grandmother	__Grandfather
__other	__other

Household Duties
Who does the cooking in the home?

__mother	__grandmother
__father	__grandfather

__other (describe_____)

Who does the cleaning in the home?

__mother	__children
__father	__grandfather
__grandmother	__other (describe_____)

Who manages the money?

__mother
__father
__other

Eating
Does the family eat dinner together?

__every day
__once of twice a week
__sometimes
__seldom
__never

When is dinner prepared?
Describe family meal times:

Religious Belief

__Roman Catholicism	__Voodooism
__Evangelical Christianity	__Atheism
__Muslim	__Animism
__Buddhism	__Other
__Hinduism	

Religious Practice
__faithful participation   __limited participation
__somewhat faithful participation   __non-participation

View of God
__sovereign involved in daily life
__distant not involved in daily life
__non-existent

Education
__little or no education
__high-school secondary school or equivalent education
__post-secondary / technical/ trade school education
__university education
__graduate / post-university/ professional education
__post graduate school

Occupation
__prior to immigration
__present occupation
__how many jobs and what kind
__goal for the future

Housing
__rent   __included in occupation
__own   __other
__share

Immigration Status
__legal   __illegal
__green card   __over-stayed visa
__student visa   __crossed border
__refugee   __other
__visitor visa
__citizen

Born in the United States
　　__2nd generation
　　__3rd generation
　　__4th generation

Community Connections
　　Where do they people go to meet friends?
　　__cultural club
　　__restaurant
　　__tavern
　　__sports field arena
　　Are primary friendships within culture group?

WORKS CITED

Anderson, Douglas L., and David Yaukey. 2001. *Demography: The Study of Human Population.* Prospect Heights, Illinois: Waveland Press, Inc.

Bakke, Ray. 1997. *A Theology As Big As The City.* Downers Grove, Illinois: Intervarsity Press.

_____. 1987. *The Urban Christian: Effective ministry in Today's Urban World.* Downers Grove, Illinois: Intervarsity Press.

Balda, Wesley D., ed. 1984. *Heirs of the Same Promise: Using Acts as a Study Guide for Evangelizing Ethnic America.* Arcadia, California: National Convocation on Evangelizing Ethnic America.

Barna, George. 1998. *The Second Coming of the Church.* Nashville: Word Publishing.

Barndt, Joseph. 1991. *Dismantling Racism: The Continuing Challenge to White America.* Minneapolis: Augsburg.

Bavink, J.H. 1960. *An Introduction To The Science of Missions.* Phillipsburg, New Jersey: The Presbyterian and Reformed Publishing Company.

Beitzel, Barry J. 1985. *The Moody Bible Atlas.* Chicago: Moody Press.

Beverly, James A. 2002. "Muhammad Amid the Faiths." *Christian History,* XXI No. 2 Issue 74, 10-15.

Biography of Martha Zimmerlan, n.d. (Author unknown). Cleveland, TN: Pentecostal Research Center, Cleveland, TN. typewritten.

Callahan, Kenon, L. 1990. *Effective Church Leadership: Building on the Twelve Keys.* San Francisco: Harper Collins.

Campus Life. 2001. Carol Stream, Illinois: Christianity Today Publishing, May/June.

Carmody, Denise Lardner and John Carmody. 1998. *The Story of World Religions.* Mountain View, California: Mayfield Publishing.

Cell Group Journal. 2002. Houston: Touch Outreach Ministries Inc., Spring.

Clarebaut, David. 1983. *Urban Ministry.* Grand Rapids, Michigan: Zondervan Publishing House.

Clayton, David, 1998. "Urban Islam: The Unseen Engine in Fundamentalism." *Urban Mission* 15 No. 3, 8-14.

Comiskey, Joel. 1998. *Home Cell Group Explosion: How Your Small Group Can Grow and Multiply.* Houston: Touch Publications.

Conn, Harvie M. 1984. *Eternal World and Changing World: Theology, Anthropology, and Mission in Trialogue.* Phillipsburg, New Jersey: P & R Publishing.

Costas, Orlando E. 1995. *Christ Outside the Gate: Mission Beyond Christendom.* Maryknoll, New York: Orbis Books.

Cox, Harvey. 1995. *Fire from Heaven: The Rise of Pentecostal Spirituality and the Reshaping of Religion in the Twenty-first Century.* Reading, Massachusetts: Addison-Wesley Publishing Company.

Crawford, Oliver. 1991. *Star Trek: The Galileo Seven.* Produced by Gene L. Coon and Directed by Robert Gist. 51 min. Paramount Pictures,Videocassette.

Dawson,John. 1994. *Healing America's Wounds.* Ventura, California: Regal Books.

Drucker Peter. 1992. *Managing the Non-Profit Organization: Principles and Practices.* New York, New York: Harper Collins Business Publishers.

Dubose, Francis M. 1978. *How Churches Grow in an Urban World.* Nashville: Broadman Press.

Elass, Mateen A. 2002. "Four Jihad." *Christian History,* XXI, No. 2 Issue 74, 35-38

Gaebelein, Frank E. ed. 1976. *The Expositor's Bible Commentary. Vol 9.* Grand Rapids: Zondervan.

Glasser, Arthur F., and Donald A. McGavran. 1983. *Contemporary Theologies of Mission.* Grand Rapids, Michigan: Baker Book House.

Greenway, Roger S. and Timothy Monsma. 1989. *Cities: Missions New Frontier.* Grand Rapids: Baker Book House.

Hawthorne, Steven C. and Ralph D. Winter. 1983. *Perspectives On the World Christian Movement.* Pasadena, CA.: William Carey Library.

Henry, Rodney L. 1971. *Filipino Spirit World: A Challenge to the Church.* Manila, Philippines: OMF Publisher.

Hesselgrave, David J. 1991. *Communicating Christ Cross-Culturally Second Edition: An Introduction to Missionary Communication.* Grand Rapids: Zondervan Publishing House.

Hesselgrave, David J. and Edward Rommen. 2000. *Contextualization: Meanings, Methods, and Models.* Pasadena, CA: William Carey Library.

Hiebert, Paul G. 1985. *Anthropological Insights for Missionaries.* Grand Rapids: Baker Book House.

Hiebert, Paul, Daniel Shaw, and Tite Tienou. 1999. *Understanding Folk Religions: A Christian Response To Popular Beliefs And Practices.* Baker Books: Grand Rapids.

Hoekema, Anthony A. 1986. *Created in God's Image.* Grand Rapids: William B. Eerdmans Publishing.

Holladay, William L. 1988. *A Concise Hebrew and Aramaic Lexicon of the Old Testament.* Grand Rapids: Eerdmans.

Holloway, Gerald. 1992. *Maximizing Opportunities: An Amazing True Story of One of the World's Most Successful Churches and of One Family Discovering God's Will.* Cleveland, Tennessee: Pathway Press.

Howard, Michael C. 1986. *Contemporary Cultural Anthropology.* Little, Brown and Company: Boston.

"Islam 101: Basics of Foreign Faith," 2002. *Christian History,* XXI, No. 2 Issue 74, 14.

Jones, Tony ed. 2001. *Postmodern Youth Ministry: Exploring Culture Shift, Cultivating Authentic Community, Creating Holistic Connections.* Zondervan, Grand Rapids.

Keener, Craig S. 1993. *The IVP Bible Background Commentary: New Testament.* Downers Grove, Illinois: InterVarsity Press.

Kirschner, David. 1998. *An American Tail.* Produced by Kathleen Kennedy, David Kirschner, Frank Marshall, and Steven Speilberg, and directed by Don Bluth. 81 min. Universal Home Video Inc. Videocassette.

King, Martin Luther, Jr. 1993. *I Have A Dream.* New York, NY.: Harper Collins Publishers.

Kraft, Charles H. 1979. *Christianity In Culture: A Study in Dynamic Biblical Theologizing in Cross-Cultural Perspective.* Maryknoll, New York: Orbis Books.

Laguerre, Michel S. 1998. Diasporic *Citizenship: Haitian Americans in Transnational America.* New York: St. Martins Press.

Lewis, Robert, and Rob Wilkins. 2001. *The Church of Irresistible Influence.* Grand Rapids: Zondervan.

Lingenfelter, Sherwood. 1998. *Transforming Culture: A Challenge for Christian Mission Second Edition.* Baker Books: Grand Rapids.

Lingenfelter, Sherwood G., and Marvin K. Mayers. 1986. *Ministering Cross-Culturally: An Incarnational Model for Personal Relationships.* Baker Book House: Grand Rapids.

Linthicum, Robert C. 1991. *City of God, City of Satan: A Biblical Theology of the Urban Church.* Grand Rapids: Zondervan.

Livingstone, Greg. 1993. *Planting Church in Muslim Cities: A Team Approach.* Grand Rapids: Baker Book House.

Malphurs, Aubrey. 1998. *Planting Growing Churches For The 21st Century: A Comprehensive Guide for New Churches and Those Desiring Renewal.* Baker Books: Grand Rapids.

Maxwell, John C. 1998. *The 21 Irrefutable Laws Of Leadership: Follow Them and People Will Follow You.* Nashville: Thomas Nelson Publishers.

May, F.J. 1990. *The Book of Acts in Church Growth.* Cleveland, TN.: Pathway Press.

Middleton, J. Richard and Brian J. Walsh. 1995. *Truth is Stranger Than It Used to Be: Biblical Faith in a Postmodern Age.* Intervarsity Press: Downers Grove, IL.

Morris, Leon. 1986. *New Testament Theology.* Grand Rapids: Zondervan.

Morison, Samuel Elliot. 1994. The *Oxford History of the American People.* New York: Meridian.

Morrison, Joan, C. and Fox Zabusky. 1993. *American Mosaic: The Immigrant Experience in the Words of Those Who Lived It.* Pittsburgh: University Pittsburgh Press.

Neumann, Mikel. 1999. *Home Groups for Urban Christians.* Pasedena, California: William Carey Library Publishers.

Nida, Eugene A. 1960. *Message and Mission: The Communication of the Christian Faith.* Pasedena, California: William Carey Library.

Oritz, Manuel. 1996. *One New People: Models for Developing a Multiethnic Church.* Downers Grove, Illinois: InterVarsity Press.

Perry, Dwight ed. 2002. *Building Unity in the Church of the New Millennium.* Moody: Chicago.

Quinn, Robert E. 1996. *Deep Change: Discovering the Leader Within.* San Francisco: Jossey-Bass Inc.

Rainer, Tom S. 2001. *Surprising Insights from the Unchurched: and Proven Ways to Reach Them.* Zondervan: Grand Rapids.

_____. 1993. The *Book of Church Growth: History, Theology, and Principles.* Nashville, Tennessee: Broadman Press.

Richards, Lawrence O. 1975. *Christian Education: Seeking to Become Like Jesus Christ.* Zondervan: Grand Rapids.

Richardson, Don. 1976. *Peace Child.* Ventura, CA: Regal.

Sellner, Edward. 1990. *Mentoring: The Ministry of Spiritual Kinship.* Notre Dame, IN.: Ave Maria Press.

Shenk, Wilbert R. ed. 1983.. *Exploring Church Growth.* Grand Rapids: William B. Eerdmans.

Smith, Donnie W. 1994. *The Undiscovered Harvest: Ministering to America's Immigrant People.* Cleveland, Tennessee: by the author.

Spradley, James P. 1980. *Participant Observation.* New York: Harcourt Brace Jovanovich.

Stanley, Andy. 1999. *Visioneering: God's Blueprint for Developing and Maintaining Personal Vision.* Sister, OR: Multnomah Publishers INC.

Stott, John R. 1979. *The Message of Ephesians.* Downers Grove, Illinois: InterVarsity Press.

_____. 1971. *Basic Christianity.* Downers Grove, Illinois: Inter-Varsity Press.

Sweet, Leonard. 1999. *Soul Tsunami.* Grand Rapids: Zondervan Publishing House.

Synan, Vinson. 1997. *The Holiness Pentecostal Tradition: Charismatic Movements in the Twentieth Century.* Grand Rapids: Eerdmans.

Tenney, Merril C. ed. 1976. *Vol.1: Pictorial Encyclopedia of the Bible.* Grand Rapids: Zondervan Publishing House.

_____. 1976. *Vol.2: Pictorial Encyclopedia of the Bible.* Grand Rapids: Zondervan Publishing House.

"The Peopling of America pre-1790." *Ellis Island.* 2000. The Statue of Liberty Foundation, Inc. Internet on-line. Available from http://www.ellisisland.org. [1 December 2006].

"The Peopling of America 1880-1930." *Ellis Island.* 2001. The Statue of Liberty Foundation, Inc. Internet on-line. Available from http://www.ellisisland.org. [1 December 2006].

Tomasi, Lydio F. ed. 2001."Dateline Migration: National." *Migration World Magazine*, No. 3, 12.

Tomlinson, A.J. 1984. *The Last Great Conflict.* Cleveland, Tennessee: White Wing Publishing.

Towns, Elmer, and Warren Bird. 2000. *Into the Future: Turning Today's Church Trends into Tomorrow's Opportunities.* Grand Rapids: Fleming H. Revell.

Tumulty, Karen. 2001. "Courting a Sleeping Giant: The Biggest U.S. minority group, Hispanics have yet to flex their political muscle." *Time Magazine*, 11 June, 74.

Wagner, C. Peter. 1990. *Church Planting for a Greater Harvest.* Ventura, California: Regal Books.

_____. 1984 *Your Church Can Grow: Seven Vital Signs of a Healthy Church*. Ventura, California: Regal Books.

Wall, Bob, Robert S. Solum, and Mark R. Sobol. 1992. *The Visionary Leader: From Mission Statement to a Thriving Organization, Here's Your Blueprint for Building and Inspired Cohesive, Customer-Oriented Team*. Rocklin, California: Prima Publishing.

Washington, Raleigh and Glen Kehrein. 1993. *Breaking Down Walls: A Model for Reconciliation in an Age of Racial Strife*. Chicago: Moody Press.

Witherington, Ben. 1998. *The Acts of the Apostles: A Socio-Rhetorical Commentary*. Grand Rapids: William B. Eerdmans Publishing.

"World Pop Clock." 2003. Internet on-line. Available from http://www.uscensus.gov [6 December].

Ziglar, Zig. 1977. *See You At The Top*. Gretna, Louisiana: Pelican.

About the author

―――――∞∞∞―――――

Sean O'Neal has traveled throughout the world working among many people groups including African American, Romanian, Hungarian, Bulgarian, Pakistani, East Indian, Latino, Korean, West Indian, American Born Caucasian, Filipino and Haitian. Sean has worked as local church youth pastor, urban missionary, consultant, conference speaker, local church pastor, and currently serves in regional church leadership. While serving as the Senior Pastor of the Narragansett Church of God in Chicago the church experienced exciting growth in attendance including ministry among 12 different ethnic groups, the planting of two new church congregations including a Latino ministry primarily reaching first and second generation Mexican people, and a Bulgarian Church. Sean earned the Bachelor of Arts degree from Lee University in Intercultural Studies, a Master of Arts degree in Urban Ministry from Trinity Evangelical Divinity School, and the Doctor of Ministry degree in Urban Missions from Westminster Theological Seminary.

Sean is a licensed church consultant, speaker, coach, teacher, and workshop leader. He enjoys helping church congregations identify ways in which they may re-vision their church developing strategic and effective methods for reaching all people of every ethnicity and culture in their community (becoming missional). Reaching them includes activities and ministries that strive to redeem the whole person and provide lift in their lives. Sean also has sincere passion to plant churches, train church planters, and facilitate the planting of churches in the pre-Christian 21st century world.

Contact Information:

Sean S. O'Neal, D.Min.
email: sean@bridges2people.com
Website: www.bridges2people.com